ON THE COURTHOUSE LAWN

ON THE COURTHOUSE LAWN

Confronting the Legacy of Lynching
in the Twenty-first Century

SHERRILYN A. IFILL

BEACON PRESS, BOSTON

BEACON PRESS
25 Beacon Street
Boston, Massachusetts 02108-2892
www.beacon.org

Beacon Press books
are published under the auspices of
the Unitarian Universalist Association of Congregations.

10 09 08 07   8 7 6 5 4 3 2 1

Composition by Wilsted & Taylor Publishing Services

Library of Congress Cataloging-in-Publication Data

Ifill, Sherrilyn A.
   On the courthouse lawn : confronting the legacy of lynching in the twenty-first century /
Sherrilyn A. Ifill.
      p. cm.
   Includes bibliographical references and index.
   ISBN-13: 978-0-8070-0988-8 (pbk. : alk. paper)
   ISBN-10: 0-8070-0988-1 (pbk. : alk. paper)
   1. Lynching—United States—History. 2. Lynching—Maryland—History. I. Title.

HV6457.I45 2007
364.1′34—dc22   2006016618

All URLs noted herein were checked for accuracy prior to publication. However, Beacon Press assumes no responsibility for the longevity, accuracy, or appropriateness of any external or third-party Web sites referred to in this book.

For N, A, and J,
who make me dream of a better world,
and for Ivo,
with whom I share all my dreams

CONTENTS

The experiences that moved me to write this book are sprinkled over my seventeen years as a civil rights lawyer. First, at the NAACP Legal Defense and Educational Fund, the nation's premier civil rights law firm, and later as a law professor, I have represented communities struggling with the problem of race. As a civil rights lawyer, my job has been to translate those problems into cognizable legal claims. Early on, I discovered that this was no easy task. My clients' claims of discrimination often represented the culmination and crystallization of decades, sometimes centuries, of halting, painful, and mostly unsuccessful attempts to negotiate a place of dignity, equality, and power within their communities. And in relating this complex and painful history to me, my clients—from Oklahoma to Maryland—inevitably told me something about lynching.

Until recently, few Americans, black or white, fully realized the widespread and pervasive reality of lynching in our nation's history. Now, thanks to some excellent books published in the last few years and an exhibit of lynching photos that has toured the country since 2001, those who want to know about this dark chapter in American history know that during the first half of the twentieth century lynching was, as historian Frank Shay observed, "as American as apple pie." Even more powerful, the lynching of James Byrd in Jasper, Texas, in 1998 and that of Matthew Shepard in Laramie, Wyoming, a year later compelled blacks and whites in communities throughout the United States to recall their own history of lynching. From Utah to Minnesota to Florida, long-repressed memories of this uniquely American form of terrorism were fanned into flame.

But as the collective memory of systematic racial terrorism awoke throughout the country, communities found that no formal mechanisms existed to assist blacks and whites in coming to terms with the legacy of lynching. Some discovered that talking about lynching was a surefire way to surface long-simmering racial conflicts. President Clinton's call to have a national conversation on race in 1994 and his appointment of the One America Commission to explore the issue of race might have provided an opportunity to face this difficult history, but lynching was strangely absent from the commission's agenda, and that body's work—some of it quite impressive—was largely unknown to most Americans.

In the course of my work, I have been amazed to discover how often and how pervasively racial violence figures into the history of small towns and cities throughout the United States. For example, I first heard about the 1921 Tulsa Race Riot, in which whites burned down the prosperous black section of town known as the Black Wall Street, from clients I represented in a voting rights case in Oklahoma and Tulsa Counties in 1991. Although I included allegations about the Tulsa Race Riot in my legal complaint in that case as evidence of the history of discrimination in Tulsa County, it was difficult at the time to find confirmation that this racial pogrom had ever happened. Because of the work of lawyers and historians, and because of the courage of elderly survivors of the Tulsa Race Riot, we now know about this act of racial terrorism and about the deliberate attempt by some whites in Tulsa to cover it up.

I learned about the Maryland lynchings in almost the same way. I was looking into the history of discrimination on Maryland's Eastern Shore—a body of land on the eastern side of the Chesapeake Bay that connects Maryland, Delaware, and Virginia. The clients I represented were African Americans who had been the victims of discrimination in state highway siting decisions in and around Wicomico County, Maryland. It took a while before I understood that there had been two lynchings, one in 1931 and another in 1933. My clients talked only about one, melding the facts of the two lynchings together in a single gruesome and terrifying story. And it took a great while longer for me to learn that in that same two-year period several other black men had narrowly averted being lynched, and that lynching had a long and powerful history on the Shore that extended back to the nineteenth century.

Two things struck me early on about the way blacks and whites talked about the lynchings. First, I was taken with how "present" the lynchings were for blacks. This should not have been surprising. As writer Ishmael Reed recently observed in the *New York Times,* "Stories of lynchings are a key feature of the black oral tradition." Even blacks in northern states, where lynchings rarely occurred, can share vivid stories about lynching. This is largely because of the courageous reporting in black papers like the *Chicago Defender,* the *Amsterdam News,* and the *Baltimore Afro-American* during the 1930s and 1940s, which enabled black readers nationwide to experience the horror of lynching and its violent aftermath. When Mamie Till, the mother of fifteen-year-old Emmett Till, who was lynched in Mississippi in 1955, insisted on an open casket for her son's Chicago funeral, the ten thousand blacks who streamed by his casket were overcome by the hideous reality of violent white supremacy, reflected in the mangled face of the fifteen-year-old boy. In effect, black Americans share a kind of communal memory of lynching that is not bound by region or by time.

So although the Eastern Shore lynchings had occurred more than a half century ago, for many African Americans the lynchings were a defining moment in their racial history. Blacks were particularly eloquent about the fact that hundreds, maybe thousands, of whites had watched the lynchings—some participating, some cheering, some shocked, but none intervening. It was not so much the eight or nine men who dragged twenty-three-year-old Matthew Williams from his hospital bed to hang him on the courthouse lawn in Salisbury in 1931 or the twenty who broke down the door of the jail in Princess Anne to hang, drag, and burn twenty-seven-year-old George Armwood on the street in 1933 who were fixed in the minds of the blacks I spoke with. It was the participation or presence of average whites—law students, businessmen, waiters, shopkeepers, laborers, police officers, and most of the Wicomico High School football team—that blacks remembered. For many blacks on the Shore, this was the lesson of lynching passed down from generation to generation: ordinary whites were not to be trusted.

Most blacks with whom I spoke had heard about the lynchings when they were children, eavesdropping on "grown folks'" hushed conversations. So vivid were these stories that these children, now grown up, could describe the lynching in great detail and with, I discovered, surprising accuracy. Edward Taylor, a retired school principal and later county councilman in Wicomico County, had so deeply internalized the description of the 1931 lynching of Matthew Williams he'd heard as a child that he grew up believing that he'd actually seen the lynching. It was not until he was a grown man that he realized he was not even born when the lynching occurred.

More than any other incident of racial violence, lynching evokes particularly resilient memories in African American communities. Orlando

Patterson, in his searing study of lynching, *Rituals of Blood,* has suggested that it is the memory of the smell of burning flesh that stays encoded in the memory, longer even than the visual image of the lynched body. Walter White, the great antilynching crusader and NAACP president during the 1930s and 1940s who was so fair-skinned that he was able to pass as a white man and observe the aftermath of several lynchings, said that it was the participation of white children in lynching, as torturers or as excited observers, that seared the horror of the act into his brain.

Perhaps it is the gruesome nature of the lynching ritual act itself that becomes indelibly etched onto the collective psyche of a black community for generations—the hanging, the dismembering, the burning, the dragging. In her biography of Fannie Lou Hamer, *This Little Light of Mine,* Kay Mills describes an incident in the late 1950s when northern civil rights workers tried to persuade black sharecroppers in Sunflower County, Mississippi, to register to vote. The sharecroppers were reluctant, and they described a hideous double lynching that had occurred in the county more than fifty years earlier. Their story of the lynching was so lurid and horrific that the civil rights workers thought it must have been half fantasy. But later the activists learned that the 1904 lynching of Luther Holbert and his wife was fact and not fiction. Holbert was believed to have murdered twenty-one-year-old James Eastland, the son of a prosperous plantation family in the county. While one thousand white spectators watched, the Holberts' fingers and toes were cut off and large corkscrews were bored into their flesh. After a prolonged torture, the Holberts were burned alive. Three other black field workers who reportedly looked like Holbert were also killed that day by members of the posse organized to search for Holbert. The lynching of the Holberts and its macabre details had so entered the consciousness of the black community in Sunflower County that even fifty years later its image had the power to keep many blacks from attempting to register to vote.

Given the power of one particularly brutal lynching to discourage blacks from political participation after fifty years, one can imagine how a regular pattern of lynching might have destabilized and retarded the economic, educational, and political development of a black community. When one takes into account that nearly five thousand lynchings took place in the United States between 1885 and 1960, it becomes clear that the damage caused by lynching in black communities throughout the United States is both widespread and deep. Indeed, more than the poll tax, the grandfather clause, and Jim Crow segregation, lynching and the threat of lynching helped regulate and restrict all aspects of black advancement, independence, and citizenship in many small towns for half a century. The fact that lynching was often accompanied by a kind of racial pogrom, in which in addition to beating and murdering blacks, whites burned black businesses and homes and chased blacks out of town, suggests that the economic harm alone to black communities is staggering.

During my time on the Eastern Shore I was also struck by the very different way that whites described the Shore lynchings. Often in the vaguest terms, whites would confirm that yes, there had been a lynching—two, in fact. But where blacks had often identified a family member—grandfather, uncle, or other relative—who heard the lynching, saw the body the next day, or knew the lynched man, whites consistently professed to know very little about the lynchings. In my interviews there were disturbingly few exceptions. And almost to a person, nearly every white person insisted that the lynchers were from "out of town." Salisbury whites claimed that those who lynched Matthew Williams in 1931 were from Princess Anne, and Princess Anne whites suggested that those who lynched George Armwood in 1933 were from Virginia.

I found this silence by whites and their detachment from the lynchings quite extraordinary when contrasted with the rich and detailed "memory" of blacks. By all accounts, between 500 and 1,000 people, predominantly white, witnessed some portion of the lynching of Matthew Williams in Salisbury in 1931. In a town that in that year had only 9,000 white residents, this means that perhaps 10 percent of the town's white population saw the lynching. Yet sixty-eight years later, when I talked with residents, very few whites admitted that they or their families had any personal recollection of the lynching. And so this event, which had constituted a defining racial moment in the black community, had virtually no contemporary significance for whites.

I discovered that the disparate reaction of blacks and whites to the history of racial violence had international significance. It mirrored a similar phenomenon then being played out in South Africa. Whites, who had benefited over centuries from a system of legalized white supremacy in that country, by 1998, when I visited the country, professed an astonishing level of ignorance about and detachment from apartheid. Apartheid had not been dead four years, but in 1998 it was difficult to find average white South Africans who would admit to having ever supported apartheid. And to this day most whites in South Africa on whose behalf the government committed the most hideous atrocities claim not to have realized the extent of their government's misdeeds.

In 1998, however, South Africa's Truth and Reconciliation Commission (TRC) was making the job of forgetting difficult for whites. In televised sessions, black South Africans were coming forward to tell what they had suffered. In graphic terms they described how they were tortured, how their loved ones were killed, and how their communities were dismantled. Even more revealing, some whites came forward to admit their participation in these atrocities. Seeking amnesty from prosecution for their criminal acts, members of the South African police and security forces admitted committing the most heinous acts of terror. And many of them made it clear that the orders to visit this terror upon black communities and activists came from the highest levels of the white power structure.

Even when individual whites would not come forward to give an accounting of their participation in apartheid-era crimes, the TRC held hearings that exposed the complicity of the nation's primary institutions in promoting apartheid's abuses against the majority-black population. In proceedings called "institutional hearings," the commission called the judiciary, the business community, the faith community, and the media to account for their actions during the apartheid era. The results of these hearings—on the complicity of the media in covering up human rights violations committed by security police, for example—were devastating. The hearings and the courageous testimony of white and black reporters revealed overt acts of complicity, of horrific racism and brutality, even within the corridors of media institutions, and an almost complete abdication by most media outlets of internationally recognized journalistic standards and ethics. Particularly telling were hearings in which the institutional actors refused to show up or participate. So it was with the hearings on the judiciary. The failure of the judiciary to respond to the invitation of the TRC spoke volumes and still stands as a stain on the legitimacy of judges appointed during the apartheid era, many of whom remain

on the bench. Despite the absence of the judges, the hearings on the judiciary went forward nonetheless, with devastating testimony from lawyers,
academics, and legal observers. In each institutional hearing, South Africans were compelled to face the systemic nature of apartheid and the way
it had infected all of the country's important institutions of civil society.

I was then, and remain still, deeply impressed by the task the South
African TRC undertook. Like every process, it had its flaws, not the least
of which was its failure, as Mahmood Mamdani has written, to hold to account the beneficiaries of apartheid—those average white South Africans
for whom the government committed its gross atrocities against blacks.
Likewise, the failure to ensure that sufficient funds were made available for
meaningful financial reparation to victims represented an immense and
easily anticipated structural flaw in the creation of the TRC. Nevertheless,
South Africans were doing something that Americans had never done:
confronting in detail the devastation caused by racial terrorism. They were
naming names, identifying institutions, creating a record, and acknowledging the demand for reparation. And they were attempting to engage in
a real conversation about how to move forward as victims and perpetrators,
as oppressors and the formerly oppressed.

This book is an attempt to begin to imagine such a project for American communities beset by a history of racial terrorism. The project of
reconciliation and reparation for lynching is urgently needed. As I discovered, and as the accounts here demonstrate, the aftereffects of lynching
continue to shape and mold the communities where these acts occurred.
As Archbishop Desmond Tutu, the chair of the TRC wrote, "The past re-
fuses to lie down quietly." The terror visited upon African American communities on the Eastern Shore in the 1930s has not just disappeared into
thin air. It lives in the deep wells of distrust between blacks and whites, in
the sense that blacks still must keep their place and that both blacks and
whites must remain silent about this history of lynching.

The lynchings made possible the maintenance of all-white political
control in many counties on the Shore until the 1980s and in some cases
the 1990s, decades after blacks had been elected to public office in other
parts of the state. Blacks were not elected to the governing bodies in many
counties on the Shore until the ACLU filed a series of voting-rights cases
in the 1990s. The black community in Salisbury, where Matthew Wil-

liams was raised and later lynched, was targeted for destruction soon after the lynching to make way for a highway. The white community's perpetual fear of a black uprising after the lynchings may have made the decision to physically split the black community with the new highway an easy one. The construction of Route 13 scattered much of the existing black community and uprooted churches and a score of black businesses. Route 13 cut through the black community like a scythe, the road standing like an open wound through what had once been a vibrant black district. Over the next sixty years the town would approve the construction of two more major highways, one plowing through the remaining black community, and the other adjacent to it. The black Salisbury of Matthew Williams's day has been dissected twice over and encroached upon by twisting highways. Each time, the community has struggled to retain its cohesiveness and the integrity of its institutions. Finally, in 1993 one black neighborhood fought back, aggressively suing the town and the state. I joined the team of lawyers working on the case in 1994. But the impunity with which white local officials were able to physically dismantle parts of the black community over the course of sixty years, and the community's powerlessness to resist these plans for so long, seemed to reflect the effectiveness of enforcing white supremacy through terror.

The white community was also affected by the lynchings. The Eastern Shore, like many white communities where lynchings occurred, closed ranks to protect the lynchers and to fend off criticism from the outside. In response to vehement and prolonged criticism from the Baltimore and Washington, D.C., press over the lynchings, white residents of the Shore boycotted the sale and distribution of Baltimore newspapers and attacked trucks delivering goods from Baltimore and Washington, D.C. Shore whites developed what one scholar has called a kind of regional hyperconsciousness—a deep sensitivity to criticism, especially by outsiders, and a fierce protectiveness of their local institutions, customs, and leaders. This self-imposed economic and cultural withdrawal from the most prosperous, diverse, and progressive regions of the state helped Shore whites remain for decades among the most educationally deficient and economically depressed in the state of Maryland. According to the 2000 Census, the percentage of residents living in poverty in counties on the Western Shore stood between 2.5 and 3.6 percent, whereas in lower Eastern Shore counties like Wicomico and Somerset, the percentage of residents living in poverty stood between 8.7 percent and 15 percent respectively. High school dropout rates for whites exceeded those for blacks in some Eastern Shore communities. In Somerset County, where 41 percent of the population is African American, nearly 10 percent of those over twenty-five years of age have a less than ninth-grade education.

Whites also remain strangely caught up in a continued bond of complicity—pleading ignorance or faded memories to avoid at all cost talking about a shameful part of their history. White children, now elderly, who witnessed these lynchings experienced a unique trauma reinforced by years of silence within their families and communities. Surprisingly, few have been willing to talk about what they saw and how it affected them.

The conversation about lynching I imagine is not of the town hall variety; nor is it meant to compete with other national reparations or litigation efforts or attempts to criminally prosecute those directly responsible for the lynchings in Maryland or in other states. The TRC process I propose is meant to address the harm done to the victims of lynchings who are often forgotten: the community. The dialogue and reconciliation efforts would be intensely local, on the ground where the effects of lynching are still felt. More than just conversation, local individual and community groups and institutions would be empowered to do the work of reconciliation, identifying for themselves appropriate forms of reparation. Rather than being bound to the narrow conception of reparations that dominates discussion of this issue at the national level, local reparation initiatives might take the form of public apologies; expunging the records of or issuing pardons to black lynching victims who were accused of or convicted of crimes they did not commit; the creation of monuments or commemorative public spaces in the community; placing gravestones on the unmarked burial sites of lynching victims; mandatory school programs on the local history of lynching; reopening criminal investigations into lynchings; financial compensation for lynching victims' descendants and for those whose family homes or businesses were destroyed in the aftermath of lynching; and institutional reform focused on the legal system and the media. I discuss these forms of reparation in the second part of this book.

Truth-telling, as the experience of the South African TRC has taught us, is also a critical form of reparation. A truth and reconciliation process for lynching would create the conditions in which for the first time blacks and whites would collaboratively retell the complex history of the communities in which they live. I like to imagine, for example, that President Clinton's call for a national conversation on race had begun in his beloved hometown of Hope, Arkansas, which in the early 1920s, as few people realize, was known by some as the lynching capital of the South. There were three lynchings in an eighteen-month period between 1920 and 1922 in Hope, a time when the former president's colorful and independent mother, Virginia, was a young woman. What, if anything, had the president heard about these devastating events from his family and neighbors in Hope? How had these acts of racial terror shaped the town and the relationships between and among blacks and whites there? Do blacks remember the town of Hope with the same dreamy sense of nostalgia as the former president, or is there another narrative about Hope, waiting to be told? What kinds of reconciliation efforts or forms of reparation might give voice and acknowledgment to another narration about Hope, Arkansas?

I use Hope, Arkansas, only as an example, just as in this book I focus on the Eastern Shore of Maryland, not because Hope or the Eastern Shore is particularly unique or because the men who were lynched and the others who were nearly lynched were extraordinary in any particular way. In fact, it is the ordinariness of the lynchings and near lynchings that makes them especially useful for this study. It is simply enough that those who were lynched on the Eastern Shore—Matthew Williams and George Armwood—and those who were nearly lynched—George Davis, Euel Lee, and Isaiah Fountain—were men, some with loving families, surrounded by a community of fellow blacks whose dreams and ambitions were undermined for decades by the threat of this most gruesome form of racial violence and that this pattern was repeated in hundreds of communities throughout the United States for seventy years.

The title of this book, *On the Courthouse Lawn,* is meant to invoke both the physical and the symbolic. It refers to the site where so many lynchings took place, both in Maryland and throughout the country. But it is also meant to belie the myth that lynching was a secret barbarity, unknown to a majority of the populace. Lynching was a public crime, in which hundreds and sometimes thousands of whites were complicit. And it is this characteristic of lynching that should compel us to face this American form of racial terrorism and to begin to assess the long-term effects of lynching on black and white communities.

This book proceeds in two parts. I first explore the history of lynchings and near lynchings on the Shore during the 1930s. Although some of these events have been recounted in local history books, their treatment has never given substantial attention to how the lynchings were experienced by the families of lynching victims and the black communities where they lived. I regard the contribution of this perspective as critical to an understanding of the long-term effects of lynching on the relationship between blacks and whites in towns where lynchings occurred. Moreover, no account of these events has linked the history of lynching to contemporary racial conflicts and to the current condition of white and black communities on the Shore.

The second part of the book draws on the larger international conversation about racial reconciliation to imagine how communities like those on the Shore might confront the history of lynching and find ways to ameliorate the effects of these devastating events on black and white communities. Again, while I apply these techniques to the communities beset by lynching on the Eastern Shore of Maryland, I do so only to ground the discussion in a specific context. Communities throughout the United States where nearly five thousand men, women, and boys were publicly hanged, burned, and tortured must each in turn confront their own history and take up the project of truth-telling and reconciliation.

Rather than just propose the concept, I suggest in this book *how* the reconciliation process I envision might unfold, drawing on restorative justice techniques in use from Australia to Baltimore. Finally, I invite communities to think creatively and pragmatically in the development of meaningful forms of reparation that respond to the particular and lingering effects of racial violence in their individual community.

Ultimately, this book is hopeful but pragmatic. It makes the case that the history of racial terrorism continues to shape the relationship between and among blacks and whites in communities all over this country. If we are honest, we know that it is this history—not that of affirmative action or busing—that lurks in the dim, gray area of distrust, fear, and resentment between and among blacks and whites. It is there—where overwhelming anger, insistent denial, shame, and guilt lie—there, where our reconciliation efforts must be targeted.

There is unfinished business in communities throughout this country, where the reality of lynching and racial pogroms has never been fully confronted, where the historical complicity of ordinary citizens in condoning racial terrorism continues to undermine the chance for trust and racial reconciliation, and where the participation of local institutions in upholding violent white supremacy continues to taint their legitimacy. I believe that communities can themselves take charge of the project of healing, reconciliation, and reparation. Some have already taken halting steps in this process in places like Duluth, Minnesota; Atlanta, Georgia; and Tulsa, Oklahoma. I discuss these efforts at the end of the book as well. These efforts should be supported by and shared with other communities that have yet to take the courageous and challenging step of unearthing the skeletons in their past. In this book I attempt to offer something of a road map or, maybe better, a menu of options from which communities can choose as they undertake this important task. I am aware that many communities will not accept this challenge. But others will, prodded along by activists, clergy, civic groups, and individuals—black and white—who want something more for their communities and their children than lives lived behind walls of racial silence. This book is meant for them.

PART I

A SEASON OF MADNESS: TWENTIETH-CENTURY LYNCHING ON THE EASTERN SHORE

CHAPTER I

A CONVERSATION ON RACE: LYNCHING AND THE COURTHOUSE LAWN

Driving or walking along the main road in downtown Easton, Maryland, it is clear that town planners put thought and creativity into this small city's central district. It is an inviting area, dominated by two-story eighteenth- and nineteenth-century brick buildings that house specialty stores, attractive pubs, and watering holes. Several restaurants in the district offer surprisingly urbane fare in well-appointed rooms, and the wait-staff and bartenders are friendly, professional, and welcoming. One feels at once a sense of history, the warmth of a small town, and a very deliberate touch of the modern and sophisticated. The window of Albright's gun shop on Washington Street features upscale outdoor wear and an advertisement for Caesar Guerini guns, billed as "fine Italian shotguns designed for the American shooter." It is all there in a five- or six-block radius—the library, the police station, the tourism office, the restaurants, and the historic Avalon Theatre. And like in small towns all over Eastern Shore, the county courthouse lies at its center.

The Talbot County Courthouse is an old, immaculately maintained red brick building with white-painted detailing. Modern renovations have connected the western wall of the courthouse to a large renovated brick and glass jail facility. Although the jail is more modern-looking than the courthouse to which it is appended, it stands slightly recessed from the front wall of the courthouse, and so manages not to distract from the quaint, historic appeal of the courthouse facade. On a sunny, temperate day, downtown Easton's charm is in full effect, and one can see in it a kind of model for other Eastern Shore towns that have tried, with considerably less success, to transform their fading and shabby downtown districts into charming tourist attractions.

But Easton is more like her sister towns on the Shore than her superior physical layout suggests. Indeed, during the first weeks of March 2004, Easton's physical charm was eclipsed by a fierce and ugly racial debate that, ironically, challenged the integrity of this town's appealing facade. At issue was, in essence, a struggle over the racial meaning and content of public space in downtown Easton. The controversy centered around a proposal to erect a statue of Frederick Douglass on the lawn of the County Courthouse. Douglass is Talbot County's most prestigious and perhaps only internationally known native son. Born as a slave in the county, Douglass went on to become the most dynamic antislavery advocate of the nineteenth century. In fact, it was Douglass's firsthand experience as a runaway slave and his description of the conditions of slavery on the Eastern Shore that helped make his voice a unique and personally compelling force for the freedom of enslaved blacks. As a young man, Douglass had been held in the jail next to the Talbot County Courthouse after his first and unsuccessful attempt to escape. During the week that he was held in the jail, white slave traders taunted him daily with the prospect of being sold to Georgia or, worse, Florida—a fate commonly understood to mean brutal conditions and an early death for a slave. But Douglass was not sold South. Instead, he was returned to Baltimore, where he had been enslaved years earlier. While working as a slave at the Baltimore shipyards, Douglass managed to escape—this time successfully—to New York. He became an author and a mesmerizing orator, speaking out against the injustice of slavery with a personal passion that more famous white abolitionists of the day could not match. Douglass became known all over the world and traveled throughout Europe, speaking against slavery. Once back in the United States, he remained an influential public figure for the abolitionist cause throughout the Civil War, advising President Lincoln and in his later life serving as U.S. marshal for the District of Columbia and as the U.S. minister to Haiti. Douglass may also have been the first black male feminist in public life, championing the cause of women's suffrage. He was the only man to speak in favor of women's suffrage at the first women's convention in Seneca Falls, New York, in 1848. Douglass returned to Talbot County in 1877 and delivered an address in the Talbot County Court-house, and several more times thereafter, for a reconciliatory meeting with his former slave master and with the sheriff of the jail. In all, Douglass remains one of the most respected figures in U.S. history. His home in Washington, D.C., where he lived for the last twenty years of his life, is now a museum, administered by the National Park Service. It sits on a hill in Anacostia, a black neighborhood, and boasts an extraordinary view of the Capitol Building. But in Talbot County, where Douglass lived for the first twenty years of his life and where he had been enslaved, there is no public monument commemorating his life or birthplace save for a plaque obscured by trees at the entrance of a small, thirty-foot bridge on the northern edge of the county, which describes Douglass as a "Negro Patriot."

Despite Douglass's extraordinary life and Talbot County roots, bitter factions erupted in the county along racial lines in support of and opposi-tion to honoring Douglass with a statue on the lawn of the courthouse.[1] A white veterans' group opposed the statue, citing a county "tradition" limit-ing monuments on the lawn of the courthouse only to veterans who "had given their lives for their country." Walter Black, president of the local NAACP chapter, and other black supporters of the Douglass monument derided this so-called tradition, which they contended no blacks had heard of until they attempted to erect a statue honoring Douglass.[2]

There are, in fact, only two monuments on the Talbot County Court-house lawn, and both honor veterans. The Vietnam Veterans memorial is not technically on the lawn of the courthouse but is positioned more accu-rately at the southeast corner of Dover and Washington Streets at the en-trance to the lawn of the courthouse. Made of granite, the two six-foot-tall rectangular panels of the monument list the names of soldiers from Talbot who died in that conflict between 1960 and 1973 and depicts a soldier as-sisting his wounded colleague as a helicopter (presumably a rescue chop-per) circles overhead. The second war memorial is located squarely on the east lawn, directly in front of the courthouse. Its position is prominent and unavoidable as one approaches the entrance. Thirteen feet high, it features the statue of a young boy holding a flag atop a granite monument that reads "To the Talbot Boys, 1861–1865, C.S.A." On the sides of the monument are etched the names of eighty-four men from Talbot County who during the Civil War joined the Confederate army and lost their lives. The "C.S.A." on the front of the granite base stands for Confederate States of America. Erected in 1913, when many leaders in the county were still Civil War veterans who'd served on one side or another of the conflict, the monument to the Talbot Boys in 2004 became a symbol to supporters of the Douglass monument that whites remained unwilling to face the county's past and to give public and tangible recognition in the county's public space to honor local black heroes.

Veterans' groups, dominated by whites and supported by several white County Council members, rejected the notion that the issue had any racial dimensions. "Skin color isn't an issue for veterans," one white local veterans' leader declared, ignoring the stunning irony of his statement in the context of the Confederate soldiers' monument.[3] Alternative sites for the placement of a Douglass memorial were bandied about. Some veterans expressed support for the monument if it were placed outside the library located behind the courthouse. County Councilman Thomas G. Duncan, in an emotional statement, charged that veterans were being disrespected by efforts to infringe on the "special place" traditionally reserved for their honor. The courthouse lawn itself was described in soaring terms by those opposing the Douglass monument as both "sacred" and "hallowed ground."

Arguments in favor of the Douglass monument were also passionately and forcefully advanced by African Americans. For them, the courthouse lawn indeed had tremendous symbolic significance as a place of prominence and of the very issues for which Douglass had fought during most of his life. As Moonyene Jackson-Amis, the only black member of the Easton town council and the energetic leader of what would become known as "Fred's Army," put it, "The courthouse stands for justice, equal justice."[4] An African American columnist writing in the *Baltimore Sun* challenged the veterans' arguments on its own terms. He contended that the white veterans' effort to limit the courthouse lawn to honoring war heroes as a basis for excluding a statue of Douglass highlighted the historical irony of racism. Douglass reportedly wanted to accept a commission to join the Union army, but he was prevented from doing so by the Lincoln administration because of fear of white reaction.[5] Now, 150 years later, white veterans were using Douglass's status as a nonveteran to keep his statue off the courthouse lawn. Moreover, Douglass had helped to recruit hundreds of black soldiers to serve in the Union army. Two of his sons served in the 54th Massachusetts Colored Infantry—the army unit depicted in the movie *Glory*.

For blacks in Talbot County, the fact that Confederate soldiers who had fought *against* their country on behalf of the seceded Confederacy of states are honored on the courthouse lawn seemed insult enough—an insult magnified by the fact that Maryland had never even been part of the Confederacy. Walter Black of the NAACP remarked, "Think about today if we had someone who fought against the U.S. government. They might be called terrorists now. But here we had the 'Talbot Boys.'"[6] As another black member of the coalition supporting the Douglass monument said of the Talbot Boys, "They certainly didn't fight for my freedom."[7]

What became known as the "courthouse incident" bitterly divided the community in Talbot. The County Council president Philip Carey Foster lamented, "This issue has so polarized our community that people are afraid to express an opinion for fear of being labeled a racist or unpatriotic. I can't think of a decision that has bothered me more or kept me awake more."[8] Another County Council person called the debate "the most emotional issue" she'd faced as a member of the council.[9] The county's NAACP chapter planned to lead a protest through downtown Easton if the council voted against the Douglass statue. For blacks in Talbot, the fact that the County Council that would decide this issue was all-white, and that it had never had a black member, now seemed a grim reminder of the consequences of minority underrepresentation in Talbot County government.

But lost in this controversy was the particular irony of the argument advanced by the white veterans' group and their supporters that the courthouse lawn was a "sacred" public space.[10] Indeed, those on both sides of the issue, white and black alike, seemed to accept the premise that the Talbot County Courthouse lawn is, as one white county councilman put it, "hallowed ground," reserved for the commemoration of great figures in local history.[11] In fact, the courthouse lawn in many Eastern Shore counties, including Talbot, has a more complex history than that suggested by the hyperbole of the veterans' groups. Between 1900 and 1935 courthouse lawns on the Eastern Shore were routinely the sites of lynchings or near lynchings, involving the participation of hundreds and sometimes thousands of white onlookers.

The most infamous of these courthouse lynchings were, of course, the Williams and Armwood lynchings of the early 1930s in Wicomico and Somerset Counties. Both men were dragged to the courthouse for all or part of the ritual surrounding their gruesome murders. But the courthouse as a site for lynchings on the Eastern Shore extended back into the late nineteenth century as well, including the lynchings of Isaac Kemp in Princess Anne in 1894 and Garfield King in Salisbury in 1898. That the courthouse was often located directly next to the jail from which lynching victims were often taken in part explains the site outside the courthouse as a frequent location for lynching. But as in the case of Matthew Williams, who was dragged three blocks from the hospital in Salisbury to the courthouse lawn in Wicomico County, lynchers often deliberately sought out the grounds outside the courthouse.

What in the early 1900s was often referred to in the local press as "lynch law" was often regarded by whites as just that—a form of law that had as much legitimacy as the formal, codified laws of the state's justice system. In fact, for many on the Shore who believed that the formal justice system was elitist and stacked against them, lynch law was *more* legitimate. Lynch law did not remove trials to a faraway venue to ensure an impartial jury, exclude confessions merely because the black suspect had been beaten by police, prolong investigation of a crime when everyone knew who'd done it, throw out convictions because blacks had been excluded from jury service, or permit appeals on technical grounds. Lynch law was uncompromising, and rather than being imposed by forces from without, it was managed and enforced by the community itself. Moreover, lynch law was swift—a quality that Shore residents appear to have held at a very high premium. References to the importance of "speedy" justice abounded in local papers during this period, although in many cases black men in the formal justice system were arrested, indicted, and convicted in less than two weeks when they were suspected of committing violent crimes against whites.

The courthouse lawn, therefore, was a very deliberate choice of venue for lynching. Lynch mobs used the location to assert what they regarded as a legitimate and necessary rebellion against the elitist trappings of the formal legal system. The hanging and charred black body on display outside the courthouse symbolized to the lynch mob and their supporters the independence of the local white community from the dictates of Annapolis and Baltimore. For rural whites, the battle for independence from the cultural norms of big cities might be a relic from the Civil War days, but in the early part of the twentieth century it still seemed worth fighting for.

Given this history, how would the debate about the Douglass statue have been transformed if the project's supporters had rejected outright the veterans' group's characterization of the courthouse lawn as "sacred" ground? What if supporters of the Douglass statue had argued that this characterization of the public space outside the courthouse reflected, as did the Talbot Boys monument, an unbroken tradition of white racial ownership of critical public spaces? Might the discussion about the Frederick Douglass statue have been transformed into a more productive, albeit still painful, dialogue about race, reparation, and the county's public spaces? And might this public dialogue have resonated with other counties on the Shore where black men were lynched on the courthouse lawn, but where similarly there are no markers, commemorative plaques, or other indications that this public space historically served as the locus for acts of racial exclusion and violence? Could the proposed Frederick Douglass monument in Talbot, with its undeniably powerful representation of black manhood, have constituted a form of reparation for the wound that lynching sought to inflict on black manhood and black citizenship on the Eastern Shore?

Although the history of lynching outside the courthouse never came up as part of the county's formal deliberations, elderly blacks talked about it among themselves and with members of the pro–Douglass monument coalition. They remembered hearing from their parents that a lynching, attended by hundreds of whites, had taken place on the courthouse lawn in the early part of the century. Certainly lynch mobs had converged on the courthouse lawn in Talbot several times during that period. But most elderly blacks were undoubtedly referring to the largest incident of mob violence in Talbot County's history—the near lynching of Isaiah Fountain. Fountain's lynching was narrowly averted, but the Talbot County Courthouse lawn was anything but "hallowed ground" on Easter Monday in 1919. On that evening, nearly two thousand whites assembled outside the

Talbot County Courthouse on the first day of Fountain's trial. A week earlier Fountain had been arrested and indicted for the rape of Bertha Simpson, a fourteen-year-old white girl. Simpson told police that as she walked home from high school along a road in Trappe, Maryland, a black man in a buggy overtook her and forced her to get in the buggy with him. She alleged that the man threatened her and raped her. A local doctor confirmed that Simpson had been raped.

The Isaiah Fountain case was one of the most notorious on the Shore during the early part of the twentieth century, and it threw Talbot County into the state spotlight. The case was remarkable for several reasons. First, Fountain was no cowering, timid farmhand. He hired himself to work on white-owned farms, yes, but he also owned a small farm himself, a horse, some livestock, and a buggy, which would figure prominently in questions about whether young Bertha Simpson had identified the right man. Fountain contended that he was not even on the Shore on the day of the attack on Simpson but had gone to look for his wife in New Jersey. He maintained his innocence at his trial and by all accounts was a forceful presence on his own behalf in the courtroom. His testimony was not shaken on cross-examination.[12] But as it was during the Jim Crow era, Fountain's self-possession probably worked against him with the all-white jury, and certainly with the townspeople of Easton. Those who were able to get in to observe the proceedings on the first day of trial reported back to their neighbors who were milling about on the courthouse lawn that Fountain displayed an "arrogant and sarcastic attitude." He appeared to participate actively in his own defense, making suggestions to his counsel as they questioned witnesses.[13] These reports probably stoked the ugly mood of the crowd outside the courthouse. To the whites in attendance, Fountain's demeanor suggested not only that he was unrepentant for a crime the town had already determined he was guilty of but, even worse, that Fountain was neither overwhelmed nor intimidated by the proceedings, which would most certainly end in a conviction and death sentence. As one reporter remarked, "Nothing seemed to ruffle him in the least."[14] This stance of control and poise, at a time when Fountain had to have known that his life hung in the balance, challenged Easton whites. Fountain did not play the role of the frightened black defendant in a script that was familiar to whites during this period. Thus the satisfaction and sense of power that whites might have drawn from the trial were undermined by Fountain's unwillingness to play along.

Perhaps whites even suspected that Fountain's demeanor reflected something more offensive to them than a guilty man's arrogance. Fountain refused to conceal his contempt for what was an elaborate, but ultimately empty, proceeding. The outcome, whatever the testimony or evidence presented, as everyone knew, was preordained. The "sarcastic smile" that observers insisted "was seen on [Fountain's] face most of the time"[15] probably reflected his response to what was, for all intents and purposes, an elaborate show trial. Fountain's stance was one of emotional detachment from a proceeding in which he had no power, no real voice, and for which he had little respect. Thus even after the guilty verdict was announced, white-owned papers reported that Fountain's "pose of indifference was maintained."[16]

Simpson's identification of Fountain as her attacker was so filled with contradictions that it would not stand up in court today, or perhaps even in 1919, but for the fact that Fountain was black. Simpson initially described her attacker as having a mustache, which Fountain did not have. She told police that the buggy that the assailant was driving was new. Fountain drove a ramshackle old buggy.[17] In fact, when Simpson was taken by the local sheriff to look at different buggies in an attempt to identify the one driven by her assailant, she initially pointed to the buggy of another black man, named Andrew Mills. Mills reportedly had lent his buggy to yet another man, named Richard Wells, on the afternoon of the attack. Wells was never arrested, according to the sheriff, because "the popular clamor was for Fountain."[18] Wells left town the next day and did not return until Fountain's trial and conviction. Fountain's lawyer suggested that Ben Butler, the state's attorney (local prosecutor), prevented the sheriff from following these and other leads that might have turned up another suspect. In fact, State's Attorney Butler refused to permit Sheriff Stichberry or anyone but himself to be present when Simpson allegedly identified Fountain as her attacker, in Butler's private office at his home.[19] Sheriff Stichberry, who had been in charge of the criminal investigation of the case, was never even called by Butler to testify at trial, an extraordinary departure from routine criminal-prosecution trial practice.[20] Fountain reportedly told black reporters of the *Afro-American* that he had a history with the white state's attorney, who months earlier had threatened to "get" Fountain after he was released from serving a one-year term for driving an unshod horse.[21]

Fountain's case was also extraordinary because Fountain refused to be lynched. When he exited the courthouse on the evening of April 21, a large angry crowd of nearly two thousand whites had assembled on the lawn, swarming around the then six-year-old statue of the Talbot Boys. Some in the crowd showed that they had ropes. Others had knives. Stichberry kept Fountain close to him as he pushed his way through the crowd to lead Fountain to the jail next door. As the sheriff and Fountain reached the jail, the crowd began to press forward. Several reached out to grab Fountain. The sheriff quickly ordered his deputy to bring Fountain into the jail while the sheriff attempted to negotiate with the crowd. The deputy pushed Fountain into the jail and returned, perhaps to the door, to provide backup for Sheriff Stichberry. Fountain, apparently lacking confidence in the sheriff's crowd-control skills, squeezed his way through the small window of an office at the back of the jail and ran for his life. The local judge and sheriff organized a massive manhunt, deputizing 250 local men to find Fountain. Most were hunters, and the thrill of the hunt was on full display. The newly deputized men were given a small red ribbon to affix to their lapels, denoting their importance and license to hunt down Fountain. The local newspaper, the *Easton Star-Democrat,* published the names of those who were deputized in a glowing article describing the hunters' bravery and sense of civic duty. The paper was careful to note, after listing the names of all of the deputized men, that "two colored men volunteered also."[22]

Knowing and seeking to avert the likely outcome of 248 armed white men hunting for a black man accused of raping a white girl in Talbot County, Judge William Adkins, the presiding judge in the case, offered $5,000, a king's ransom in 1919, as a reward for Fountain's safe return.[23] The search for Fountain must have been like something out of a Hollywood movie. Roadblocks were set up; teams of bloodhounds led parties of men through the woods on Fountain's trail. The hunters increased the level of excitement by spreading the rumor that Fountain was "bristling with artillery,"[24] although there was no suggestion as to how he could have obtained firearms during his flight, nor was there evidence that Fountain was inclined to be homicidal. Nevertheless, local deputized men brandished whatever weapons were available to them, imagining, perhaps with a small thrill, that they would be in mortal peril were they to meet up with Fountain.

Life came to a virtual standstill in Talbot as all of the county's excitement and focus were directed toward the search for Fountain. Little is known about what these days were like for the black community in Talbot, but it is not hard to imagine. White hunters stopped every car traveling in the county and drew their pistols and rifles whenever a black man was inside. Two and a half days later, Fountain was found hiding in a barn on a farm in Delaware, unarmed, hungry, and exhausted.[25] Judge Adkins's decision to announce a sizable reward for the return of Fountain may have saved Fountain's life. He was returned to Easton to complete the trial.[26] The reward money was split among eight men.

Governor Evan Harrington insisted that a battalion of the state militia be sent to Easton to ensure that the trial would be conducted without interference from the mob. He called Judge Adkins and informed him that troops would arrive later that evening. What Talbot Countians would have perceived as an "invasion" by state police might well have set off violent resistance among local residents, who by this time were hypersensitive to the negative depiction of their county in Baltimore papers over the Fountain case. But Adkins, a popular local figure, deftly managed the presentation of the governor's order to the townspeople. Assembling the 250 or so men who'd been deputized during the search for Fountain, he asked that they "give approval to the Governor's wish" that state militia troops be deployed in Easton to secure Fountain's safety.[27] Adkins characterized the "Governor's wish" not as "a reflection on the citizenry of the county, but [as] the intention of...preventing ruffianism on the part of *other than* Talbot countians."[28] Adkins's effort to placate the townspeople worked, and "permission" was given to bring in outside officers. The state militiamen arrived in the predawn hours of the following day and were stationed at all entrances to the courthouse and jail with drawn bayonets.[29] The militiamen were augmented by twenty-five members of the Baltimore Police force. No one, except Fountain, the attorneys, the jurors, and those having business with the court, was permitted to enter the courthouse.

Isaiah Fountain's trial resumed the next day. Bertha Simpson arrived to testify in a wheelchair. The jurors returned a verdict of guilty after five minutes of deliberation.[30] Judge William Adkins sentenced Fountain to death by hanging.

In 1919, on the Eastern Shore of Maryland (and perhaps in most places in the United States), the fate of a black man would, by this point, have been sealed. But unlike other black men accused of raping white women during this period, who often survived being hung by a mob only long enough to be hung on the gallows by the state, Fountain's court-appointed attorney was a brilliant Baltimore lawyer who had made a name for himself by challenging injustice. Eugene O'Dunne had run unsuccessfully for the district attorney's office in Baltimore City but was best known for heading up a commission appointed to investigate conditions at the Baltimore City penitentiary. His 1912 report to the governor exposed inhumane conditions at the jail including torturous punishments, unsanitary living quarters, inedible food, and a complex system of graft and corruption organized by the warden.[31] O'Dunne raised arguments that few white lawyers were willing to make on behalf of black defendants in those days. He challenged the venue of the trial and in essence argued that the local prosecutor had improperly influenced the victim's identification of the buggy driven by the man who overpowered her. Even more impressively, O'Dunne argued on appeal after Fountain's conviction that Fountain had not received a fair trial before an impartial tribunal as guaranteed under the Constitution because of the atmosphere of mob violence that had pervaded the trial.[32] The judges of the Maryland Court of Appeals agreed with O'Dunne's argument.

According to the court, the mob that gathered on what would eighty-five years later be referred to as the "hallowed grounds" of the Talbot County Courthouse lawn tried to "take [Fountain] from the custody of the officers of the law and lynch him, this purpose being openly declared by members of the crowd, some of whom were armed with various weapons and provided with ropes."[33] As a result, the court found that the impartiality of the jury had been unalterably tainted. The court found it "difficult to imagine that the jurors could have remained in ignorance of the presence, temper and conduct of the crowd on the Court House grounds through which they passed repeatedly on their way to and from sessions of the Court."[34] The record also showed, the court noted, that the jurors were "informed of the flight of the prisoner to escape the violence of the crowd" and heard the court "offer... a reward of $5,000 for [Fountain's] recapture and safe return" and suggest to the sheriff that local men be deputized to find Fountain. Based on all of this evidence, the court concluded that "[t]he conditions under which the appellant was tried were such as to make it almost impossible for the issue upon which [Fountain's] life depended to be impartially considered and decided by the jury."[35]

Local newspapers nevertheless blamed the Court of Appeals' decision on the influence of big-city newspapers in Baltimore, which had carried stories of Fountain's near lynching and escape on their front pages. Despite the record in the case and the Court of Appeals' findings, the local *Easton Star-Democrat* insisted that "at no time was Isaiah Fountain in danger at the hand of the people of Talbot County. At no time has there been an armed mob about the court-house." Earlier editions of the paper conceded that there had been a mob, but a "foreign mob," which had come "from outside the borders of the county."[36]

Fountain was granted a new trial. The venue of the trial was moved to Towson, Maryland, in Baltimore County. There, he was convicted a second time and sentenced to die. Fountain maintained his innocence throughout the period he spent on death row, and when his execution date approached, he insisted that he be executed wearing a purple robe and crown, to analogize his innocence to that of Jesus Christ.[37] In a last desperate attempt to retain control over his fate, Fountain tried first to hang himself and then to slash his own throat two hours before his execution. His suicide attempt was thwarted by prison guards.[38] Fountain was hung on a gallows in the Talbot County jail on July 23, 1920, the jail where Frederick Douglass had been held eighty-three years earlier as a runaway slave. On the night before his execution, a crowd of three hundred to four hundred men again assembled on the courthouse lawn and made their way to the jail. Some used a log as a battering ram and unsuccessfully attempted to storm the jail to get at Fountain.[39] By the day of his execution, Fountain had no property to leave to his absent wife. Eugene O'Dunne had not taken the Fountain case on a pro bono basis. Fountain's farm and other possessions had been sold to pay O'Dunne's fees and expenses.[40]

TRUTH, REPARATION, AND PUBLIC SPACES

The story of Isaiah Fountain's desperate escape from the Talbot County mob that gathered to lynch him on Easter Monday 1919 never made it into the divisive discussion on whether a statue of Frederick Douglass should be placed on the courthouse lawn. Instead, after two heated public hearings, the County Council divided 3–2 in favor of the monument, and plans are moving apace to have the Douglass monument built and unveiled by 2007. Resentment, expressed covertly and passive aggressively—in controversies over the height of the monument (not to be taller than the Talbot Boys monument), over the selection of the artist, and over other details associated with the project—lingers. But the public debate has ended. And yet, what have the residents of Talbot learned from this debate about their pretty little town? Are the tensions that exploded over the Douglass monument merely lying dormant until a future effort to honor African American history is proposed for a prominent location in the town?

Public spaces have yet to become part of the formal reparation or racial-reconciliation conversation for black Americans. It is a curious omission because in towns all over the United States, and not only on the Eastern Shore, public spaces were used to enforce the message of white supremacy, often violently. Lynching, particularly in the twentieth century, was most often an explicitly public act. The examples of this practice are legion: the hanging of four blacks from the Moore's Ford Bridge in Georgia in 1946;[41] the lynching of Anthony Crawford outside the fairgrounds in Abbeville, South Carolina, in 1916 after he was first paraded through town with a noose about his neck;[42] the hanging of three black men from a downtown lamppost in Duluth, Minnesota, in 1920;[43] the burning of Will Turner in a city park in Helena, Arkansas, in 1921;[44] the hanging of a black janitor by University of Missouri students from a bridge in Columbia, Missouri, in 1923;[45] the hanging of a black man from an oak tree in the public square in Bastrop, Louisiana, in 1934.[46] All of these incidents—and they represent only a fraction of the thousands of other such lynchings —are examples of the intensely *public* nature of lynching. Even those who did not attend lynchings, as most blacks in a community most assuredly did not, were compelled to witness the results. Lynch mobs routinely dragged the bodies of their victims to the black section of town to terrorize the black community. The gruesome and mutilated black body was meant to convey a message, and the public display of that body in a public space, sometimes for hours or days, was the means by which whites let blacks and other whites know that white supremacy would be protected in that jurisdiction at all costs. White Southern writer Ellen Douglas, in her revealing memoir, *Truth: Four Stories I Am Finally Old Enough to Tell*, describes her mother's horrified reaction when in 1922, driving for the first time into Hope, Arkansas, where the family would live for many years, they saw the body of a lynching victim hanging from the town's water tower.[47]

Compelling communities to recognize the public nature of lynching serves a vital purpose. Communities, in order to forthrightly address the reality of lynching, must be prepared to recognize and grapple with the role of ordinary members of the community in supporting or condoning this act of racial terrorism. Most lynchings were not secret murders carried out in the woods without the knowledge of white community members. The central location of lynching and the role of hundreds or thousands of white spectators undermine the desperate effort of some to recast lynching as a covert act carried out by a few bad apples, ruffians, or out-of-towners. Instead, the responsibility for lynching sits squarely at the door of every member of a community who watched, who listened, but who failed to interfere, who refused to identify the lynchers, or who participated in the conspiracy of silence in the weeks, months, and years following a lynching. As historian W. Fitzhugh Brundage has remarked, although "some spectators may have been shocked and disgusted by the violence they witnessed … it was their visible, explicit, public act of participation and not their ambiguous, private sentiment that bound the lynchers both socially and morally."[48]

Several years ago, on a trip to the Sachsenhausen concentration camp in Germany, this point was powerfully brought home. Sachsenhausen is located in what later became East Berlin but which is now just a district on the far eastern edge of the city. After the fall of the Berlin Wall, it became possible for Westerners to visit this former concentration camp where political prisoners, homosexuals, Jews, and other identified enemies of the Nazi state were imprisoned and killed. The S-Bahn stop leaves visitors about one and a half miles from the camp, and the walk there on a warm day seems long and dusty. I remember remarking to my husband, "In America, some enterprising person would have come up with a minibus or van service to the camp." But the longer I walked, the more it became clear why in America our insight often falls victim to eager entrepreneurship. The route to Sachsenhausen meandered through a residential district, on sidewalks past ordinary homes, quaint pubs, and buildings that had clearly survived the war. And it occurred to me: this is the same walk that the prisoners took once they left the train. They too had to walk through the town to make it to the camp. The prisoners must have been tired, bedraggled, and frightened. But more important, they must have been *seen*, seen by the townspeople, the shop owners, and the local merchants. Seen by mothers with their babies, boys on bicycles, and old men smoking pipes on the street. Herein lay the value of the long, dusty, meandering walk to the camp. Perhaps on purpose, or perhaps just because a population as used to walking as Germans are would find it impractical to run a bus line for such a relatively short distance, those in charge of opening the Sachsenhausen camp as a museum and commemorative space had compelled visitors to absorb its most important lesson before ever setting foot on the grounds of the camp. Sachsenhausen did not exist as a secret. Perhaps residents of the town did not know all of the details of what took place in the camp, but they knew enough, and they did very little. Likewise, acknowledging lynching in key public spaces in towns throughout the United States would compel townspeople and visitors to reflect on the complicity of ordinary people in systematic violence.

Some communities where public lynchings occurred have begun to organize projects designed to create commemorative public spaces as part of a reconciliation process. In Duluth, Minnesota, after months of marches and community conversations, a group of black activists in 2002, supported by hundreds of community members, created a commemorative monument at the site where three young men were lynched before a crowd of ten thousand whites in 1920.[49] Even in Maryland's state capital of Annapolis, a plaque was commissioned for the place on St. John's College where Henry Davis was lynched in 1906. Also in Annapolis, a plaque was erected over the gravestone of John Snowden, a black man executed in 1919—a few months before the trial of Isaiah Fountain—for the murder of a pregnant white woman. In the black community, the belief in Snowden's innocence has passed down through several generations. His death was widely regarded as a "legal lynching," and members of Snowden's family had sought a gubernatorial pardon for nearly twenty years. After reviewing the records of the case, in 2000 Governor Parris Glendening granted a posthumous pardon to Snowden.[50]

Perhaps the most intriguing and comprehensive approach to integrating public spaces into reconciliation efforts is taking place in South Africa. Government-sponsored Legacy Projects are designed to address in a deliberate, thoughtful, and systematic way Afrikaners' historical use of public monuments to reinforce the white supremacist message of apartheid. The projects, which are developed by the Department of Arts, Culture, Science and Technology, are designed to erect monuments and set aside commemorative public spaces that "acknowledge the previously neglected, marginalized and distorted South African heritage."[51]

In 1998, for example, black South African leaders participated in a ceremony in Durban for the inauguration of a new monument to commemorate the loss of three thousand Zulus in the Battle of Blood River, one of the fiercest military battles between black and white colonial powers in the history of that nation. To commemorate their victory at the 1838 battle, Afrikaners erected a bronze monument on the site where the battle took place in KwaZulu-Natal. For Zulus, the Battle of Blood River is no less significant. It represents the important role of the fiercely proud and unrelenting Zulu nation in attempting to hold on to its freedom and land in nineteenth-century South Africa. Then-deputy president Mbeki explained that the two monuments would "help reconcile conflicting historical interpretations" of the Battle of Blood River by "commemorating the participation of both sides."

The Legacy Projects also recognize that in a country with such a long and intense history of racial oppression, there is very little consensus among blacks and whites about historical events. An event such as Blood River, regarded by Afrikaners as a great victory for pioneering Afrikaner forces, is for Zulus the ground upon which the blood of three thousand of their tribesmen was shed in the defense of their land. Because oppressed and marginalized racial or ethnic groups are often ignored in the official history written by those in power, Legacy Projects can help give voice to the untold stories of the oppressed.

A particularly compelling example of the potential of these projects to help blacks share in the official record of history is the planned recognition of black African casualties of the Boer War, regarded by Afrikaners as a seminal event in their battle to defeat British colonial forces for control of the territory of South Africa. The particularly vicious fighting that oc-

curred during this turn-of-the-century war has defined the relationship and traditional enmity between Dutch-descended Afrikaners and
British-descended white South Africans. But as many blacks point out,
twenty thousand black African lives were lost during the Boer War. For
the Afrikaners and the British, the loss of African life in the Boer War has
been a mere footnote to what they regard as the larger and more significant
conflict between the two battling white colonial forces.

Legacy Projects and other reconciliation efforts directed at creating a
shared ownership of historically significant public spaces are not without
controversy. When few Afrikaners attended the ceremony unveiling the
new monument at Blood River, both Thabo Mbeki, then the deputy president, and Chief Mangosuthu Buthelezi of the Zulu tribe expressed disappointment at the lost opportunity for reconciliation. Rather than viewing
Legacy Projects as sharing historically significant public spaces, many
Afrikaners regard these efforts as a "takeover" or displacement of white
history. Likewise, many whites in Talbot County viewed the plans to create a memorial to Frederick Douglass as a threat to their conception of the
courthouse lawn as a "sacred" space set aside to honor white war heroes.

A Legacy Project focused on recognizing the history of lynching in
public spaces on the Eastern Shore would powerfully reclaim the public
space for the shared history of blacks and whites in the region, and it would
represent a commitment to honestly facing the region's complex and disturbing racial history. Such an effort would be particularly compelling
on the Shore because lynch mobs claimed so many of the region's public
spaces during the first third of the twentieth century. Yet that history is
masked by white ownership of the terms in which public space is defined
and developed.

In the fall of 2003, the *Baltimore Sun,* in its Sunday travel section,
published an article that described a number of Eastern Shore towns as
new real estate venues.[52] The towns listed, Trappe, Princess Anne, Berlin,
Crisfield, and Denton, were each in turn seeking to build their population
base by developing new homes and commercial property. Given the proximity of these communities to Ocean City and the popularity of water-
front retirement or second homes, the plans to jump-start the economy of
these towns seemed promising indeed. Yet the reputation of these towns
may sound a caution to some blacks in the state who might otherwise take

advantage of these lucrative new housing opportunities. Princess Anne and Crisfield were the sites of well-known lynchings in 1933 and 1907. Trappe, the town where little Bertha Simpson was attacked by a man she claimed was Isaiah Fountain, was also the town from which masked men came to Salisbury to lynch Garfield King in 1894. Berlin is the town where marauding mobs went looking for Euel Lee after the murder of the Green K. Davis family in 1930, and where in the days and weeks after those murders blacks were warned to stay off the street as bands of whites beat, chased, and assaulted black men and women.[53] And Princess Anne, of course, is the site of the George Armwood lynching, where perhaps two thousand spectators watched and many cheered the public mutilation, hanging, and burning of a black man in 1933. None of these towns bears in its public space tangible evidence that it has acknowledged and come to terms with its racially violent history. The assumption of most whites is that this history is dead, unimportant, and irrelevant to the modern reality of life on the Eastern Shore. But in fact a town's reputation as a racially violent one often lives on in the lore shared among blacks. Despite the many trips I've made to the Shore, blacks in other parts of the state routinely warn me to be particularly careful once I cross the Bay Bridge.

Decisions about where to look for a new home, where to stop late at night for gas or for a bite to eat, and where to send one's children to school are often informed by a town's historic reputation for racial violence passed down from generation to generation. The details may become lost in the telling, but the sentiment is often surprisingly intense and unchanged. But in avoiding these towns and communities, blacks may unwittingly cede to whites continued control and ownership of what may be a desirable real estate opportunity, the best schools, or just the closest gas station. And whites, unwittingly as well, may perpetuate a kind of segregation that is carried with a town's historical reputation for racial violence.

A white community's willingness to forthrightly address its history of racial violence through public plaques or markers recognizing the significance of these events is vital. More important is an opportunity for blacks to play an equal role in defining and developing the community's public spaces in ways that honestly reflect the town's history. A project that sought to reimagine public space in the context of racial reconciliation and reparation would ask: how can the community—black and white—deliberately break historical patterns of white supremacist ownership of public space? The Talbot County "courthouse incident" presented just such an opportunity. Most residents on both sides of the Douglass monument issue accepted unthinkingly the "sacred" nature of the courthouse square. Little thought was given and certainly no discussion was aired about how the community might come to a consensus about which public spaces are sacred and what the content of those sacred spaces should be. Had they done so, the attempt to lynch Isaiah Fountain and others on the courthouse lawn would have been an important and relevant part of this discussion. The Douglass monument might have been explicitly recognized as a form of reparation for the violent historical use by whites of the grounds surrounding the courthouse. The fact that Douglass became a passionate antilynching activist in the last two years of his life, publishing several pamphlets on the subject and supporting the work of antilynching journalist Ida B. Wells-Barnett, would have positioned the proposed monument honoring him as an essential way to confront the county's shameful history of racial terrorism, rather than as a kind of racial balance to the Talbot Boys monument. In fact, the legitimacy of the Talbot Boys monument on that space might itself have become the subject of discussion and review.

Much of white supremacy is about the semiotics of place. In fact, "staying in one's place" was, for decades, a kind of mannerly way of describing the crude requirements of white supremacy. During the Jim Crow era, the "place" for blacks was understood to be below, behind, after, and under that of whites. Efforts by blacks to vote, to attend white schools, to use facilities designated for whites by law or custom, were all deemed to violate the boundaries of racial place. But the connection between white supremacy and "place" is not just metaphysical. In the contemporary physical landscape, continued white control of the terms in which public space in multiracial communities is defined and developed is a vestige of white supremacist notions of racial place. When some veterans in Talbot County suggested that the Douglass statue be erected on the lawn of the Easton Library located *behind* the courthouse, or alternatively at the library in the neighboring town of St. Michaels, located ironically on *Back* Street, blacks demanded a different place: front and center, in the heart of the charming little town of Easton, outside the town's most important building. The battle for the Douglass statue has been won, although "Fred's Army" is still faced with the daunting task of raising hundreds of thousands of dollars for the development of the project. But there is a larger battle, a more ambitious one, which has yet to be engaged in in the town of Easton and in towns throughout this country. That battle is really a challenge—a challenge to each community to do the hard work of healing the public space, of repairing the wounds of white supremacy that still stand open and untreated on the prettiest street in town.

Nowhere is the challenge of confronting the past greatest than in those Shore counties where lynching occurred. The last of the Shore lynchings —indeed, the last recorded lynchings in Maryland—were of Matthew Williams and George Armwood, who were lynched in 1931 and 1933 in Wicomic and Somerset Counties, respectively. I now turn to those lynchings and to the effect of the lynchings on the communities where they occurred. The brutality of the lynchings, the terror visited on the black community, and the widespread complicity of hundreds and perhaps thousands of whites in condoning this form of racial terrorism illustrate the enormous but compelling need for a truth and reconciliation process.

The courthouse lawn outside the Talbot County Courthouse, where some residents seek to erect a statue of Frederick Douglass. The monument to the Talbot Boys is in the foreground.

CHAPTER 2

MOB RULE ON THE SHORE, 1931–1933

Although Maryland has a geographically diverse lynching record, with lynchings recorded in thirteen of the state's twenty-five counties, the Eastern Shore has per capita been the site of a disproportionate share of the state's lynchings. Somerset County has led the state in the number of lynchings. Of the seven recorded lynchings on the Eastern Shore, four took place in Somerset County. Wicomico County follows, with two recorded lynchings. Most of the Shore lynchings—and indeed most of the lynchings in the state—took place in the last twenty years of the nineteenth century. But by the early 1930s conditions were ripe again for lynchings on the Shore.

Where matters of race were concerned, the Eastern Shore of Maryland was not, in 1931, very different from the rest of the South. "The Shore," as the region is known in Maryland, had long been regarded by those living on the western side of the Chesapeake Bay as having more in common with southern states like Virginia than with Baltimore, the state's most populous city. Stretching across 130 miles from north to south and sharing borders with both Delaware and Virginia, Maryland's Eastern Shore lies between the Chesapeake Bay on its western border and the Atlantic Ocean on its eastern border. The counties that make up the Shore, because of their proximity to and reliance on the bay, have long been united in a unique culture that for some time developed in virtual isolation from the rest of the state. Before 1956, when a suspension bridge was built to connect the Shore to Maryland's capital city of Annapolis, the trip from the Shore to Baltimore was a long drive north into Delaware and then west and south, or by ferry across the choppy, cold bay waters. As a result, Maryland Shore residents often felt themselves to have more in common with residents of Virginia and Delaware, who lived only a stone's throw away. When the region faced daily criticism in the Baltimore, Washington, D.C., and Philadelphia press following the Armwood lynching in 1933, the suggestion was circulated among Shoremen, and taken quite seriously by some, that the Shore should secede from Maryland and join with the other regions of the Shore to create the new state of Delmarva, the name given to the peninsula where Delaware, Maryland, and Virginia meet.

The rest of Maryland, by contrast, or the Western Shore, as Eastern Shore folks call it, has long had an uneasy and uncertain sense of where it lies on the all-important north-south divide. Many Marylanders, particularly those in Baltimore, felt more kinship with the interests of Philadelphia and Washington, D.C. (the latter having its own conflicted southern identity). Maryland was never a member of the Confederacy, but that may be only because President Lincoln sent forces into Maryland early to quell its rising Confederate sympathies in 1861. Certainly, Maryland was a slave state. The Fells Point neighborhood at the Baltimore Harbor boasted one of the biggest and most lucrative slave-selling markets in the Southeast. And the two most famous former slaves in U.S. history, Frederick Douglass and Harriet Tubman, were both enslaved on the Eastern Shore of Maryland. For most of the last 150 years, Maryland has been characterized by a kind of racial schizophrenia. It is a state capable of at once launching a Thurgood Marshall, the great civil rights litigator and Supreme Court justice, and a Spiro Agnew, the governor and later vice president known for his race-baiting oratory; birthing a Frederick Douglass, the escaped slave who become the most brilliant and compelling antislavery orator and author of the nineteenth century, and a Roger Taney, the chief justice of the U.S. Supreme Court who wrote the infamous 1850 decision in *Dred Scott v. Sandford,* declaring that blacks "had no rights that the white man was bound to respect." Maryland was the laboratory for some of the NAACP's early litigation victories challenging the doctrine of separate but equal in education and the site of some of the fiercest white response to civil rights protests in the 1960s. It was the first state to pass a law outlawing interracial marriage and miscegenation in the 1700s, and its courts were the first to order integration of its flagship state law school in 1937.

Despite these contrasts, Maryland has largely enjoyed the reputation of being a progressive state. The 1930s were no exception. The governor of the state, Albert Ritchie, was considered a star of the Democratic Party and a likely presidential candidate. His response to the Eastern Shore lynchings ended his chance at the presidency, however, and by 1934 his political career was over.

Common to all residents of the Shore, whether from Maryland, Virginia, or Delaware, was the centrality of the bay to their livelihood. Oystermen, crab pickers, watermen, and scores of businesses were dependent on the Chesapeake Bay and its tributaries. The sense of solidarity between residents of this region was unusually strong. With their livelihood dependent on a common natural resource, Shore residents believed in literal terms that their boats rose or fell together. This perhaps explains why when Matthew Williams was lynched in 1931 and George Armwood in 1933, Shore residents closed ranks against criticism aimed at them from all over the country.

The geographic isolation of the Shore had unfortunate consequences for blacks, who constituted 15 percent of the Shore's population in 1931. Across the bay, Thurgood Marshall was headed off from Baltimore to law school at Howard University in Washington, D.C. The *Afro-American*, owned by John Murphy, was an influential weekly black paper. "The *Afro*," as it was known, chronicled the lives of black debutantes and college students at Morgan State and Hampton Universities and reported on the leaders of local fraternal lodges and meetings of preachers and bishops in the African Methodist Episcopal Church. Even divorce and seduction scandals reported in the *Afro* gave the impression that blacks were living lives as exciting and complex as those of whites. Frederick Douglass High School, one of only two black high schools in Baltimore, was regarded as a premier educational institution, whose students put on yearly plays such as *Sleeping Beauty*, performed entirely in French.[1] The Baltimore chapter of the NAACP through the 1930s and 1940s was the prime engine pushing the NAACP's antisegregation litigation offensive. Headed by the indomitable Lillie Carroll Jackson, the only woman, it was later said, who could scold Thurgood Marshall about his drinking and smoking habits, the Baltimore chapter became, through the 1930s and the 1940s, the crucible in which many of the organization's early civil rights litigation victories were nurtured. Jackson's daughter Juanita Jackson returned to Baltimore from college in Philadelphia just before lynching fever took hold of the Shore. Young Juanita Jackson's activism as a founder of the Baltimore City-Wide Young People's Forum would lead her in 1934 to testify before Congress in favor of a federal antilynching bill. Walter White, the then-president of the NAACP, enjoyed a cordial and familiar relationship with the Democratic governor of Maryland, Albert Ritchie. In sum, although Baltimore was still deeply segregated, and many blacks lived at or below the poverty line, a vibrant black middle-class community and a sense of black progress thrived in the heart of the city. Things could not have been more different on the Eastern Shore.

There, rigidly enforced Jim Crow laws and practices relegated most blacks to servile positions with low wages. Most were either laborers or domestics. An extremely small middle class existed, composed of teachers, doctors, and small business men who served the black community. But even those who were poor enjoyed the benefits of a close-knit community that looked after its own. Black children were provided with a sense of security and remained largely insulated from the difficulties of life under Jim Crow. Progress for blacks on the Shore was slow, and when it came it was not the result of boycotts, sit-ins, or overt activism. Determined residents fought within the system, finding what inroads they could to advance the lives of their children. Adele Holden recounts in her memoir, *Down on the Shore*, the dogged determination of her father, Snow Holden, an auto mechanic, to create an opportunity for blacks to go to high school in Worcester County in the late 1930s. In nearby Salisbury, Maryland educator Dr. Charles Chipman worked for years to build a new high school for black students. The building of the new Salisbury high school is one of the great stories of black determination in the years before favorable Supreme Court decisions and the aggressive activism of the civil rights movement. The land for the school was purchased by the African American community in 1930, after a decade of raising money through bake sales, musical productions, and church offerings.[2] Accumulating $25,000, the community, after purchasing the land, deeded it to the County Board of Education with the caveat that the property be used only

for the "public education of the African Race of Wicomico County, Maryland." The school opened to great fanfare as a thirteen-classroom high
school on Lake Street in Salisbury in 1930. Elzey Brown, who lived in
rural Wicomico County, voluntarily operated a bus service to bring students from the outlying areas of the county to the high school. Dr. Chipman, who had been trained at Howard University and the University of
Chicago and had come to Salisbury as an educator in 1919, coordinated the
purchase and development of the land for the school. Chipman ultimately
served for forty-six years as the elementary and high school principal in
Salisbury.

Not all efforts by Shore blacks to improve their condition were non-
confrontational. In September 1931, after their wages were lowered from
thirty-five cents to twenty-five cents a gallon, black women in the crab-
picking industry went on strike in the town of Crisfield in Somerset
County.[3] Their action suspended sales of crab and crippled the town's most
important industry. This aggressive stance by black women laborers no
doubt alarmed the white population. Local papers reported that the strik-
ers visited several plants where wages had been similarly dropped and
encouraged their workers to strike as well. Whites were surprised by the
direct nature of this action by black workers. Their failure to credit the
willingness of Shore blacks to fight for better conditions no doubt contributed to the ease with which some whites were willing to believe rumors
of "Communist infiltration" of black communities on the lower Eastern
Shore and to submit to fears of a potential "black uprising" after the lynching of Matt Williams in December of that year.

These actions by black residents to obtain better working conditions
and access to education were exceptions to the prevailing reality for blacks
on the Shore in the 1930s. The rule was a rigid system of Jim Crow, in
which whites effectively maintained rigid control of the parameters of
black economic, political, and educational progress.

The Depression fell hard on the Eastern Shore, a region already marked
by poverty and limited opportunities for economic advancement. These
were, after all, what historian T. H. Watkins has called the "the hungry
years," when destitute families were broken by poverty, when in the cities
the homeless "wandered the streets like particles in liquid suspension,
seeking shelter however they could," and when those in some of the most
remote rural areas "lived off dandelions, pokeweed and blackberries."[4]

Many whites in the early 1930s were experiencing the kind of economic despair in which a majority of blacks had lived since the turn of the twentieth century.

Somerset County was in particularly difficult economic straits by the fall of 1933. A devastating hurricane decimated the corn and fruit crop in late August.[5] The county was reportedly unable to pay schoolteachers their salaries that year, and unemployment was a serious enough problem that the county opened a reemployment office in the town.[6]

For blacks on the Shore, as elsewhere, the Depression years were acutely painful. There were few opportunities for blacks to better themselves educationally. Even in towns with high schools, many blacks simply had to leave school in the seventh or eighth grade to assist their families as wage earners. Black teachers were better off than most laborers but earned only half the salary of their white counterparts. Black laborers in the fruit-packing industry and black watermen had to be satisfied with subsistence wages. Indigent blacks even had to overcome obstacles to receive relief. In perhaps a crude foreshadowing of the welfare reform work plans of the 1990s, black women who received free flour from the Red Cross in 1931 were required, in exchange for this small charity, to work as domestics in white homes.[7]

Many scholars of lynching have speculated that the reality of unrelenting economic despair among whites set the stage for the spread and proliferation of lynching in small towns during the 1930s. It is certainly true that the 1930s marked the decade in which lynching had the most widespread geographic diversity, perhaps reflecting the effect of a nationwide economic depression on the inclination of whites even outside the South to vent their frustration, anger, and fear in racial violence. A November 1933 issue of the *Afro-American* featured a remarkable front page dominated by stories about three separate lynchings that had recently occurred: one in Missouri, another in California, and a third in South Carolina.[8] Sherwood Anderson, in his 1930 essay "Look Out, Brown Man!" grimly foreshadowed the rise of lynching in the Depression years when he cautioned: "These aren't good times for a Negro man to be too proud, step too high. There are a lot of white men hard up. There are a lot of white men out of work. They won't be wanting to see a big proud black man getting along. They'll be lynchings now."[9] His prediction might well have been written with the Eastern Shore of Maryland in mind.

THE LYNCHING OF GEORGE ARMWOOD,
PRINCESS ANNE, MARYLAND, OCTOBER 1933

By the time George Armwood was dragged from the jail in Princess Anne and lynched before a crowd of two thousand, blacks on the Shore were well acquainted with the reality of mob violence. Lynching blacks had been in practice on the Eastern Shore of Maryland since before the Civil War, when lynch mobs conspired to murder free blacks suspected of assisting runaway slaves.[10] After the Civil War, lynching occurred with some regularity on the Shore. And even when the lawless brand of mob-run lynching abated, the public and often gruesome execution of blacks convicted of crimes against whites no doubt satisfied the appetite for lynching. One particularly gruesome quadruple execution in 1869 in Princess Anne took place near the site where nearly sixty-five years later George Armwood would be mutilated and burned. Four black men between the ages of nineteen and twenty-six were convicted of mutiny and murder aboard an oyster schooner at the mouth of what was then called the Big Annamesie River. Convicted in a series of trials, the four were taken to a gallows erected outside the jail in Princess Anne on a cold March afternoon. A large crowd, estimated at five thousand men, women, and children, gathered to witness the event. Nearly three thousand were believed to have traveled from surrounding cities and towns to witness the event.[11] The execution was not a quick affair; nor did it differ in its macabre details from later accounts of mob lynching. Apparently the gallows had been in use since before the Civil War. They were ramshackle and unreliable, as one of the four young convicts soon found out.

The trap was then sprung and they all fell through the door, writhing and kicking in a horrible manner. The body of Rounce was so heavy that he broke his neck instantly. Bailey died with a short struggle. Wells also died almost instantly. But the death of Wilson, poor wretch, was the most heart-rending and terrible. The noose about his neck was very loose and he did not lose his consciousness when he fell, but knew for four or five minutes where he was sprung through the trap. He broke loose the pinions which tied his arms, and held himself up by the body of Anderson, next to him. There was a cry of shame from every one present. Finally, the dying negro hoisted himself up like a gymnast, fully six feet, to the platform of the scaffold, and a man ran up and kicked him off, when he swung to and fro, the most terrible groans coming from his throat all the time like a wild beast. Then he hoisted himself again on the platform, when the same brute ran up on the scaffold, and pressing the noose choked him fiercely, all the while the boy struggling fiercely with him. A universal wail of sorrow went up from every black throat at him. After choking him the boy was swung off again to die like a dog.[12]

The steady diet of gruesome, public killings of young black men was a staple of life on the Eastern Shore until well into the first part of the twentieth century. Although lynching did not occur on the Shore with the frequency that it did in Mississippi and Alabama, it happened with a disturbing regularity, with just enough consistency to serve as an effective caution to blacks in every aspect of their lives. Data collected by the Maryland State Archives identifies four other lynchings on the Eastern Shore in the twenty-year period between 1890 and 1910. In the 1890s, three black men were lynched in three separate incidents. Each was suspected of murdering a white townsperson.[13] James Taylor, who was believed to have been involved in the 1892 murder of a white doctor, was lynched by a mob in Chestertown. In 1894 Isaac Kemp was lynched in Princess Anne after townspeople suspected him of murdering Edward Carver. Four years later Garfield King, accused of killing a white man, was taken by four whites from the jail in Salisbury. King was clubbed, hung, and shot at least fifty times before a crowd of one hundred whites.[14] His clothes were torn from his body. King had graduated from the Princess Anne Academy, now the University of Maryland, Eastern Shore, and was apparently well regarded in the town. James Reed was lynched by a mob in Crisfield in 1907 after he was suspected of shooting and killing a policeman.

But in addition to these lynchings, racial murders and near lynchings on the Shore contributed to the climate of racial terror during the early twentieth century. These incidents often evoked the same sense of terror as completed lynchings. One of the most notorious racial murders was the public stabbing of Stephen Long, a highly respected black school principal from Pocomoke City in Worcester County. Long was walking on the street with his young adopted daughter when a white man, William

Pilchard, accosted him. As they struggled, Pilchard's brother John rushed over from a nearby store and stabbed Long in the stomach. Long's death reverberated throughout the African American community from the Eastern Shore to Baltimore.[15] That John Pilchard was later acquitted of murder and received only a three-year sentence for manslaughter intensified what African American poet and Shore native Adele Holden in her memoir describes as "the pain of justice denied."[16] Only two years earlier, Isaiah Fountain was nearly lynched by a crowd of two thousand whites who had assembled on the courthouse lawn in Easton, Maryland, during the first day of Fountain's trial for raping a white girl. Rather than face certain death, Fountain mounted a daring escape from custody, eluding recapture for three days and prompting a massive manhunt on the Shore.[17] Ultimately Fountain was tried, convicted, and executed (see chapter 1).

The Eastern Shore of Maryland saw a fairly steady pattern of lynchings, near lynchings, and racial murders during the early part of the twentieth century. In each case, no white person was tried and convicted for murder. In most cases hundreds—and sometimes thousands—of white members of the community watched and encouraged the lynchers. White jurors refused to indict suspected lynchers, white witnesses declined to identify members of the lynch mob, and local law enforcement refrained from arresting lynchers. In all, blacks on the Shore lived in an environment in which the white community could be expected to band together to publicly mutilate and murder black men, and in which the legal apparatus in the community could be counted on to ensure that these murders would go unpunished. When a black man was accused of a violent crime against a white victim, he could expect a hideous death by lynching, or in the case of a nonviolent crime, a disproportionately long prison term in the state penitentiary.

By 1933 blacks on the Shore had lived for two tumultuous years in a climate of mob violence. In addition to the lynching of Matthew Williams, blacks knew that mobs of three hundred to five hundred men had swarmed throughout four counties on the Shore looking for Euel Lee and George Davis in 1931. Both men survived only because local law enforcement quickly spirited them to Baltimore for safekeeping. Neither man was ever returned to the Shore. Lee had been accused of murdering an entire white family in Worcester County, and Davis had been charged with attempted assault on a young white woman in Kent County, Maryland. In January 1932 Davis was sentenced to sixteen years in prison after a one-day trial that had been moved to Elkton, Maryland, to avoid mob interference. Lee, whose 1932 trial had been moved to Towson, Maryland, was convicted once and then, after that verdict was thrown out by the Court of Appeals, was convicted a second time. His attorney, Bernard Ades, a white Communist lawyer from the Baltimore branch of International Labor Defense—the organization that was representing the Scottsboro boys in Alabama—had put up a spirited defense of Lee, challenging the failure of Towson officials to include blacks on juries. This charge was the basis upon which Lee's first conviction had been thrown out by the Maryland Court of Appeals. White Shore residents were furious about the Lee case. By October 1933 Lee was on death row, with an execution date looming in a few weeks. But white Shoremen were not satisfied with Lee's imminent legal execution. The popular feeling was that Lee had somehow escaped justice on the Shore. In fact, many contended that the 1931 lynching of Matthew Williams was an expression of white Shoremen's frustration over the Euel Lee case. But even in the fall of 1933, when Lee's execution was only weeks away, articles in local newspapers continued to vilify the legal system that had permitted Lee to have two trials and a successful appeal. What whites on the Shore regarded as the long delay in Lee's execution was a sign that the formal legal system was tipped in favor of black defendants once they were removed from the Shore. And it seemed as though the wounded pride of whites on the Shore, who had been denounced as barbarians in newspapers in Baltimore and Washington, D.C., over the Matthew Williams lynching, would not be assuaged until they had proved that they were unrepentant and unafraid to take the law into their hands by lynching a black man.

Given this recent history, on October 17, 1933, when George Armwood was returned to the custody of Eastern Shore authorities from a Baltimore jail where he had been held for safekeeping, it could not have been a surprise that a determined lynch mob began to form within hours of his arrival. Armwood, aged twenty-three, was a plain young man of medium height and a chocolate brown complexion. He had the solid build of a laborer and was known to work hard on various farms throughout Somerset County. His primary employer was a white couple, Mr. and Mrs. John

Richardson. Armwood had worked for Mrs. Richardson before her marriage.[18] According to Armwood's mother, when George finished school—reportedly in the fifth grade—the Richardsons asked "that George be given to them."[19] This kind of arrangement, in which desperately poor and powerless blacks "gave" their children to whites as laborers, was not unheard of in the rural South during this period. Given the very few employment opportunities for poor blacks during the Depression, the decision to "give" one's child to a white family in exchange for assurances that the child would be fed and clothed was a pragmatic option for some black women in Mrs. Armwood's position.

After his death, many blacks reported that George Armwood was believed to be "slow" or "feeble." In an interview with the *Afro*, George's mother described George's mental condition as "not the best."[20] It is difficult to determine whether this was true or whether claims about Armwood's diminished mental capacity was a post hoc way to justify the lynching. The claim that a lynched black man was mentally impaired appears with suspicious frequency in lynching accounts from throughout the South. Black leaders sometimes made these claims about lynching victims as well, perhaps to advance the idea that a "normal" black person would not permit the kind of violent crime that provoked whites to commit a lynching. The *Afro-American* ran a surprising editorial on October 28, 1933, describing the failure of the state to place "unbalanced Negroes" in "an institution for the sub-normal at the expense of the State" as the "root of the evil" that resulted in recent Maryland lynchings.[21]

It was also rumored that Armwood had assaulted Zelpha Wilson, a young black woman, a year or so before the attack on Denston. He was freed by local authorities and the charges were dropped, according to published reports, after his white employer—most likely John Richardson—stepped in on his behalf and obtained his release. Such was the nature of racial justice on the Shore in 1933. The rape of a black girl could go unpunished, and a black suspect could be released on the "word" of his white employer. Although Richardson may have saved Armwood from prison in 1932, in 1933 Richardson may have embroiled Armwood in a scheme that ultimately resulted in Armwood's grisly murder at the hands of a white mob.

Contemporaneous interviews as well as those conducted decades later with local blacks raise the possibility that it was John Richardson who conspired with Armwood to rob Mary Denston. Denston was known to carry money obtained from property that her family rented to tenants. The plan was for Armwood to snatch her purse and bring it to Richardson. But either Armwood was an incompetent thief or Denston was an unusually plucky eighty-two-year-old. She fought Armwood, who ripped her dress in the process and then fled in a panic. Whether this story is an accurate account is far from clear. Feeble or not, when Armwood ran from the screaming Denston, he had to have known the kind of trouble he was in. He ran to the home of the one person he thought could help him—the person who had helped him in the past, John Richardson.

For George's mother, Etta Armwood, the night of October 17 must have been torturous. To her knowledge, her son's life had been saved by the sheriff's decision to take him to Baltimore. But Etta Armwood would most likely have known that this was only a temporary reprieve for George. The best she could hope for was a long prison term for George after a summary trial before an all-white jury. Just a year earlier another black man, George Davis, had been convicted of attempted assault on a white woman in Kent County, about ninety miles from Princess Anne. Lynch mobs had looked for Davis in four Eastern Shore counties before he was taken for safekeeping to Baltimore. But after his one-day trial, Davis had received sixteen years in the penitentiary. So twisted was the justice system when black men were accused of crimes against white women that Davis's sixteen-year sentence was perceived as a victory for the defense, and in a way it was. The prosecution had sought the death penalty, but the three-judge panel refused to impose that sentence for attempted assault. In fact, one judge on the panel deciding Davis's case dissented from the decision to even impose the sixteen-year sentence. This was a highly unusual move for a local judge to make, and therefore in and of itself raised doubts as to whether Davis was guilty.

But George Armwood could not hope for a similar "victory." He was accused of actually assaulting Mary Denston. The county sheriff had organized hundreds of men into a posse to search through the woods for Armwood. Local police had arrived at Etta Armwood's Manokoo, Maryland, home brandishing weapons. Without explanation, they searched her dilapidated two-story home. After a fruitless search, the police told Etta

Armwood that George was accused of attacking a white woman. When they did not find George at her home, they left after receiving a tip that he was at the Richardson farm south of Pocomoke City, near the Virginia border. George was captured, arrested, and taken from the Richardson home. According to Etta Armwood, on their way back from the Richardson farm, police beat George while they brought him across a field near her home. The police were so brutal that Etta Armwood thought that they might kill George right then and there, and in a panic she ran to the attic of her home.[22] But although the police beat George with their fists and guns, they did not kill him. He was arrested and taken to the jail at Salisbury in Wicomico County, rather than Princess Anne, where lynch mobs were already forming. By the time Armwood was in the Salisbury jail, lynch mobs were reportedly headed to that town. Captain Edward Johnson called the governor's office to ask if he could move Armwood to Baltimore. Fearing the imminent arrival of the mob, Johnson moved his prisoner first to Cecil County on the Western Shore and then, after receiving a call from the governor, to Baltimore.[23] Only two years earlier, in separate incidents, the decision to move prisoners to Baltimore had saved three black Eastern Shoremen accused of committing crimes against whites from lynch mobs.

But Armwood's future was still uncertain. Even if his case made it to trial, his life might not be spared. In those days, black men were often given the death penalty for raping white women. The Scottsboro boys' case in Alabama had riled up white southerners' obsession with avenging interracial rape. Moreover, lurid rumors embellishing the story of the attack on Denston were circulating around Princess Anne, casting Armwood as a beast who had to be destroyed. In one story, Armwood was said to have bitten off Denston's breasts. In this climate, even if he survived his trial, Armwood would be dead within a year—hung by the state rather than by a howling mob. But on the night of October 17, Etta Armwood, her seventeen-year-old daughter, Irema, and George's younger brother, Clifford, did not know that George would be denied even that year's reprieve and the relative dignity of a state execution.

What Etta Armwood also did not know was that the local prosecutor, State's Attorney John B. Robins, and the local circuit judge Robert F. Duer were pressured by local townspeople. Shoremen were still smarting over

—Acme Photo.
Seventy-one-year-old Mrs. Mary Denston, the victim of a criminal assault which whipped an Eastern Shore mob to lynching fury, is
shown at left. Above is George Armwood, 28-year-old Negro, who
was killed after he is said to have confessed the crime. With him is
Lieut. Ruxton Ridgley, of the Maryland State Police, who first reported to Gov. Ritchie the danger of mob violence.

*George Armwood, accompanied by state police officers, on his way to
the Baltimore City jail for "safekeeping." Within twenty-four hours,
he would be returned to Somerset County and lynched.*

earlier instances in which black prisoners had been taken to the Baltimore
City jail for safekeeping. Euel Lee's removal to Baltimore after being accused of killing a white farm family in Worcester County in 1931, and his
lawyers' subsequent no-holds-barred two-year battle to save Lee from the
gallows, had stuck in the craw of Shore people. Lee's lawyer, Bernard
Ades, was a member of International Labor Defense, an organization reputed to be Communist and that represented the Scottsboro boys. Ades

was white, Jewish, and northern, and at every turn he exposed the racism of the justice system in Maryland. He'd successfully gotten Lee's first conviction for the murder of the Green Davis family overturned because of the exclusion of blacks from juries in Baltimore County. He raised, as grounds for the reversal of Lee's second conviction, the issue of the maintenance of Jim Crow practices in the courthouse, including segregated bathrooms and water fountains. The Court of Appeals denied the second attempt to overturn the Lee conviction. Instead, Lee was sentenced to death. In fact, on October 17 Lee was on death row, his execution scheduled for October 27. Within hours it would become obvious that Lee's imminent legal execution would not satisfy the desire of Shore residents to exact their own form of justice against George Armwood.

It was 2:00 a.m. on October 18 before Somerset police officers arrived back in Princess Anne with George Armwood. Later that day, in the afternoon, the town was beset by murmurs of lynching. Frank Spencer, a white man from California who was visiting a friend in Princess Anne, told reporters of the *Afro-American* that all afternoon he encountered crowds milling about downtown Princess Anne talking of lynching Armwood.[24] Spencer reported that a twenty-year-old white woman, a relative of Denston, was downtown all day "inciting the mob on to lynch Armwood." Williams Street—the main street downtown—was crowded with automobiles.

By about 7 p.m. that evening, there could be no question that the mob assembled outside the jail was dangerous. It numbered about three hundred men, women, and boys who began to taunt and hurl insults at the state police guarding the jail. State policeman Edward Johnson requested the help of the local American Legion office. The legion refused to help, the commander of the post reportedly stating that the legion would not come "to protect . . . a Negro." In a letter sent to the commander of the legion post two days after the lynching, NAACP counsel Charles Hamilton Houston, himself a veteran and a legionnaire, excoriated the local legion and demanded that "vigorous and persistent" action be taken to punish the legion post commander.[25] There is no record of any action being taken against the local legionnaires.

Word of the gathering mob had reached Judge Robert Duer as he prepared to attend a dinner with a friend. The judge was in a bind. Earlier in the day he'd had a rather contentious and awkward conversation with the governor, Albert Ritchie. After learning that Judge Duer and Sheriff Daugherty had ordered the return of Armwood to the Eastern Shore, a furious Governor Ritchie had put a call through to the judge. He sought assurances from the judge and from the state's attorney that Armwood would be kept safe. Ritchie made it clear to Duer that he held the judge responsible for whatever happened to Armwood. Despite rumors of lynching running throughout the town, both Judge Duer and State's Attorney Robins assured the governor that there would be no lynching. By 8 p.m. Judge Robert Duer knew that he had made a terrible mistake.

Now, as the crowd swelled outside the jail, Judge Duer, who a day earlier had ordered Armwood returned to the Shore because he feared the rebuke of his white constituents, knew that he would have to face the ire of the governor if Armwood were lynched. On his way to dinner, Duer stopped by to address the mob. He implored the crowd to disperse and to let the legal system deal with Armwood. The crowd heckled the judge, warning that Armwood would not become Euel Lee. Duer reminded the crowd that he was "one of them" and held them "on their honor" not to interfere with the legal process.[26] Several in the crowd continued to heckle him. In fact, Duer was not "one of them." He was a judge and therefore represented the very legal system that many Shoremen believed had permitted Euel Lee and his white Jewish lawyer, Bernard Ades, to ridicule the Shore. Duer's bid for reelection was a scant thirteen months away. It was an election he was fated to lose.

When the crowd refused to disperse, Duer went on to his dinner party. After the lynching, Duer stated that at the time the crowd "did not strike me as being a determined crowd, but rather curiosity seekers." Perhaps for this reason he did not call the governor or other authorities to ask for reinforcements. He admitted later that he had been "badly mistaken."[27]

The crowd began to throw stones and bricks at the police, and several men grabbed a telephone poll to use as a battering ram. There was pandemonium outside the jail. Inside, there was turmoil of a different sort. The Princess Anne jail is a boxy, brick two-story structure. Administration offices were located on the first floor. Prisoners' "cages"—as they were called—were on the second floor. In those cages, black prisoners were caught in the grip of terror. Several blacks assembled in a common area

climbed on top of the cages. All feared that the lynchers would be indis-
criminate and take any black man they saw. It is perhaps impossible to
imagine the naked fear of every black man on the second floor of the prison
as the battering ram struck the thick wooden door of the prison again and
again until it gave way. A howling crowd of whites ran up the stairs looking for Armwood. At the inquest held a week later, the black prisoners
were no less afraid. One by one they testified that they did not recognize
any of the men who took Armwood.[28] One prisoner who was in the same
cell with Armwood testified that he did not see anything.

Armwood had lain down on the floor and put his mattress over his
head.[29] He was taken from his cell begging for mercy. Almost immediately
he was stabbed by a member of the mob. He was dragged into the hall by
his feet and down the stairs to the first floor. His head hit every one of the
metal steps while being pulled down to the first floor. This cruelty may
have mercifully rendered Armwood semiconscious. When he was dragged
outside the jail, the crowd began to kick and pummel him. A young man,
seventeen or eighteen years old, jumped on Armwood's back and cut off his
ear. A rope was placed around his neck. Armwood was dragged through
the streets to the neighborhood where Judge Duer lived. The crowd then
hung him from a tree near Duer's home. It is likely that Armwood was still
alive although not conscious when he was hung. As he hung from the tree,
his body "twitched." The crowd continued to beat him. A woman rushed
in and "hit him in the stomach with a big stick."[30] The crowd then dragged
Armwood back to the corner of Prince and Williams Streets outside the
courthouse, doused his body with gasoline, and burned him.

Clarence Mitchell, who later became an influential lobbyist for the
NAACP, was a twenty-two-year-old cub reporter for the *Afro-American*.
When word reached Baltimore on October 18 that Armwood was likely to
be lynched that night, Mitchell set off by car with several other *Afro* reporters for the Eastern Shore. They were too late to catch the ferry and
had to endure a six-hour drive. Before Mitchell left Baltimore, a colleague
at the *Afro* gave him a gun for his protection. Mitchell had never handled
a gun before, so he set it under the passenger seat of the car. By the time
the *Afro* reporters arrived the next morning, George Armwood's body
lay smoldering in a downtown lumberyard near the Washington Hotel.
Mitchell's moving account of what he saw that morning as he bravely
walked amid groups of still-excited whites gripped black readers through-

*Irema and Etta Armwood, George Armwood's sister and mother,
after hearing of the lynching.*

out the state. With his press pass identification on his hat, Mitchell observed Armwood's body and talked with whites about the lynching. He
described the gruesome condition of Armwood's corpse and the macabre
excitement of unrepentant whites as twin horrors:

> The skin of George Armwood was scorched and blackened while his
> face had suffered many blows from sharp and heavy instruments. A
> cursory glance revealed that one ear was missing and his tongue,

between his clenched teeth, gave evidence of his great agony before his death. There is no adequate description of the mute evidence of gloating on the part of whites who gathered to watch the effect upon our people.[31]

Under the caption "George Armwood a la Maryland," the *Afro* ran the only known picture of George Armwood after he was lynched. The *Afro*'s photographers had covered Armwood's genitals with some sacks that were nearby. His skin was crisp and bubbled up like bacon. His face was a horror. After this valiant reporting in the *Afro*, Mitchell's brother Parren Mitchell recalled that Clarence was unable to hold down food for several days after the lynching.

Black residents, particularly children on their way to school, saw Armwood's body as it lay in the lumberyard on that Thursday morning. Roma Jones, then a secondary school student, passed George Armwood's body as he walked to school with black friends. Asked seventy years later to recall what he did after he saw the body in the lumberyard, Jones replied, "What could you do? You went on to school."[32]

THE LYNCHING OF MATTHEW WILLIAMS, SALISBURY, MARYLAND, DECEMBER 1931

If the Armwood lynching can be said to have been predictable after his return from the jail in Baltimore, the lynching of Matthew Williams two years earlier, on December 4, 1931, certainly was not.

It had been more than twenty years since the last lynching on the Shore. In Wicomico County, the last lynching had been in 1898, when Garfield King was dragged from the jail in Salisbury and then shot and hung on the courthouse lawn. The day Williams was lynched was an unseasonably warm Friday. Many whites in town were excited about the football match between Wicomico County High School and Delmar High. The Delmar team trounced the Wi-Hi team soundly, but a celebratory dinner was being held nevertheless for the home team in the Wicomico Hotel. The hotel, a prime source of employment for both blacks and whites, was located at the corner of Main and Division, directly across the street from the courthouse. A group of seven or eight young black men, including Howard Purnell, James Stanley Pinkett, and James Harrison

Webb, worked there as bellhops and cooks. They are believed to be the only blacks who witnessed the lynching of Matthew Williams.

Christmas was only weeks away, and the local papers reminded shoppers of how many days they had left to purchase Christmas presents. Local businesses held welfare drives, in which employees contributed funds to provide for needy families during the holiday season. The number-one song in the country was Guy Lombardo's version of "Goodnight Sweetheart." The Arcade Theater was showing the latest Mary Astor film, and rumors circulated in papers nationwide that the "It Girl," actress Clara Bow, had secretly married her costar Rex Bell.

If one looked carefully behind the cheerful holiday facade, one could see that the ingredients for lynching were carefully stacked like kindling and firewood. All that was needed was a spark to set off the conflagration. By the fall of 1931, the Scottsboro boys' case was in full swing. This incident, in which nine black boys were accused of raping two white women on a train in Alabama, had become a nationwide cause célèbre. For most white southerners, and most likely a good number of northerners as well, the Scottsboro incident dramatized and legitimized their belief that black men, if given the opportunity, would not hesitate to rape white women. For these whites, the case presented a vindication of the notion that blacks had to be dealt with swiftly and brutally where the "honor" of white women was concerned, in order to deter black men from giving in to what whites regarded as their natural impulse to assault white women. For blacks, the railroading of the nine young men in trials marked by rampant due-process violations exemplified the injustice of the southern legal system and its obsession with the taboo of interracial sex. Most blacks believed that the white girls on the train had either never been sexually involved with the black boys or had done so consensually. This view was later vindicated when the girls were alleged to be prostitutes and one of the girls recanted her original charge of rape. Blacks regarded the Scottsboro trials as a legal lynching, and the NAACP, which joined the International Labor Defense lawyers in representing the young men, held fund-raisers throughout the nation to raise money to appeal the hasty convictions that had been handed down by all-white juries. Duke Ellington gave a benefit concert for the "boys'" defense in Washington, D.C., in October 1931. The event was prominently advertised in the Baltimore *Afro-American*.

Earlier in the year, the lynching trope had been given a cinematic boost as well. Horror movie fans had just experienced what was universally regarded as one of the most effective and chilling films of that genre, *Dr. Jekyll and Mr. Hyde.* The film, in which the mild-mannered Dr. Jekyll drinks a potion that unleashes the bestial part of his nature, tapped into southern whites' fears about the seemingly docile black servants, farmhands, laborers, and domestics in their midst. Stories that alcohol unleashed black men's lust for white women were common during this period. After the film's release, white newspapers routinely described black men accused of raping white women as "fiends," the term used to describe the rapacious Mr. Hyde in the film.

And finally, Jack Johnson, the former heavyweight boxing champion who had goaded whites for twenty years with his unrepentant and serial associations with white women, married yet another white woman in October 1931, whom he brazenly introduced to the world at the opening of his nightclub in Los Angeles.

But despite this backdrop, there were still no overt signs that the town of Salisbury would erupt into full-scale racial violence on the evening of December 4, 1931. In fact, many blacks hoped that Eastern Shore whites had calmed down considerably since October. Then, marauding bands of whites had scoured jails on the Shore looking for Euel Lee, a sixty-year-old farmhand who was accused of murdering a white farm family in Berlin, Maryland, near Ocean City. Just a month later in November, lynch mobs were out again, this time looking for twenty-seven-year-old George Davis, a black farmhand accused of attempted assault on a young white woman in Kent County. Davis, like Lee, was taken to Baltimore as well. Both of these cases had had white Shore residents up in arms and decrying the justice system for permitting the removal of the men to Baltimore and denouncing the attempt by Lee's lawyer to change the venue of his trial. But by December it was hoped that agitation over the two cases had died down.

Just as the warm December afternoon gave no sign of the turbulence and violence that would grip the town by nightfall, so too was Matthew Williams an unlikely figure to be at the center of a murder and lynching. Williams had no history of violence or instability. In fact, although both were young black men working at menial jobs to make their living, there were few other similarities between George Armwood and Matthew

Williams. Williams was the nephew of a respected and middle-class black family. Along with his older sister Olivia, Matt had been taken in by his grandmother Mary Handy and her husband after Matt's mother, Annie Handy, died of pneumonia in 1912. He went to school until his grandfather died when Matt was fourteen years old. Like many young men in those days, Matt had to leave school and work to help support the family. When his grandmother died, he lived with his mother's sister Addie Black and her husband, Thomas Black Sr., on Isabelle Avenue, in the black district of Salisbury. Matt grew up in a comfortable, close-knit family with his cousins Viola, Thomas Jr., Preston, Edna, and Mary Black.

Given the high level of unemployment on the Shore in 1931, Matt was fortunate to have held a more or less steady job for years. He'd worked since he was a teenager for one of the most popular and well-regarded employers in town, Daniel J. (D. J.) Elliot. Elliot owned a lumberyard and box factory, where laborers made boxes for local fruit to be shipped to the Western Shore. Elliot lived in an attractive house on Park Avenue, with his wife, Lottie, and his son, James. His two daughters, Laura and Alice, had already married and were living with their husbands, Laura in South Carolina and Alice in Salisbury. As the Depression hit and jobs became scarce, Elliot tried to keep on as many of his employees as possible, shifting many to part-time work and juggling employee schedules so that they could at least remain employed. Williams worked at the factory as a laborer, and if there was no work there, then at the Elliot home doing odd jobs. By all accounts Daniel and the entire Elliot family were quite fond of Williams, and he of them. This fact made it hard for many to believe, even after he was lynched, that Williams could have shot and killed Elliot.

Williams was a serious young man, especially about his money. He'd reportedly saved $56 by the time of his death, a considerable sum for a young black laborer in 1931. After his murder, no trace of the money was ever found. Williams did not drink or hang out with girls. He attended several churches, most often the John Wesley Methodist Church. His only frivolous indulgence seemed to be his hair. He was one of the few young black men in town to have processed hair, which he had touched up regularly at the Apex Hair salon on Isabelle Street.

What happened on the afternoon of December 4, 1931, still remains unclear. Williams's aunt Addie Black said that Matt ate lunch at her home as usual and seemed to be in good spirits, playing with his cousins as he often did. At about 2 p.m., Matt announced that he was going over to the factory to work. Within several hours Daniel Elliot had been shot and killed in his office, and Matt Williams had suffered two gunshot wounds.

We know that Elliot was in his office on the telephone with a business partner, Thomas Chatham, when a shot rang out. The coroner described the wound that killed Elliot as a gunshot to the left side of the head. Chatham heard a shot and then heard the line go dead. He called the police station. At the same time Elliot's secretary also heard the shot. She never heard any voices. At this point, the story of what actually happened in Elliot's office diverges dramatically.

The official story—told by the state's attorney, Sheriff G. Murray Phillips, and the local press—goes like this. Matt Williams, angered over low wages, walked up to Daniel Elliot, put the muzzle of his gun to Elliot's left temple, and shot him. Williams then allegedly turned the gun on himself, grazing himself in the temple. Elliot's son, James, ran into his father's office. Williams, who was only wounded, got to his feet and stumbled out of Elliot's office and into the lumberyard. James Elliot picked up Williams's gun and fired at Williams, hitting him in the leg and chest. Daniel Elliot was dead. Matt Williams was believed to be near death. But by the time he arrived at Peninsula Hospital, it was clear that Williams's wounds were only superficial. He was put in a straitjacket and his head was heavily bandaged, the bandages covering even his eyes. While Williams was lying in his hospital bead, semi-comatose and straitjacketed, State's Attorney Bailey and Sheriff G. Murray Phillips questioned Williams—or so they claimed—and Williams said, in a turn of phrase quite uncharacteristic of him, "I got my man," indicating that he had killed Elliot.

But both at the time of the event and in the subsequent seventy years, many people, white and black, who have been interviewed about the Elliot murder acknowledged the existence of another widely believed story of what happened in Daniel Elliot's office—that Elliot's son, James, shot both his father and Williams. The prevailing view is that Williams gave James Elliot the money he'd saved on the agreement that James would repay the sum. When James refused to return Williams's money, Williams took the matter to the elder Elliot, with whom he was close. Daniel Elliot reportedly berated his son and demanded that he repay Williams. James

Elliot was supposed to return Williams's money on Friday, December 4, 1931. Instead he arrived with a gun. He shot his father and Williams, concocting the story that Williams had shot Daniel Elliot and then turned the gun on himself. In the late 1970s Joseph L. Sutton, an elderly waterman living in Dorchester County, summarized the story as it was understood by many in the community to his biographer:

> I heard a white man from down there was telling it. . . . He said, "He didn't shoot that man" . . . didn't nobody shoot him but his son and put it on this colored fellow. And the colored fellow had been workin' for this man, the man had some kind of lumberyard, I think. "Well," he say, "he'd been workin' for him ever since a boy. . . . We know he didn't shoot him. And they always give him everything he wanted." And [the son] was spoiled! And he was the one that killed his father.
>
> And after they had lynched this fellow, well, they say the majority of them then down there spoke of it, they said the same thing, said, "Wasn't nobody but his son." He killed his father and then shot this colored fellow so he wouldn't be there to be against him. Then he said this colored fellow had killed his father and he took the gun away from him and shoot him.[33]

What is known for certain begins again in the early evening, when groups of white men congregated on street corners around the courthouse square, talking about the Elliot murder. Many believed that Williams had died at Peninsula Hospital, but others clearly did not. Charles Hearne, a law student at the time, was told by an older man in town to come back to town by 7 p.m. that night "if he had any red blood in his body."[34] The lynching was being planned. Hearne, like many other whites, came back later that evening to watch. He observed the lynching from the balcony of the Wicomico Hotel.

At about 7:30 p.m. the *Salisbury Times,* then located on Main Street several blocks from the courthouse, learned that Williams was alive. It issued a special bulletin, posted in the window of the paper's offices, announcing that Williams was alive and was expected to recover. This was all that the crowd needed to hear. As word spread that Williams would live, the cry "Let's lynch him" went up and men began running toward Peninsula Hospital. The crowd gained in strength as it approached the front entrance of the hospital. Once there, the crowd was met by several police officers, including Police Chief N. H. Holland and Deputy Sheriff John Parks, who blocked the entrance to the hospital. The mob then went to a side door, where they met the hospital superintendent, Nurse Helen Wise. She told the lynchers, "Well if you must take him, take him quietly."[35] Williams was spirited out of a window on the first-floor "Negro Ward" of the hospital. The two other black patients in the male section of the hospital's Negro Ward, Rufus Jernigan and Jacob Conquest, could only watch and listen in horror. By the time a grand jury was called to investigate the lynching of Matthew Williams, Conquest would be dead, and Jernigan had disappeared.

As Williams was dragged toward the courthouse, the crowd grew. White residents flocked out of their homes and businesses and joined the mob's procession. Williams was heavily bandaged about the face and was still wearing a straitjacket, a precaution the police had deemed necessary despite the seriousness of Williams's injuries. As Williams struggled to remain on his feet, one member of the mob repeatedly stabbed him with an ice pick. He was dragged the rest of the way. By the time the mob arrived with the either dead or unconscious Williams, one witness said, "His buttocks did not have God's bit of skin left on them."[36]

At the Wicomico Hotel across from the courthouse, workers and guests had heard the commotion. The Wicomico High School football team was having a dinner after its (losing) game against Delmar High School. The players poured out of the dining room to join the crowd.[37] Employees and spectators assembled on the balcony to see what was going on. Among those on the hotel balcony were four or five stunned and terrified black men, all of whom worked as bellhops or cooks at the hotel. James Stanley Pinkett, the bell captain at the hotel and the grandfather of current Salisbury City Councilwoman Eugenie "Shanie" Shields, found a phone and called a neighbor in the black community, since there was no phone in his home. He asked the neighbor to get word to his wife, Roxie, that he was trying to make his way home. He instructed the neighbor to warn blacks to stay indoors. Pinkett then went down to the street to try to find a way home amid the howling crowd, which by now had slung a rope over a tree in front of the courthouse and hung Matthew Williams. A white taxi driver whom Pinkett knew motioned to him to quickly get in the cab and offered to give him a ride home. Pinkett took the ride and made his way back to his family.[38]

James Harrison Webb, a cook at the hotel and grandfather of Walter Black, a Talbot County NAACP president in 2004, heard one member of the exultant mob cry out, "Anybody want a nigger sandwich," as Williams was dragged by. Howard Purnell, a bellhop at the hotel who had been a classmate of Williams, also saw the lynching. He never spoke of what he saw that night.

After Williams was hoisted up and down several times, his body was dragged again, this time to the bridge at the corner of Willow and Lake Streets on the outskirts of the black community.[39] At a lot near Poplar Hill, in front of Rosen's store, Williams's body was tied to a lamppost, drenched with gasoline, and set on fire.[40] As one witness explained, "So all the colored people could see him."[41]

Black men who happened to be on the street were terrified. Two of them, John Allison and Harold Fisher, jumped into the Wicomico River and tried to swim home after several mob members pointed at them and cried, "Get those niggers."[42] Other blacks hid under the porches of white homes. Some were hidden by whites.[43] All in all, for blacks who had the misfortune to be downtown that Friday evening, it was a night of terror.

Back at the Williams home, Matthew's aunt Addie Black fainted when she heard that her nephew had been taken from the hospital and lynched. She had been preparing to go to the hospital and visit Matt when she heard the news.[44] Earlier in the day, when she first heard about the Elliot shooting, Black had sent her daughter Mary to see Matt at the hospital. Mary had rushed to the hospital, and after waiting for some time, was told either by hospital officials or the police that she could not see Matt. No explanation was given. When Black regained consciousness, she was terrified. Convinced that "the mob would attack me and my family," she wanted to pack up quickly and leave town.[45] Her husband, Thomas Black, refused to leave and insisted that they wait at least until arrangements could be made for securing Matt's body and having a proper funeral. Matt's body had been taken to the outskirts of town and dumped. Black contacted the sheriff's office and asked that they arrange to have Matt's body collected by the town's black undertaker.

In America in the 1930s, death was an even more segregated experience than life. As the town's black undertaker, James Stewart would have handled all deaths in the black community. Despite Stewart's vast experience, Matt Williams's corpse must have presented a challenge. The upper portion of Williams "was completely charred beyond recognition. The hair and skin was burned off completely, leaving a skull covered with soot. The eyes were destroyed, leaving only the black holes"[46] A quiet service for Williams attended only by family members was held in a room at the Stewart Funeral Home.

In the weeks that followed the lynchings, Shore whites almost uniformly blamed the lynchings not on the mob but on frustration over the slow pace of the Lee and Davis cases that fall, in which blacks had been arrested for committing violent crimes against white victims. The failure of the legal system to promptly bring these men to "justice," said Shore whites, resulted in the December 4 explosive violence against Matthew Williams. The facts, however, belie this claim. In fact, Euel Lee and George Davis, the men accused of the crimes in Worcester and Kent Counties, had themselves narrowly escaped lynch mobs. By the time Williams was lynched in December, Lee and Davis were alive only by virtue of having been spirited to the safety of the Baltimore City jail, in each case just an hour ahead of marauding Shore whites carrying ropes.

THE CASE OF EUEL LEE

At the time of the Green K. Davis murder, Euel Lee was a fifty-eight-year-old farm laborer. Very little is known about his past before he came to work on the Davis farm in the fall of 1931. He stayed at a boarding house in Ocean City owned by a black woman named Martha Miller and arranged for his clothes to be laundered by a black washerwoman named Mattie Johnson. According to Lee, he had been raised by a family of whites, who called him Orphan Jones. He is believed to have served time in a Pennsylvania jail for manslaughter. He was not known to have a family, although after his execution, a man purporting to be Lee's son went on a speaking tour for the International Labor Defense, the Communist-affiliated organization that provided for Lee's legal defense.

Lee was either a homicidal sociopath or an elderly farmhand framed for committing a gruesome murder. Whatever the truth, within hours of the discovery of the bodies of the Green Davis family, whites on the Shore were convinced that Lee was the former.

Davis owned a farm where he grew fruits and vegetables, which he sold at a roadside produce stand near his home. His wife, Ivy, assisted with the farm, along with his two daughters, Elizabeth and Mary. The girls were students at Buckingham High School in Berlin, Maryland.

When Davis did not show up at his produce stand for two days, and the two girls did not go to school, Charles Howe, the Davises' neighbor, became alarmed. Accompanied by another neighbor, he approached the Davis home and entered through the kitchen door. In the upstairs bedrooms, he discovered a gruesome scene. The Davis family had been killed in their beds by shotgun blasts at close range. The faces of Mr. and Mrs. Davis appeared to have been bludgeoned as well. The bedroom drawers were ransacked. The floor of the kitchen and bedrooms was covered with kerosene.

Word of the murders spread like wildfire through the town. A crowd of men went to the Davis house. The local police almost immediately called Baltimore City to obtain the assistance of detectives there. Suspicion almost immediately centered on Lee. According to some accounts, Green Davis had told others that Lee had threatened him. According to these accounts and to witnesses at the trial, Lee believed that Davis had failed to pay him for a day's work. This controversy over a day's wages was said to be the motive for Lee's slaughter of the Davis family. In a confession made later at the Baltimore City jail, Lee claimed that he had given Green Davis $250 for safekeeping and that Davis had stolen the money.

Other witnesses suggested that Lee had a growing animosity not just toward Davis but also toward Davis's wife and daughters, who Lee claims referred to him in derogatory, racist terms. Lee told a neighbor of Green Davis's that Mrs. Davis "had too much coon in her mouth."[47] Yet another witness, ironically named Coon Cooper, testified that several days before the murders Lee had said that "[Green Davis's] wife was always saying nigger, nigger, and he didn't want to be called nigger, because he was not a nigger, he was a colored man."[48] In his confession to the Baltimore police, Lee stated that the Davis girls "had too much coon and nigger in their mouths."[49]

Local police drove to Ocean City and apprehended Lee, who reportedly blurted out, "I didn't kill anybody." There is no question but that Lee was assaulted during questioning by police. Some accounts suggest that Lee was savagely beaten, stomped, and punched and that his bloody shirt was changed before he was led out of the police station. Pictures of Lee leaving the station show him with a bandage on his forehead and a swollen mouth.

Crowds had begun to gather after word of the Davis family murder spread around Worcester County. When it was learned that a suspect was in custody, crowds moved purposefully toward the jail. Anticipating trouble, police had moved Lee to the jail in Salisbury in nearby Wicomico County. But it was soon learned that determined mobs were making their way to Salisbury. State police wisely decided that Lee must be removed from the Shore. He was taken by ferry to the Baltimore City jail. This was to be his home for the next two years until he was executed there in October 1933.

At the Baltimore jail lawyers for the International Labor Defense (ILD) contacted Lee and arranged to represent him. The ILD had already gained national notoriety for their aggressive representation of the Scottsboro boys. The ILD's tactics and brand of lawyering were confrontational. Their effort was always to expose systemic injustice, not just provide representation for individuals. Exposing racial discrimination in the justice system would, ILD lawyers believed, encourage blacks to support communism as a more egalitarian alternative. The clash between the ILD's lawyering and the Maryland judicial system was contentious. Without question, Lee's ILD lawyer, Bernard Ades, zealously represented his client. The ILD's representation of Lee saved his life for two years and resulted in a landmark decision from the Maryland Court of Appeals affirming the unconstitutionality of jury selection practices that excluded blacks. It also resulted in Ades's being investigated by the FBI and ultimately suspended from the federal bar for five months in 1934.[50]

In November 1931 Ades's representation of Lee nearly cost Ades his life. On a trip to Worcester County to address the question of who would represent Lee—Ades or Lee's local appointed counsel—a mob of whites attacked Lee and his associate on the way to his car. Ades was hustled to the jail by Judge Joseph Bailey and several police officers, where he was held for safekeeping. The crowd then attacked Ades's car, rendering it useless for a return journey to Baltimore.[51]

The violent attack outside the courthouse in Snow Hill persuaded Ades immediately to seek a change of venue for the trial on the grounds that Lee could not get a fair trial on the Eastern Shore. The petition clearly had merit. Mobs had harassed and beaten blacks on the streets of Berlin in the week following the Davis murder,[52] prompting responsible white businessmen to circulate a petition denouncing the violence. Local police had been concerned that outraged mobs might try to storm the jail in Worcester, so they moved Lee, first to Wicomico and then to the Baltimore City jail.

Neither Ades nor Lee would ever return to the Shore. The Eastern Shore judges of the First Judicial Circuit refused to grant the change of venue that Ades sought. They contended that Lee could get a fair trial on the Shore and ordered that his trial be held in Dorchester County, about fifty-five miles west of Snow Hill. Ades appealed the Circuit Court's decision. His petition to the Court of Appeals appealing the Circuit Court's decision denying the change of venue gained currency after the lynching of Matthew Williams in December. The Maryland Court of Appeals did not overturn the Circuit Court's decision outright, but strongly suggested that if Lee were tried on the Shore, a conviction would be overturned on the grounds that a mob atmosphere had tainted the verdict.

The Circuit Court got the message. Lee's case was transferred to Towson in Baltimore County. There he was tried and convicted. The jury deliberated for thirty-four minutes. But Ades, with the assistance of Stanley Levinson, another ILD lawyer, successfully challenged the verdict on the grounds that African Americans were excluded from jury service in Towson. In fact, it was conceded at the trial that no African American had been selected to serve on a jury in Towson in the twenty-six years preceding the Lee trial. In a landmark decision, the Maryland Court of Appeals threw out Lee's conviction on the grounds that the exclusion of African Americans from jury service in Baltimore County violated Lee's constitutional right to be tried by an impartial jury of his peers.[53] The decision rocked the Shore and the state. Lee's challenge exposed discriminatory jury practices not on the Shore but in Baltimore County. For whites on the Shore, the idea that a Communist lawyer had been able to thwart what they regarded as speedy justice (meaning the execution of Lee) was untenable. The charge that "Communist interference" was to blame for the racial violence that beset the region from 1931 to 1933 became a kind of mantra in Shore newspapers.

The reprieve for Lee was brief. He received a new trial in Towson, and was again convicted. Appeals of this conviction were rejected. Lee was executed at the Baltimore jail on October 28, 1933, ten days after George Armwood was lynched in Princess Anne by a crowd that shouted, "We ain't gonna have no Euel Lee in Somerset County." Lee's last words before ascending the gallows were "I forgive everybody."[54]

GEORGE DAVIS SURVIVES

Twenty-seven-year-old George Davis looked about seventeen years old. His boyish appearance and hesitant demeanor may have saved his life.[55] Davis had been arrested and ultimately convicted of "attempted criminal assault" on a young white farm wife, Elizabeth Lusby, in Kent County, Maryland. Prosecutors took the extreme step of seeking the death penalty, insisting that Lusby had "gone through the agonies of hell" even though "the act was not completed." The three-judge panel that heard his case and convicted Davis rejected the death penalty and imposed instead sixteen years in prison. It was a long sentence for a case in which it was conceded that no actual assault had taken place. The court went out of its way to suggest that Davis's intentions toward Lusby were most likely not violent. One judge on the panel even dissented from the conviction. In 1941, when the last known reference to Davis appears in the records of the Baltimore Penitentiary transferring him to "The Farm" at Hagerstown, George Davis was still alive.[56]

Davis had worked for Edgar Lusby on a farm near Kennedyville in Kent County but had been recently discharged. According to the account provided by Mrs. Lusby and her husband, Davis entered Mrs. Lusby's bedroom in the early morning of November 21, 1931. He sat on the bed and asked Mrs. Lusby if she would intervene on his behalf and persuade Mr. Lusby to rehire him. Davis is then alleged to have grabbed Mrs. Lusby and torn her nightgown. Mrs. Lusby screamed and fell off the bed. She and Davis struggled. The Lusbys' one-year-old baby began crying in the next room. A panic-stricken Davis fled the room and ran down the stairs. Mrs. Lusby bolted the door. Davis returned to the house a moment later and from the landing of the stairs called up to Mrs. Lusby and apologized for frightening her. He then fled. When Edgar Lusby returned from the barn, he found his wife in a hysterical state.[57]

Davis was old enough to know that his life was in danger. He went to his uncle Edward Davis and tried to borrow some money so that he could get out of town. When his uncle refused, Davis hitched a ride on a truck and fled to Delaware.[58] In the meantime, Kent County authorities had contacted police in Delaware and had coordinated a manhunt. Davis was apprehended by Delaware police and turned over to the custody of Kent County officials. Little is known about Davis's treatment at the hands of the police, but it is said that he signed a confession in the presence of Sheriff John Vickers of Kent County, admitting to the attempted assault.[59]

By the time Davis was in the custody of the Chestertown police, lynch mobs had begun to gather in town. But Sheriff Vickers had anticipated mob violence and had arranged for Davis to be taken by a deputy to the jail at Easton in Talbot County. When seven hundred men arrived at the jail in Chestertown, Sheriff Vickers could truthfully assure them that Davis was not there. When the mob refused to disperse, the sheriff permitted a delegation of the mob, led by Mrs. Lusby's brother, to inspect the jail. Finding that Davis was not there, the mob split into two teams and set off to search the jails at Elkton, in Cecil County north of Kent, and to Centerville, in Queen Annes County. In Easton, Sheriff George Carroll also heard that mobs might be headed to his jail. A little after midnight, Carroll and a deputy transported Davis to Baltimore.[60] Sure enough, at about 1:00 a.m., a contingent of the mob arrived and surrounded the jail in Easton. Deputy sheriffs permitted a delegation of the mob to search the jail. Once assured that Davis was not there, the crowd left. In all, on the night of November 23–24, the mob had searched jails in four counties looking for George Davis. Had he been found, it is doubtful that his boyish demeanor would have saved him from death by lynching.

AT THE HANDS OF PERSONS UNKNOWN

No one was tried or convicted for the lynching of Matthew Williams or George Armwood. The state's attorneys refused to even consider convening a grand jury to indict members of the mob who attempted to lynch Euel Lee and George Davis. More than one hundred witnesses were called before the grand jury after the Williams lynching. Forty-two witnesses were called before the grand jury in the Armwood case. In both instances, the men were found by the jury to have died "at the hands of persons unknown." Both in and out of the courtroom witnesses and spectators to the lynchings insisted that the lynchers were strangers who had come from out of town. The conclusions reached by these juries were consistent with the history of lynching investigations in Maryland. In the fourteen cases of reported lynchings in Maryland beginning in 1885 and ending in 1933, no suspected lynchers were ever indicted.[61]

CHAPTER 3

A CONSPIRACY OF SILENCE: ORDINARY PEOPLE AND COMPLICITY IN LYNCHING

It is the nucleus of ordinary men that continually
gives the mob its initial and awful impetus.
W.E.B. DUBOIS

PRESENCE

To imagine how many people saw all or part of the lynching of Matthew Williams, it may help to put the figures in context. If one thousand people witnessed the lynching of Matthew Williams, that would constitute nearly 10 percent of the white population of Salisbury in 1931. If two thousand people witnessed the lynching of George Armwood, that figure would account for about 10 percent of the current population of Somerset County and nearly 20 percent of the current population of Princess Anne. These figures, even if slightly inflated, suggest that several thousand people among the various Eastern Shore towns either observed or heard firsthand accounts of the lynchings. Still another several hundred (and perhaps many of the same) individuals were part of the roving lynch mobs that searched for George Davis and for Euel Lee. This means that participation in and knowledge of lynching among Eastern Shore whites was widely dispersed—a fact that Eastern Shore blacks would have known.

Without question, the participation of a crowd of spectators constituted a key part of early twentieth-century lynchings. Until the late 1930s, lynchings were often observed by thousands of people. One lynching in 1916 in Waco, Texas, attracted a crowd of fifteen thousand.[1] Ten thousand were on hand to watch the lynching of three black men hung from lampposts in Duluth, Minnesota, in 1920.[2] It is the presence of spectators, the open and audacious criminality of this distinctly public murder, that gives lynching its particular terror. No effort was made by perpetrators of most lynchings to conceal their identity or to hide the bodies of the lynching victims. Instead perpetrators posed for photographs next to the victims' smoking and charred remains. Bodies of victims were dragged through the streets openly and notoriously, or left hanging for hours and sometimes days, as a warning to black community members. The willingness of lynchers to act publicly is tremendously significant. It reflects the lynchers' certainty that they would never face punishment for their acts. The willingness of the crowd to participate in lynching—to cheer, to yell their encouragement, or just to stand and watch without intervention—is perhaps equally terrible.

The image of the lynching crowd, preserved in photos and macabre postcards and provided in newspaper accounts, presents a strangely democratic picture. Rather than portraying stereotypical rough-necked hillbillies, many lynching photographs show crowds that represent what can best be described as a cross section of the white community. Lynching crowds are, for the most part, remarkably diverse, made up of farmers and clerks, teachers, students, businessmen, the elderly, women, and, unfortunately, children. The lynching of Matthew Williams was observed by the two publishers of the local newspaper, one of whom reportedly "saw prominent officials... watching the action from the sidewalk in front of the Wicomico Hotel."[3] The entire Wi-Hi football team had enjoyed a postgame dinner at the hotel, and many members joined the throng observing the lynching.[4] Law student Charles Hearne observed the lynching from the balcony of the Wicomico Hotel.[5]

Shopkeepers, secretaries, truck drivers, and businesspeople were all part of the crowd that saw the lynching. In fact, as the leaders of the mob dragged Matthew Williams from the hospital to the courthouse lawn, "groups... ran from stores, from offices and from dwellings" to witness the hanging.[6] Lynching required the cooperation of educators, religious leaders, political leaders, law enforcement, shopkeepers, and countless others.

Helen Wise, the nurse on duty at the Peninsula Hospital, where Matthew Williams was held, told the crowd, "Well if you must take him, take him quietly."[7]

Children were also present at the lynchings. A young boy was hoisted up to throw the rope over the bough of the tree on which Matthew Williams was hung. One witness to the lynching was most startled by the number of women and children in attendance. A young girl who tried to turn away from the burning body of George Armwood was scolded by her mother and compelled to watch Armwood "being barbecued."[8]

The presence of children at lynchings is a deeply troubling phenomenon that seems nevertheless to have been common practice. Walter White, the great NAACP president and antilynching crusader, described "the warping of the minds of Southern children [as] by far the worst aspect of lynching."[9] Lynching photographs often show young boys, and in several cases girls, no older than nine or ten placed at the front row at hideous lynchings.[10] Children actively participated in some lynchings, carrying kindling or taking part in the ritual itself. In a Texas lynching in 1917, white oil-field workers compelled a ten-year-old white boy who carried water to the workers to castrate a black lynching victim.[11] Other children were just mute observers. Compelled by family members, and following the mores of the adults in their community, white children were in the unique position of being both victims of and participants in lynching. Suffice it to say that the presence of children ensured that the experience of lynching—the knowledge of the ritual, the memory of the brutality, the smell, the shared purpose of the crowd—was carried forward into subsequent generations. The effect of lynching on white children, and the particular contribution that whites who observed lynchings as children can make to a community's reconciliation process, will be further explored in chapter 7.

Of the crowd of five hundred to a thousand people who saw all or part of the lynching in Salisbury in 1931, only three individuals are believed actively to have tried to stop the Williams lynching. Daniel Eliot's son-in-law, E. R. White, is reported to have stood facing the mob outside the courthouse and implored them to stop.[12] A local businessman, Alexander Grier, driving in his car on Division Street, is also alleged to have tried to stop the mob as it moved from the hospital toward the courthouse. Yet another man, John Downing, described as the head of one of Salisbury's banks, made his way into the crowd and, after Williams was hanged, asked that the body be given to the sheriff rather than burned. Each man was rebuffed in his efforts by the crowd. The action of each of these men was courageous and stands in stark contrast to the vast majority.[13]

George Armwood's lynching was similarly "well attended" by a diverse group of people from Princess Anne and other Somerset County towns. Again, truck drivers, shopkeepers, businesspeople, and students were part of the lynching crowd of perhaps two thousand that observed all or part of the Armwood lynching. A young man cut off Armwood's ear as he emerged from the prison. A woman poked Armwood in the stomach as his body was hung. Later, during the night, as Armwood's body lay abandoned and mutilated on the streets, additional residents and curiosity seekers came to view the body.

The harvesting of lynching victims' body parts is perhaps the most grisly aspect of the lynching ritual. Some townspeople kept fingers of lynching victims in bottles and displayed them with macabre delight. For years after the Armwood lynching, rumor among local blacks had it that a white man named Bonneville kept Armwood's ear in a bottle of grain alcohol. One lynching participant reportedly cut off and hoarded Matthew Williams's toes.[14] Pieces of the rope used on both Armwood and Williams were kept by townspeople and displayed in the days after the lynching. William Denston, the son of Mary Denston and a Pennsylvania traffic policeman who was present at the Armwood lynching, displayed for reporters a piece of the rope he'd taken as a souvenir.[15] Desperate for relics of the lynching, men began cutting up the wooden plank that had been used as a battering ram. Tear-gas canisters used by the state police were also a coveted prize.[16] Historian David Roediger has estimated that in this way "several million early 20th century whites witnessed a lynching or touched its relics."[17]

The presence and acquiescence of the crowd is the aspect of lynching that has produced among blacks a deeply held and long-term suspicion of whites, which resonates to this day. It hardly matters whether those who watched lynchings were active or passive participants. As Fitzhugh Brundage observes in his work *Lynching in the New South*, although "some spectators may have been shocked and disgusted by the violence they witnessed ... it was their visible, explicit, public act of participation and not their ambiguous, private sentiment that bound the lynchers both socially and morally." The strength of these bonds is exemplified by the fact that after a lynching, witnesses called to testify before a grand jury regularly insisted that they recognized no one in the crowd. Thus, lynching victims were routinely found to have suffered "at the hands of persons unknown." The refusal of passive members of the lynching crowd to assist in the prosecution of active lynchers undermined any claim to diminished culpability or complicity in the lynching.

PASSIVE POSTLYNCHING COMPLICITY: SILENCE

When ten-year-old Clinton Adams told the deputy sheriff that he had seen the lynching of two black couples who were shot to death under the Moore's Ford Bridge in Walton, Georgia, in 1946, the burly sheriff, whom Adams looked up to like a surrogate father, told the boy, "From this day forward, don't you ever say that again."[18] This story is not uncommon. Despite the open and almost bacchanalian revelry of lynching, what invariably followed was days of silence. Those who had witnessed the lynching never talked about it, not even among themselves. For obvious reasons, the few blacks who saw lynchings remained silent. The bellhops and cooks at the Wicomico Hotel who saw the lynching of Matthew Williams whispered it to their wives but never spoke of it openly, for fear of violent reprisals. Seventy-five years after the lynching, Howard Purnell told me that he'd seen the entire lynching, that Matthew Williams was a classmate of his, and that it was the worst thing he'd ever seen. Purnell had been with James Stanley Pinkett, the bell captain of the hotel and Purnell's best friend, on the balcony of the hotel overlooking the courthouse lawn. James Harrison Webb had also been part of this group. These black men, in addition to witnessing the horror of their neighbor's brutal murder, must have feared for their own lives, and each had to find a way home that night through the hollering, bloodthirsty crowd. It must have been a night of unspeakable horror. But Purnell, a dignified and proud man, refused to say anything about the lynching. Despite my repeated attempts over several years, Purnell took his eyewitness account of the lynching to his grave.

Whites, for different reasons, also joined a conspiracy of silence. In silence there was safety—safety from potential prosecution for the lynchers, yes, but more important, safety from the danger of facing a difficult truth: that the quiet, close-knit little town that regarded itself as Christian and its residents as civic-minded and neighborly also could be bestial, cowardly, and lawless. After the Matthew Williams lynching, the decision to be silent came from the top. On December 5, the day after the lynching, the *Salisbury Times* set the tone by imposing a news blackout on the lynching. Instead, the paper published "A Statement" explaining its decision *not* to report on the lynching. Reporting the facts of the lynching would, wrote the paper's editors, "be superfluous." The editors encouraged residents to instead "co-operate in speeding up a return to absolutely normal and harmonious conditions."[19] Silence was couched as a form of civic duty and an expression of regional loyalty. The lynching itself was referred to as a "demonstration."

On the Sunday morning after the Williams and Armwood lynchings, white church leaders in Salisbury and Princess Anne were largely silent about the melee that had overtaken their towns just a few days earlier. That many of the parishioners seated in the pews had undoubtedly either participated in or witnessed a hideous public murder was not regarded as an opportunity for spiritual challenge by clergy in Wicomico and Somerset Counties. In fact, white ministers were united and adamant in their determination *not* to mention the lynchings in their sermons. The pastor of the First Baptist Church, Rev. Frank K. Brasington, stated that he had been assured by his parishioners that the lynch mob that killed George Armwood was not made up of Princess Anne residents.[20] The pastor of the Manokin Presbyterian Church, Rev. J. Paul Trout, announced before Sunday his intention to "refer to violence in the community, but not to the Armwood killing." The pastor of St. Andrew's Church, where Judge Duer was a prominent member and vestryman, explained that he would "preach 'the word of God' without reference to the death of Armwood." After Matthew Williams was lynched in Salisbury, the pastor of Trinity Methodist Episcopal Church reportedly "did not believe this was the proper time to address his audience" on the topic of the lynching, as "the community had suffered a strain."[21]

The reaction of the rest of the state and the country to the Williams lynching made it impossible for Shore residents to maintain absolute silence. H. L. Mencken's column entitled "Eastern Shore Kultur" denounced the Shore as "a lush stamping-ground for knavish politicians, prehensile professional patriots, and whooping soul-savers" who had "succumbed to its poor white trash."[22] Ministers from Baltimore and other parts of the state spoke out forcefully against the lynching.[23] The lynching was national news, and the condemnation of the Eastern Shore was, in many instances, vicious. And so silence was broken for the limited purpose of responding to Mencken's searing denunciation of the Shore. But beyond defending the honor of the Shore and blaming delays in the Euel Lee case on Communists' interference, whites had little or nothing to say about either the Williams or the Armwood lynching.

Certainly, whites did not talk about who was involved in the lynching and whether they would be brought to justice. Instead, in the days and weeks after the lynching, whites closed ranks to protect their neighbors and acquaintances from prosecution. More than one hundred witnesses were called before the grand jury investigating the Williams lynching, yet none could identify members of the lynch mob. Many insisted that the lynch mob members were not from Wicomico County. In a pattern repeated in Eastern Shore investigations of lynch mobs over the years, witnesses from Wicomico thought that lynch mob members were from Somerset County. Two years later, when the Somerset County grand jury heard testimony from forty-two witnesses in the Armwood case, several suggested that residents from Wicomico and Worcester were responsible. Both Wicomico and Somerset residents were the instigators and most active participants in both lynchings. In Princess Anne, even after state police officers in sworn testimony identified nine men as leaders of the lynch mob, a local grand jury issued no indictments for Armwood's murder.

Decades later Judge Alfred Truitt Jr. interpreted the silence that followed the Williams lynching—including the decision by his father and uncle to not report on the lynching in the town's newspaper—as a reflection of a kind of stunned disbelief that many whites experienced. According to Truitt, most responsible residents of Salisbury felt a sense of "chagrin." They were simply shocked and ashamed that the lynching had happened.[24] More than likely, Judge Truitt is right. In the days after the lynching whites would have been grappling with the fact that many of their neighbors and acquaintances were capable of the kind of hideous violence and depravity displayed on the night of December 4. But an understandable "shock" in the first days after the lynching fails to explain why that silence continued through grand jury hearings and testimony. Nor does it explain why the lynchings were almost never discussed in any detail within white communities in Wicomico over the next seventy years.

On the day after George Armwood was lynched in Princess Anne, whites talked rather openly about the event. Small groups of whites laughed and joked about the previous night's happenings. One man remarked, "It would have cost the State $1,000, I guess to hang that man. It only cost us 75 cents."[25] But after the first day, talk of the lynching evaporated. Those who had openly proclaimed that they were at the lynching had, by the time the grand jury was convened, changed their stories. No one recognized anyone who had been there.

State's Attorney Robins, who'd spent the night of the lynching at his home in Crisfield, refused to make any comment the day after the lynching. Judge Duer issued a statement conceding that he had been "badly mistaken" in assuming that the crowd that he addressed was made up of "curiosity seekers" rather than murderers. The local police were talking, but only to reassure the public that they did not recognize any of the lynchers. The town sheriff, Luther Daugherty, who had stood at the door of the jail when the mob attacked, announced the day after the lynching that he thought that all of the lynchers were from Virginia. Nearly every local official—from the jailer to the local judge to the coroner to local eyewitnesses—repeated this claim. And this became the official story. The lynching was committed by outsiders. The universal adoption by local leaders and townspeople of this patently untrue but comforting story justified for white residents their determination to maintain silence in the ensuing weeks. The lynching was not really about their community, and so there was nothing to talk about.

COMPLICITY AND LYNCHING'S BENEFICIARIES

To understand why whites felt compelled to participate in the conspiracy of silence after the lynching, it is important to remember that whatever the event that sparked mob violence, lynching was a tool of white supremacy. Other tools used during this period included the poll tax and other forms of voting disenfranchisement, sharecropping, segregation, employment discrimination, antimiscegenation laws, and so forth. Lynching was the violent analogue to these other methods of oppression. Lynching enforced white privilege, Jim Crow, and white domination of the political, educational, and economic advancement of the community through terror. The horror of lynching reminded blacks that, as a last resort, violent reprisals could be exacted for breaches of the social order. This means that, at least in the short term, ordinary whites—even those who would never have joined a lynch mob—benefited from lynching, just as they benefited from the other tools of white supremacy.

In essence, whites' shared interest in maintaining white supremacy lay at the core of the conspiracy of silence following a lynching. As one Mississippi resident put it after a lynching in his community, "We're all neighbors and neighbors' neighbors."[26] Passive participants of lynching had more in common with the violent ruffians who pulled the rope or lit the match than with blacks or with whites who were less dependent on black labor and black subordination for the maintenance of their livelihood. And so many whites, even those secretly repulsed by the lynchings, closed ranks with their neighbors to protect the status quo.

In some southern communities, whites derived more explicit economic and political "benefits" from lynching. This was especially true in those southern counties where blacks constituted a majority or near majority of the population. Without the threat of lynching, eligible blacks exercising their right to vote would have formed significant and powerful voting blocs. Similarly, for white farming communities relying on an army of poorly paid sharecroppers to work large plantations, lynching helped ensure the maintenance of a compliant and available workforce, without which the traditional agrarian southern economy could not function for the benefit of whites. Freed from competition with black labor, entrepreneurship, political activity, and educational advancement, whites—even those who did not actively participate in lynching—derived benefits from the willingness of their more aggressive neighbors to tend to the more unsavory and violent aspects of maintaining white supremacy.

Ironically, even arguments *against* lynching in some southern jurisdictions were couched in terms of white benefit. One editor of a Tennessee paper reasoned, "The Negro is about the only dependable tiller of the soil in these parts. Competition for existence is not keen enough to force many white people into the harder work. The Negro also is very useful as a distributor of money. About all he gets goes through his fingers. Commercially, then, he is a very valuable asset. It is not good business to kill them."[27] Certainly in many communities lynching produced a phenomenon that white communities dependent on black labor neither anticipated nor desired—the migration of blacks to the North. In fact, there is strong evidence to suggest that the Great Migration of blacks from the South to the northern industrial centers between World War I and World War II was fueled at least in part by lynchings and the threat of racial violence in southern communities. A study of Georgia and South Carolina reveals that the black exodus to the North was heavier in counties that experienced severe mob violence.[28] As the author of one book on antilynching legislation put it, "The North was no Garden of Eden...but for many migrants it at least offered some hope of avoiding institutionalized violence."[29] Despite this unintended consequence of lynching, whites for the most part benefited economically and politically from the violent maintenance of white supremacy.

ACTIVE POSTLYNCHING COMPLICITY

Not all whites were passively complicit in lynching. Some actively defended the lynching of Williams and Armwood. The day after George Armwood was lynched, Baltimore *Afro* reporter Clarence Mitchell was stunned and sickened by the whites who walked through the town recounting the lynching with glee and taking their young children to view George Armwood's body, which lay uncovered and mutilated in a lumberyard.[30] Editorials and letters to the editor in local papers overwhelmingly excused the actions of white lynch mobs or accused outside agitators of "stirring up" discontent among local blacks. No editorial that appeared in any local Shore paper in the aftermath of the Williams or Armwood lynching unequivocally condemned the lynching without offering some excuse or mitigating factor. Even letters to the editor that appeared in the *Baltimore Sun* were mixed. The overwhelming majority condemned the lynchings, but some state residents, most writing from the Eastern Shore, but even some from Baltimore City and Harford County, expressed support for, or at least understanding of, the lynchings.

Affirmative efforts were made as well to control the response of the local black community. After Matthew Williams was lynched, Salisbury mayor Wade Insley called a meeting of local black leaders in what the *Afro* described as "an old Dixie custom of getting the colored leaders of the city 'in line.'"[31] The mayor advised blacks to stay off the streets and ordered that blacks close their businesses temporarily. A similar curfew was not imposed on white businesses. But the mayor promised to provide additional police presence on the main street of the town. In an official statement after the meeting, the mayor insisted that "[t]here never has been any trouble between the races here, and there is not going to be now."[32]

And of course when, in the months after the lynchings of Williams and Armwood passions had cooled a bit and Eastern Shore whites had an opportunity to fulfill their obligation to provide sworn, truthful testimony to grand juries investigating the lynchings, witness after witness refused to identify any members of the lynch mob. Whites may have further obstructed justice by intimidating black witnesses and preventing them from telling what they saw. No efforts were made to sequester black witnesses or to offer them long-term protection in exchange for truthful testimony about what they saw on the night of the lynching. Jacob Conquest, a Wicomico County resident who was a patient in the Negro Ward at Peninsula Hospital alongside Matthew Williams and an eyewitness to Williams's abduction from the hospital, was listed as a grand jury witness, but he died soon after the inquest was announced. Rufus Jernigan, another black patient in the Negro Ward at Peninsula Hospital, was called as a grand jury witness, but he mysteriously disappeared before he could testify.[33] It is hard to know whether these men were murdered or threatened, or whether Jernigan was simply savvy enough to know that his life would be in danger if he were to testify before the grand jury. In either case they could not have been expected to provide truthful testimony to the inquest without endangering their own lives and the lives of their family members. Twelve black prisoners who had suffered the horror of seeing George Armwood dragged from their prison cell at the Princess Anne jail by the howling white mob, were similarly intimidated when they were called to testify before the coroner's jury investigating the lynching. Each in turn testified that he saw nothing and recognized no one. When one black prisoner was asked whether he saw the men who entered the prison cell that night do anything, he replied under oath, "No suh." In the courtroom, the mostly white crowd erupted in laughter at the black prisoner's incredible, but wholly understandable, testimony.[34]

Perhaps the most public act of support for the lynching of George Armwood occurred when white townspeople in Salisbury violently confronted the National Guard, who were sent in to arrest four suspected lynchers. After the investigation of the lynching was taken over by Attorney General Preston Lane, twelve men were identified by state police as being active members of the lynch mob. The state police officers, several of whom had been knocked out by belligerent mob members determined to storm the jail, identified the lynchers by name. Some of the state police officers testified that they personally knew the lynchers. Upon orders of the governor, the state National Guard arrested four of the suspected lynchers. The Guard was met by a crowd of at least one thousand townsmen from Salisbury who challenged the Guard's efforts to take the suspects to Baltimore.

The battle between the townspeople of Salisbury, who were holding rocks and bricks, and the National Guard, with their bayonets drawn and tear-gas fired, is one of the most extraordinary in the history of this country. White community members were not just staying silent or refusing to identify lynchers. A crowd of one thousand local men used force to try to keep the National Guard from arresting men who'd been identified by the state police as leaders of a lynch mob. This crowd could not be explained as a "foreign mob" from "Virginia." No one had known the National Guard were coming into town. They had arrived in the hours before dawn, and no significant out-of-state contingent could have been mobilized to face the Guard on such short notice. It was local townspeople in Salisbury who sought to repulse the arrest of the suspected lynchers. When Attorney General Lane was spotted by members of the crowd, the cry went up, "Lynch Lane!" The attorney general was whisked to safety, but not before his car was pelted with rocks and bricks.

A day later, when the Somerset County state's attorney ordered the four suspected lynchers returned to Princess Anne for a habeas corpus hearing and the four men were brought before local judges, a crowd of nearly one thousand well-wishers crammed into the county courthouse and cheered the release of the four men, affirming their solidarity with the suspected murderers.

Members of the Fifth Regiment of the National Guard face off with residents of Salisbury who repulsed their efforts to arrest suspected lynchers.

BLACKS' RESPONSE TO LYNCHING:
FEAR, COMPLICITY, AND RESISTANCE

For many blacks, the crowd of white lynchers represents a shared commitment among whites to maintain white supremacy by the most violent means. And yet few whites today understand the long-term effect of the either tacit or explicit complicity of their forbears in the lynchings and near lynchings in towns throughout the United States. That blacks were aware that many of their employers, coworkers, and town leaders observed or heard firsthand accounts of Eastern Shore lynchings is an important fact. In her moving memoir about growing up on the Shore, poet Adele Holden recalls that her father's outrage about the lynching of Matthew Williams was further fueled by the casual way in which white coworkers openly confirmed their presence at the lynching in the days after the event. The complicity of average whites in joining or condoning the lynchings convinced many blacks that whites were simply not to be trusted. Snow Holden expressed the sentiment of many blacks when after the Williams lynching he concluded, "It's got to be one or two good [whites], but if push come to shove, they're not going to do no better'n keep quiet."[35]

In communities where lynchings occurred, fear kept blacks mostly silent and compliant. Lynchings were rarely single events. In many lynchings in the Deep South, whites would burn black homes and businesses after a lynching. Ripples of violence could last for weeks or even months. A week after Matthew Williams was lynched, blacks could still be intimidated with the threat of mob violence. One young black man, Lawrence Moore, was reportedly threatened on his job by white coworkers who wanted to replace Moore with one of their white friends. They told Moore that they would "set a mob on him unless he quit" his job. Moore, a native of Virginia, decided to leave the town of Salisbury.[36]

Additionally, when the mutilated body of a black man was found in the city on the Sunday morning after the Williams lynching, many blacks suspected that the man had been beaten to death by a gang of whites who had reportedly been running throughout the town menacing black residents on Saturday night.[37] Dr. A. B. Brown, the only black physician in town, who had treated Williams when he was shot at the Elliot mill, feared for his life. Brown had been in town when the lynching began and recognized members of the mob. Temporarily moving his family from their home to a safe location, Brown armed himself with a shotgun and left town for the night.[38]

More than a month after George Armwood was lynched, when the four lynching suspects were returned to Princess Anne from their one-night stay in the Baltimore City jail, members of the white crowd that assembled at the courthouse to meet them apparently forced blacks off the street and out of town.

In sum, blacks had reason to fear postlynching white violence. For this reason, some black leaders sought to mollify white anger by publicly condemning *not the lynchers* but the lynching victim. Even before the lynching of George Armwood, Dr. T. H. Kiah, the principal of the Princess Anne Academy, the local black college (now the University of Maryland, Eastern Shore), took pains to emphasize that Armwood was alleged to be "feeble-minded." Kiah also offered assurances "that no harm" would come to Armwood in Princess Anne. He was proven wrong. Charges that Matthew Williams was "slow" and "feeble-minded" also circulated after he was lynched.

In December 1933 three black leaders took the extraordinary step of writing an open letter published in the *Salisbury Times* and on the front page of Somerset County's *Marylander and Herald* in which they attributed "the entire disturbance on the lower Shore" to the outside influence of Bernard Ades, who "injected himself" into the Euel Lee case.

In a statement clearly designed to pander to whites, the three leaders—James Stewart, a prominent Salisbury mortician, the Reverend James M. Dickerson, and James L. Johnson, a retired schoolteacher—declared, "We state without fear of contradiction, that it was the tactics Ades employed in [the Euel Lee] case which caused the death of Matthew Williams and George Armwood."[39] They painted an idealistic picture of the relationship between blacks and whites in Salisbury, insisting that "[w]e enjoy the lives we live here in this beautiful Shore, graced by nature and abounding in plenty. We feel that our people here on the average are more intelligent, more understanding, more prosperous, more industrious and happier than are our people in any other section of this nation." The three ended the letter by committing themselves to work to eliminate "crime and also outside interference," and pledged that they would have other black groups adopt resolutions endorsing their statement. The statement appeared on the front page of the *Salisbury Times,* the white daily paper that had refused to report on the lynching of Matthew Williams two years earlier, under the headline "A Statement by Outstanding Negro Leaders."

The *Afro* denounced the letter penned by what they called "Three Uncle Jameses" as a "defense of the Eastern Shore lynchers."[40] But more significant, a group of nineteen black leaders from the Shore took the extraordinary step of replying to the letter, denouncing the three leaders' accommodationist rhetoric.[41] The group of nineteen included several clergymen, the town's black physician, Dr. A. B. Brown, who had attended Matthew Williams after he was shot, and Levin Purnell, a relative of Howard and also a bellman at the Wicomico Hotel. The nineteen leaders met in Salisbury and drafted a response, which they sent to the *Afro.* One person whose name had originally been signed to the letter, Dr. Charles Chipman, wired the *Afro* to explain that he had not authorized the inclusion of his name on the letter.[42] Chipman was perhaps the most prominent educational leader on the Eastern Shore. He spearheaded the construction of a new high school for blacks in Salisbury and was recognized by whites and blacks as the driving force for black education in Wicomico County.[43]

The addition of his name to the letter would have carried considerable weight.

In any case, the letter by the nineteen leaders was explosive. It responded to both the tone and the substance of the letter by the three leaders published in the *Salisbury Times* and forcefully rejected the rhetoric of the *Times* piece.

We profoundly regret and deplore the unfortunate happenings which have occurred on the Eastern Shore within the past two years and clearly realized that the resulting opprobrium cannot be removed in a day by a simple wave of the hand, a few absurd claims, prevarications or unauthorized statements. The public, outside of our own turbulent little section, are not so easily deceived. They readily see through such fabrications, as appeared in *the Salisbury Times* of December 6th, under the caption "a statement by outstanding Negro leaders" as clearly as looking through a two-inch mesh.

It would have been far more courageous and manly to have made a clean breast of the whole matter; admitting our faults, acknowledging our grievous mistake and then start out with a resolute determination to guard against the possibility of a recurrence of such violent demonstrations. Sponsor adequate measures before the Maryland Legislature and see to it that such laws are enacted as will render it practically impossible for any lawless mob to perpetuate such wild scenes again.

Such a course would have inspired a much greater confidence in our world and placed us squarely on the road of appeasing an outraged public opinion.

The countergroup went on to point out "[t]he ridiculous absurdity of [the three leaders' statement]," which, they contended, "sinks at once to the level of a travesty on common sense." Clearly charging that the three leaders had been pressured by whites to issue their statement in the *Salisbury Times*, the nineteen charged that "the 'statement' [by the three] bears all the ear marks of a command to sign on the dotted line,' by some interest which would profit most by impressing the public that the Negro on the Eastern Shore is spineless." The nineteen concluded by emphasizing that the three leaders "do not and can not speak for anyone but themselves and those to whose paper they saw fit to affix their names."

This public reply and the meeting that precipitated it represented a courageous and bold resistance on the part of Eastern Shore blacks. They refused to acquiesce in efforts to shift responsibility for the lynchings away from Eastern Shore whites. Moreover, by articulating their support for federal antilynching legislation, they adopted a platform of sorts, identifying the need for concrete measures that could help protect the lives of blacks from mob violence. These nineteen blacks must have feared or expected reprisals for this bold statement, not only from whites, but also from other blacks who would have regarded their stance as too radical and potentially dangerous. The decision to release their reply publicly and to offer an unequivocal alternative account of a black response to the lynchings is therefore all the more impressive.

Blacks also responded in pragmatic ways to the lynchings. A deep well of suspicion was created in the black community. White coworkers, a white boss, or fellow waterman could have been part of the lynching crowd. And even if they had not been part of the crowd, they would, as Snow Holden pointed out, "keep quiet." Blacks became more cautious, more insular around the whites with whom they worked and interacted. One of the most remarkable examples of this kind of black response to white complicity in lynching was described by Judge Alfred Truitt Jr., who was only five or six years old when he saw part of the lynching. Truitt was with his father, who in addition to being one of the publishers of the *Salisbury Times* was in charge of the town's civil defense. Young Truitt stood with his father near the fire station and saw the crowd drag Williams in the direction of the courthouse. Several days later, Truitt recalled, he was walking on the streets of Salisbury when he saw a young black boy with whom he was friends. The black boy stepped off the sidewalk to permit Truitt to pass, something he had not done before. Truitt asked the young boy why he deferred to him, and the boy replied, "My mama told me not to talk to you people anymore."[44] Even at that age, Truitt remembers thinking "What's going on?" In the space of one week, two young friends were reminded of their superior and inferior social status. Black parents were teaching their children to walk carefully and to trust no whites, not even white children.

CHAPTER 4

"THE LAW IN ALL ITS MAJESTY"

It is only since the Supreme Court's majestic 1954 opinion in *Brown v. Board of Education* that the courts in the United States have taken on the reputation as defenders of racial minorities. The *Brown* decision established and cemented for the U.S. justice system an international reputation for courage, impartiality, and a commitment to equality. Given the significance of that decision in ending legalized racial apartheid, that reputation is, in part, deserved. The language of the opinion, and its recognition of how racial discrimination corrodes our society, articulate the highest aspirations of a nation struggling with the long legacy of slavery.

But *Brown*, in fact, is an anomaly. In the context of the Supreme Court's long history, the *Brown* decision is a bump in the road along a path marked more consistently by the Court's embrace and reaffirmation of inequality and exclusion based on race, wealth, and gender. In fact only a year after deciding that "separate but equal has no place in public education," the Court decided *Brown II,* considered by many to be a nadir in the Court's civil rights jurisprudence. In the 1955 *Brown* decision the Court turned over the implementation of school desegregation to local judges, who were to act not immediately but with "all deliberate speed." *Brown II* set off a twenty-five-year pattern of resistance to the core directive of *Brown* throughout the United States and sounded the death knell for the promise of integrated education in our nation's schools.

In fact, the Supreme Court's tentative and ultimately status quo–reinforcing decision in *Brown II* was more consistent with its history than the soaring courage of *Brown I.* The Supreme Court and the federal courts below it were not institutions of social or political change. Before the

1950s, the legal system, more often than not, reinforced and perpetuated society's gross class and race inequities. State court systems were notoriously reactionary, especially in the South. Judges on southern courts in most states have been elected since before the Civil War, and the jurisprudence of those judges, particularly during the first half of the twentieth century, often reflected the prejudices of the voters who put the judges in office.

The criminal justice system, in particular, played a critical role in subordinating and marginalizing blacks in southern states. Blacks were regularly excluded from serving on juries in the South, especially in cases where a black defendant was alleged to have committed a violent crime against a white victim. Where blacks served as witnesses, their word was not regarded as more credible than that of an opposing white witness. Jim Crow was the custom in courthouses, with different bathrooms and water fountains for blacks and whites. Different sides of the courtroom were reserved for whites and blacks. Black witnesses were often disrespected in the courtroom, under the indifferent eye of judges. When Martha Miller, who owned the boarding house where Euel Lee lived, testified at his trial in 1932, she was repeatedly addressed by the prosecutor as "Aunt Martha."

Black lawyers in the 1930s and 1940s fought hard and valiantly for black criminal defendants in a system in which black lawyers received little respect from judges, jurors, and prosecutors, and little or no remuneration from their struggling clients. Most southern jurisdictions had no black lawyers. In high-profile interracial criminal cases, black lawyers from the big cities or from the North might be prevailed upon to represent a black criminal defendant. In other cases, white lawyers, often with Communist or Socialist Party affiliations, represented black criminal defendants in an effort to expose the racism and inequality they regarded as inherent to the capitalist system. The case of seventeen black young men taken from a train in Alabama and arrested for raping two white women—the infamous Scottsboro boys case—became a symbol of the effort by white and black lawyers to fight against the excesses of the southern criminal justice system.

There is no record of any white person ever having been convicted of murder for lynching a black person—not in the thousands of instances of white-on-black lynchings in thirty-four states. This is both a damning and a revealing statistic. It reflects across regions and over decades a colossal and unbroken culture of legal complicity in violent white supremacy. It reveals that thousands of individuals who served in the legal system—from police officers to judges to juries—participated in concerted action to subvert the rule of law and to further the cause of white supremacy. The long-term consequence of this history is the deep suspicion with which many blacks regard the legal system today. Blacks have an almost encoded memory of racial injustice in the criminal justice system—a memory passed down in families and communities. Contemporary racial miscarriages of justices—from the acquittal of the police officers who beat black motorist Rodney King in Los Angeles in 1991 to the death of African immigrant Amadou Diallo, who was shot by New York City police officers forty-one times as he attempted to produce his identification in 1999—serve to reinforce for blacks a preexisting and well-documented history of racial miscarriages of justice. When in 1993 blacks were shown on television applauding the acquittal of black former football star O. J. Simpson for the murder of his white ex-wife and her companion, many whites understood for the first time the skepticism and intense distrust with which many blacks regard the criminal justice system. What even fewer whites understood was the historical context within which blacks have developed this cynicism about one of our democracy's bedrock institutions. Lynching, and the historical complicity or indifference of legal institutions to lynching, is a critical part of this history.

The response of the legal community on the Eastern Shore to the lynchings and near lynchings of the 1930s provides an almost textbook example of the persistent and shameful collusion between and among white legal actors to insulate white criminals from legal punishment for crimes against blacks and to deny black criminal defendants the most basic due process. This history is grim. Very few whites involved in these cases demonstrated adherence to the rule of law that they had sworn to uphold as peace officers, lawyers, jurors, and judges. Some whites—few, but some, demonstrated enormous courage and integrity. They refused to yield to a racial code that compelled their silence, their inaction, or their acquiescence. It is important to recognize and explore at some length the actions of those whites who did act courageously to uphold the rule of law because their conduct undermines efforts to explain away the disgraceful conduct of those who complied with injustice as compelled by the time and circumstances in which they lived. Whites—especially those in positions of power and authority, such as judges and prosecutors—had the choice to act honorably or dishonorably. Too few chose the former. And the consequences of this choice continue to shape black and white responses to, and involvement with, the legal system in communities throughout the United States.

LOCAL POLICE OFFICERS

The Williams Lynching

The first and therefore most important legal actors to respond to real or imagined black criminality were police officers. Their action or inaction set the stage for how a black man suspected of committing a crime against a white person would be treated. Often police officers determined whether a black man would face a trial or a lynch mob. When Matthew Williams was dragged from his hospital bed on the night of December 4, 1931, a large crowd had gathered on the streets of Salisbury. Groups had been gathering and talking about an impending lynching since the late afternoon. Law student Charles Hearne was advised by an older acquaintance to return downtown later in the evening to witness what was clearly a planned lynching. Hearne later returned to town as suggested and observed the lynching from the balcony of the Wicomico Hotel. This means that rather than the purely "spontaneous" event that Chief of Police Holland described to reporters later, the lynching of Matthew Williams was openly discussed and planned soon after word got out that Williams had shot and killed D. J. Elliot.[1]

By the evening, crowds were milling about outside the newspaper offices of the *Salisbury Times*, located across the street from Peninsula Hospital, where Williams lay, seriously injured. Police officers, including Chief of Police Holland, were stationed at the hospital, guarding Williams. This suggests, yet again, that the officer suspected that mob violence was a possibility. The police had every reason to take this threat of mob violence seriously. Mobs had searched four counties in an effort to lynch Euel Lee in October and had traveled through four counties to find George Davis in November. The leader of the mob looking for George

Davis displayed a rope over his arm. Two sheriffs helped save Davis's life that night. Sheriff John T. Vickers of Kent County had Davis immediately sent to Easton in Talbot County upon his arrest. When lynch mobs arrived at the Chestertown jail, Sheriff Vickers could honestly assure the crowd that he was not holding Davis. Leaders of the crowd, including the brother of Mrs. Lusby, went through the jail to confirm that Davis was not there. Undeterred, the mob went on to Talbot County. Sheriff George Carroll hurriedly had Davis taken to Baltimore City for safekeeping. A half hour after Davis's departure for Baltimore, a lynch mob arrived at the Talbot County jail, leaving only when Sheriff Carroll permitted leaders to conduct a search of the jail to ensure that Davis was not there. In both the Lee and the Davis case the mob was dispersed only after police officers and prison wardens permitted members of the mob to search the jails at Salisbury, Chestertown, and Easton. By December every police officer in the county knew that both Lee and Davis were alive only by virtue of their presence in the Baltimore City jail, where they had been taken for safekeeping. Even Lee's white attorney, Bernard Ades, had nearly been lynched in broad daylight in Snow Hill, Worcester County. Ades had been saved by the intervention of the local judge and sheriff, who spirited Ades away from the crowd and locked him in the town jail for his own safety. Thus the stage was set for a mob effort to lynch Williams.

Although Wicomico County chief of police N. H. Holland spoke with the men who came to the hospital to abduct Matthew Williams, followed the crowd that dragged Williams to the courthouse, saw Williams hung, and stepped in after the hanging to secure the body before the crowd took the corpse away to be burned, he was unable to identify any of the lynchers. Holland contended that after Williams was hung from a tree in front of the courthouse, "there was no use for me to try to arrest anybody because I was outnumbered too much."[2] And yet there was no evidence that Holland had anything to fear from the crowd. In fact, Holland himself stated that he could not "remember whether any of them threatened me, because everything happened so fast."[3]

The Armwood Lynching

The failure of local police to protect George Armwood from lynching in 1933 was even more egregious. After all, Armwood had been taken to safety in Baltimore City immediately after his arrest. The order to bring him back was, in effect, a death sentence. Why was he brought back to the Shore? Responsibility for the order itself rests with the local state's attorney, John Robins, and the local sheriff, Luther Daugherty. No doubt under intense local pressure, they ordered that Armwood be arraigned in Princess Anne the next day, on October 18. No explanation for the urgency of this court appearance was ever offered. Sheriff Daugherty could easily have anticipated that Armwood would be in grave danger if he was returned to the Shore so soon after his arrest for the attack on Mary Denston. Daugherty could not claim, as the police had in Salisbury two years earlier, to be surprised by the determination of the mob. The Williams lynching only two years earlier had demonstrated all too clearly that Eastern Shore mobs were prepared to act murderously against black men accused of violent crimes against whites.

Moreover, throughout the afternoon of October 18 there were open discussions among townspeople about lynching Armwood. Whites standing in cliques along Williams Street and outside the Washington Hotel on Somerset Street talked excitedly and openly about the possibility of a lynching. According to one report, a young relative of Denston, the woman who had allegedly been attacked by George Armwood, was a fixture on Williams Street throughout the day, encouraging and exhorting townspeople to lynch Armwood.[4] Denston's son William, a motorcycle cop from Pennsylvania, was downtown and on hand to, as he put it later, see "every part of [the lynching]."[5] One out-of-town visitor, who later witnessed the lynching, swore in a statement that throughout the afternoon he heard discussion among groups of men who talked of lynching Armwood.[6] One such group milled about outside the jail. At least one mob member was heard to say, "Let's give him the same dose we gave Williams."[7] That same witness said that at least three police officers were present during these discussions. Across the bay, the evening edition of the October 18 *Baltimore Post* went on the newsstands at 6:00 p.m. The headline was eight columns wide and read, "Mobs Are Forming on the Eastern Shore and There Is Grave Danger That a Lynching Will Occur Tonight." As the associate editor of the *Post* testified before a congressional committee the following year, the story for the evening edition was written well before 6:00 p.m., which meant that by late afternoon even newsmen in

Baltimore had received word of the mob gathering in Princess Anne.[8] Yet local police insisted that they were unable to confirm that there were serious plans afoot to lynch Armwood.

Certainly by 1:00 p.m. Governor Ritchie in Annapolis had heard rumors of unrest in Princess Anne and talk of lynching Armwood. The governor began making a series of urgent calls to the local judge, Robert Duer, to State's Attorney John Robins, and to the state police, seeking reassurance that Armwood would be safe. Yet Sheriff Daugherty, who might have had credibility and influence with members of the gathering mob, and who in any case was charged with ensuring public safety, spent the afternoon and early evening at his home in the nearby town of Crisfield. By the time Daugherty arrived at the jail at around 7:00 p.m., the mob had already formed and solidified with the intent to storm the jail and lynch Armwood.

Accounts of lynchings reveal that mob action was averted only when local law enforcement removed a potential victim from the jurisdiction or conveyed persuasively to the members of the lynch mob that they would be shot if they proceeded with the lynching. Local lawmen were well known to members of the community and to the lynchers. A handful of cases from the South reveal that local law enforcement officers who were determined to forestall lynching in their jurisdictions used a variety of tactics to stave off mobs, ranging from humor to threats of violence. To stop a mob in Spartanburg County, South Carolina, from entering the jail yard where a black prisoner was being kept, for example, Sheriff W. J. White reportedly announced, "Gentlemen, I hate to do it, but so help me God, I am going to kill the first man that enters that gate."[9] By contrast, the presence of state officers or National Guardsmen in Princess Anne appeared to exacerbate the lynchers' sense that their murderous acts constituted a defense of their local pride and autonomy. As a result, the inaction or passivity of local law enforcement ensured that a lynching would be completed.

Unfortunately, zealous protection of black prisoners was all too rare. In many cases, local law enforcement officers appeared to be complicit with lynchers. Simply leaving the jail untended where a black defendant accused of committing a violent crime against a white person was being held could pretty well ensure that a mob would have its way. In one South Carolina lynching, the chief of police reportedly "told [the lynchers] to wait until dark and we would find the jail unlocked."[10] In another lynching in Indiana, police officers "stood on the river bank and watched the men and boys about the fire for an hour or more." Officers rarely used their pistols to stop a lynch mob, in one Texas case expressing their fear that "somebody would be hurt."[11]

And in the aftermath of lynching, local police officers, like the townspeople who attended the lynching, proved unable and unwilling to identify lynchers. When George Armwood was lynched, three local police officers were present, along with a contingent of state police. The mob assaulted several of the state police officers. There is no evidence that the local police were injured or threatened. Deputy Police Chief Norman Dryden, the jailer at the Princess Anne who handed over the keys to the jail to mobbers, testified that he "didn't see anybody [he] knew." His exhortation to the crowd took the form of a plea that they "not do anything to [Armwood] *in the jail*."[12] Dryden also took the unusual step of removing his gun "when the thing got bad" because he "didn't want any shooting."[13] Charles Dryden, another deputy sheriff, testified that he "didn't see anything." Apparently without shame, Charles Dryden testified that when the mob burst into the jail, he ran to a back room inside the jail "to get out of sight."[14] The crowd of spectators at the postlynching inquest greeted this admission with a roar of laughter.

Sheriff Luther Daugherty, who stood at the door of the jail as lynchers pounded the door with a battering ram and assaulted state police officers, claimed later that he recognized "not a one of them."[15] Sheriff Daugherty's actions during the attack on the Princess Anne jail are at first glance difficult to figure out. No witness reported that the sheriff vigorously defended the jail. In fact, most accounts suggest that it was the state rather than the local police officers who attempted to defend the jail against the mob's attack. Daugherty was outside the jail at 7:00 p.m. as the mob began its attack. Although more than a dozen state police officers were hurt trying to repel the mob, Daugherty was not. When the mob broke through the front gate, Daugherty entered the jail as well and reportedly tried to dissuade the mob from taking Armwood.

But a close reading of news accounts suggests that once the crowd had grabbed Armwood, Daugherty busied himself with safeguarding the life of John Richardson, the white man who was also held in the jail as an ac-

cessory after the fact to the Denston attack. According to Norman Dryden, once the crowd grabbed a terrified and cowering George Armwood
from his cell and dragged him down the stairs to the front door of the jail,
Dryden began thinking about the safety of Richardson. "The mob had
gone off to the left of the jail so I took Richardson and gave him to Sheriff
Daugherty," Dryden explained. As the mob cut off Armwood's ear and
dragged him to a tree to hang him, Daugherty, according to Dryden, "put
[Richardson] in an automobile and went away with him toward Crisfield,
where Daugherty lives."[16]

And Daugherty's misconduct did not end once the lynching was completed. Later on he showed little will to investigate the lynching or to identify perpetrators. At about 11:00 a.m. the next day, Baltimore detectives
who had arrived to assist in the investigation recalled that when they asked
Daugherty where Armwood's body was located, he replied "he had no
idea."[17] Yet townspeople and schoolchildren had been ogling Armwood's
charred body as it lay in the lumberyard all morning. Despite the fact that
he had faced the mob outside the jail and later inside had admonished the
mob not to take Armwood, Daugherty insisted that he did not recognize
any of the members of the mob. More important, Daugherty either deliberately or carelessly compromised his own investigation into the lynching
by publicly declaring the day after the lynching that the mob members
"were all strangers... from Worcester County and maybe from down below the line in Virginia."[18] Thus any townsperson who might have been
inclined to identify one of his or her neighbors as a member of the lynch
mob would have had to be prepared to challenge the sheriff's certainty that
the lynchers were all strangers.

The investigative skills of local police in all of these cases also left something to be desired. Strong-arm interrogation of suspects undermined the
credibility of confessions obtained from black defendants. After Euel Lee
was arrested by local police in October 1931, he was clearly beaten. Pictures
of Lee emerging from the police station and from a police car with his face
swollen and bandaged stoked suspicion among African Americans that his
"confession" had been beaten out of him. Although Lee later provided a
detailed confession under legal questioning by Baltimore police detectives,
the photograph of him after the "third degree" at the hands of local police
remained, in the minds of many blacks, as proof of his innocence, or at
least proof that one could not trust the police account of the case. Thus de-

spite Lee's convincing confession, some blacks to this day continue to regard Lee as an innocent man who was the victim of a "legal lynching."

Sheriff Daugherty's "investigation" appears not to have yielded even a quarter of the information about the lynching developed by intrepid *Afro-American* reporters. His investigation probably followed the same assumption as the investigation into Matthew Williams's lynching—police officers either failed to recognize that the black community had important and valuable information that would aid the investigation or knew that it did and deliberately ignored it. Matthew Williams's aunt and cousin were never interviewed or called as witnesses in the lynching probe, for example, although they had important information about Williams's state of mind when he left their home to go to the box factory on the afternoon of the Elliot murder. Their knowledge of Williams's temperament, his habits, and, most important, his considerable savings should all have been regarded as relevant to the grand jury's inquiry. But Williams's family was never questioned or called to appear before the jury probing the lynching. Instead, Williams's sister Olivia, who lived in Philadelphia and was likely to have little information relevant to the lynching, was called.

Contributing to the manipulation of potential witnesses in the Armwood case was the coroner, Edgar Jones, in charge of convening a jury to conduct an inquest into the lynching. The day after the lynching, he issued a statement condemning the lynching but insisting that "the instigators of the crime were not from Princess Anne." Moreover, Coroner Jones stated that "the Euel Lee case [was] responsible. If it had not been for the excitement that followed the Lee case this lynching would not have occurred."[19] Not surprisingly, the members of the coroner's jury failed to identify any perpetrators whose names could be furnished to a grand jury for indictment. Later, after Attorney General Lane conducted his investigation of the lynching, which formed the basis of the governor's decision to send in the National Guard to arrest four of the lynching suspects, Jones served as the lawyer for Irving Adkins, one of the suspected lynchers.[20]

STATE POLICE OFFICERS

Unlike the local constabulary, state police officers showed, in this period, greater adherence to ethical police practices than their local counterparts. Although their record was not unblemished, the state police in several instances performed admirably and even saved the lives (only temporarily, in some cases) of black criminal defendants. When Euel Lee was arrested, state police officers immediately surmised that Lee would not be safe on the Shore. The gruesome murder of the Green K. Davis family was shocking and deeply threatening to whites. Lee was a hired man, a laborer who performed occasional farmwork in exchange for subsistence wages. Whites were familiar with this type of person. Many whites employed blacks as laborers of some kind or another to help with farmwork or domestic chores. Lee's insurrection and explosion of violence against his employers, therefore, would have had personal resonance for Green K. Davis's neighbors. In their minds, the response to Lee's actions would have to be swift and of such a nature as to discourage other black laborers from contemplating violent reprisals against their white employers. State officers understood this reality and acted swiftly to thwart what they rightfully predicted would be a vigilante response to the Davis murders.

Likewise, Lt. Ruxton Ridgely of the Maryland state police transported George Armwood to Baltimore City after his arrest, over the objections of the local police and prosecutor. The photograph of Ridgely taking a solemn-faced but strong and able-bodied Armwood to Baltimore City that appeared in the *Sun* papers stands in stark contrast to that of Armwood's naked, burned, and defaced body on the cover of the *Afro-American* days later. And on the night of the lynching Ridgely and his deputies suffered injuries in their attempt to fend off the crowd. Thirteen officers were reportedly hurt, several of them seriously enough to warrant hospitalization, although at least one witness suggested that the injuries the state officers sustained were exaggerated.

Several of these officers courageously identified members of the lynch mob to Attorney General Preston Lane, who investigated the case. These identifications became the basis of the arrest warrants issued by Lane and the governor's order to the National Guard to arrest the men in November 1933. When he testified in favor of the Costigan-Wagner antilynching bill before Congress in 1934, Lane publicly read aloud the affidavits of the police officers who identified the lynchers as men they knew from Princess Anne and other nearby communities.

PROSECUTORS

In Maryland local prosecutors, known as state's attorneys, are charged with prosecuting crimes within the countywide district. Today and in the early 1930s state's attorneys ran for office countywide. This fact, no doubt, had an unfortunate effect on how state's attorneys conducted themselves when blacks were accused of violent crimes against whites.

The Euel Lee Case

When Euel Lee was accused of killing the Green Davis family, the local prosecutor was Godfrey Childs. Without question, if crusading International Labor Defense attorney Bernard Ades had not injected himself into the Lee case, Childs would have had an easy time of trying and convicting the elderly black laborer. Lee had no alibi, and Green K. Davis had told neighbors that he'd been threatened by Lee in the days preceding the murder. Jewelry and money from the Davis family were found in Lee's room at the boarding house where he lived in Ocean City. But Ades put Childs to his paces, and the experienced prosecutor struggled to prevail against Ades, who had never tried a criminal case before. Ades put race squarely at the center of Lee's defense. His successful petition for a change of venue off the Eastern Shore for the trial, and his success in having Lee's first conviction thrown out, proved that in many ways race was at the center of the Lee case. Moreover, Ades's defense of Lee demonstrated the structural conditions in the legal system that made it nearly impossible, without extraordinary representation, for a black defendant to receive a fair trial in an interracial murder case.

Like other prosecutors in Maryland, Childs accepted the embedded racism in the criminal justice system as a given; indeed, he may not even have recognized that it existed. And so, although Childs was aware that on the night of Lee's arrest roving mobs had visited several county jails looking for the black suspect, Childs resisted Ades's request for a change of venue. Even after Ades was set upon by a mob in broad daylight in Snow Hill, where the trial would have taken place, Childs continued to argue that Lee could get a fair trial before a jury made up of Shore residents.

The circumstances of the Green Davis family murder were reason enough to seek a change of venue. The slaying of the entire family shocked the small community. Once the murder was reported, crowds of local men gathered outside the family house and took up a vigil for several days until experienced Baltimore City detectives arrived to investigate the crime scene. Many potential jurors would have known the Davises. Their children would have gone to school with the two teenaged Davis girls. These conditions alone suggested that it would have been hard to impanel an impartial jury to decide the fate of the person accused of this hideous crime. That Lee was black, and the almost immediate formation of lynch mobs to execute him before the trial, certainly provided enough reason to believe that Lee could not get a fair trial on the Shore, and in fact that Lee would be lucky to get a trial at all if he returned to the Shore.

State's Attorney Childs tacitly acknowledged that Lee's life would be in danger on the Shore, even as he insisted that the trial remain on the Shore. Childs proposed moving the trial to Cambridge, Maryland, sixty miles west of Worcester, but still "on the Shore," a kind of political compromise designed to mollify townspeople. In Cambridge, Childs suggested, Lee would be housed on a boat on the Choptank River, surrounded by armed guards. These extraordinary measures were necessitated only by the fact that Lee's life was in danger on the Shore. But Childs offered this "solution" as though the mere necessity of these extraordinary precautions was not in itself evidence supporting Ades's motion for a change of venue. Fortunately, the lynching of Matthew Williams on December 4 convinced the Court of Appeals that in the atmosphere of mob violence, Lee could not get a fair trial on the Eastern Shore. The case was moved to Towson, Maryland, on the Western Shore, where Lee was ultimately tried and convicted. Childs later cooperated in an investigation of Ades launched by a local judge, who enlisted the assistance of the FBI in an attempt to have Ades disbarred.

The George Davis Case

The conduct of prosecutors in the George Davis case was perhaps even more disturbing. The venue of George Davis's trial for attempted criminal assault in January 1932 was also moved from the lower Eastern Shore. Davis was tried in Cecil County, rather than in Kent County, where the attempted assault against Elizabeth Lusby had reportedly taken place. State's Attorney Kent Collins sought the death penalty for Davis—even though Davis was not charged with having assaulted Lusby. In fact,

Lusby's testimony strongly suggested that Davis had never even touched her. He entered her room and frightened her, asking her to intervene with her husband to rehire Davis on the farm. But none of the lurid details of attempted rape that would normally have accompanied a report on a case like this in the local press were present here. Lusby was permitted to testify outside the hearing of the public and outside the presence of the defendant (a violation of Davis's constitutional right to confront witnesses against him), so newspapers could only speculate on the nature of the "attempted assault." Although Davis was convicted, two facts suggest that the state's attorney overcharged the case and overreached on his sentencing recommendation. First, one of the judges in the Davis case dissented from the conviction. This, in and of itself, was extraordinary and suggests that the prosecution's case was weak. Moreover, the judges who voted to convict Davis refused to impose the death penalty and instead sentenced Davis to serve sixteen years in prison.[21]

In addition to his overzealous prosecution of Davis, State's Attorney Collins's reprehensible conduct included his refusal to investigate and, if possible, prosecute those who had tried to lynch Davis. Identifying the members of the mob would have posed no problem. The mob leaders spoke with the jailers at Easton, and three leaders of the mob were taken through the jail to prove that Davis was not there. One of the three leaders openly displayed a rope. In a letter to a local paper, a resident of Kennedyville, where the assault had taken place, described with pride the mob as "represent[ing] some of the best that the Kennedyville section could produce. They were there for the purpose of administering justice for a wrong deed that had been committed on a lad they knew and respected."[22] The writer signed his name as William Collins. There was no indication that the writer had any relation to the state's attorney.

Nevertheless, State's Attorney Collins determined that there was no action he could take against the mob. Collins insisted, "The mob didn't do anything. They didn't commit any act of violence. I have no intention of trying to prosecute them." One wonders whether the charge leveled against George Davis—attempted criminal assault—would not have been an equally appropriate charge for the leaders of the lynch mob that traveled over several counties with the express purpose of lynching a man who by law was innocent until proven guilty.

The Matthew Williams Lynching

Wicomico state's attorney Levin C. Bailey impaneled the grand jury to investigate the Matthew Williams lynching and to determine whether Williams had killed his employer as a result of Communist influence or instigation. The latter charge was ridiculous, purely a rumor. But charging the jury to investigate this wild claim provided a symmetry to the proceedings that enabled Shoremen to focus on the outrage of the Elliot murder rather than just on the unspeakable act of the Williams lynching. After hearing 128 witnesses, the grand jury reported that it had found "absolutely no evidence that can remotely connect anyone with the instigation or perpetration of murder" of Matthew Williams.[23] The grand jury also found no evidence of Communist influence in the murder of Daniel J. Elliot.

The two black eyewitnesses, who were patients in the Negro Ward at Peninsula Hospital and on the list of witnesses to be called before the grand jury, never had an opportunity to testify. Jacob Conquest died before the hearing, and Rufus Jernigan disappeared.[24] The state's attorney launched no investigation into the death of Conquest or the disappearance of Jernigan.

That Judge Joseph Bailey, the uncle of State's Attorney Bailey, presided over and charged the grand jury seemed not to have raised any question of impropriety in the probe of the Williams lynching. On the Shore in the 1930s, where everyone knew the names of the leading white lawyer families—the Duers, the Baileys, the Adkinses, the Keatings—it was not uncommon for these kinds of connections to exist.

The George Armwood Lynching

Somerset County state's attorney John Robins came from a long line of prominent male family members. As the prosecutor for Somerset County, he was well regarded, as was his father before him. At every turn, Robins thwarted efforts to prevent the lynching of Armwood and later to prosecute those responsible for the lynching. It was Robins who on October 17 ordered Armwood's presence at an arraignment in Somerset County—the order that compelled police to return Armwood from the safety of the Baltimore City jail to Princess Anne. Armwood would be dead within eighteen hours of Robins's decision. Robins spent the night of Armwood's lynching at his home in Crisfield, despite reported rumors that mobs planned to kill Armwood that evening. Most important, Robins engaged in a pitched battle with Attorney General Preston Lane over how the investigation into the lynching would be conducted. At every turn, Robins gave lip service to his intention to fully investigate the lynching. But at the same time he publicly articulated his presumption that no one could be prosecuted for the lynching, signaling to potential witnesses that identifying the lynchers would be in vain. When the governor ordered the arrest of four of the lynchers, leading to a street confrontation between townspeople in Salisbury and the National Guard, Robins made clear to his constituency his intention to bring the accused lynchers back under local control. The lynchers arrived back in Princess Anne like conquering heroes, hailed by excited cries from a crowd of supporters. The habeas corpus proceeding was presided over by Judge Pattison and Judge Duer.

Later, when Attorney General Lane and the governor revealed publicly that Robins, at the time of the hearing, had in his possession the sworn affidavits of state police officers who identified the lynchers more than a week before they were arrested by the National Guard, it became clear that Robins had no will to produce an indictment. The affidavits constituted the kind of strong and persuasive evidence that in the hands of a willing and skilled prosecutor could not help but produce an indictment. For example, one state officer provided the following identification of Rusty Heath, a Princess Anne resident who was a former jailer at the Salisbury jail: "I positively identify 'Rusty' Heath as being in the crowd in front of the jail on the night of the lynching. I have known 'Rusty' Heath for 15 years. I first saw him at the intersection of the Deals Island Road and the road in front of the jail."[25] Yet another officer corroborated this identification, saying, "I can positively identify 'Rusty' Heath. I first saw him about 7:15pm [sic] at the intersection of Deals Island road and the jail road. He was the leader of the first mob (about 100 men). I grabbed him and pushed him back. The second time he was standing by the tree where Armwood was being hung."[26]

Several state officers identified William Hearn, a Salisbury truck driver, as one of the leaders of the mob. One officer "saw him directly in front of the jail, just before the battering rams came up. He was a leader. He shouted 'Let's go get him.' He came up to the door and attempted to shove us off the steps. He is very large shouldered, 6 feet 2 inches tall, 180 pounds, light or almost white hair, 28 years old, slouch hat (gray), blue coat and pants."[27] This testimony was also corroborated by several officers, one of whom said that Hearn was "in front of the jail before the main rush. This time he kept shouting, 'Let's go—come on,' just before the mob rushed. Then he ran to the jail steps, followed by the mob."[28]

Yet Robins made no effort to impanel an impartial jury (which could not have been obtained in Princess Anne) or to obtain an indictment based on this evidence. When asked whether, once the suspects in the lynching were identified, he would convene a grand jury on which black jurors would serve, Robins replied testily, "It hasn't anything to do with the case. Armwood is dead."[29]

It was only when Attorney General Lane testified before a subcommittee of the Senate Judiciary Committee on the Costigan-Wagner antilynching bill in 1934 that the full scope of John Robins's negligence was laid bare. Attorney General Lane released the affidavits from the state police officers identifying the lynchers, as well as the correspondence between Lane and Robins, which had grown increasingly acrimonious in the weeks after the Armwood lynching, as Robins refused to take action against the alleged lynchers. In one of the most astonishing exchanges, Robins, in a letter to Lane, explained forcefully his decision not to seek the arrest of the suspected lynchers. He first explained his belief that the proper legal procedure was to impanel a grand jury to seek indictments of the men before arresting them. Lane had urged Robins to arrest the men based on the sworn statements of the state police officers. Robins, the county prosecutor, dismissed the sworn identification of the lynchers provided by the state officers, writing to Lane:

> Has it never occurred to you that the testimony you furnished me is from men who were battling against a mob in the nighttime, probably under the stress of great excitement, turmoil, and confusion. Has it occurred to you that under such circumstances there may easily be a case of "mistaken identity." There were some people there that night, the sheriff tells me, who were unknown to him, and who instead of inciting people to lynch, were urging them to desist. Is it not possible, even probable, that the State troopers in fighting with their backs to the wall might have mistaken those who were attempting to

restrain the mob as being those who were inciting the mob?...Is it possible that the witnesses confused these well-intentioned people with others not so well intentioned...?[30]

This communiqué ended the correspondence between Lane and Robins. Lane chose not to answer the letter; in a letter to Judge Pattison, the chief judge of the Circuit, he stated, "It seem[ed] hardly necessary for me to comment upon the right of the sheriff or any other peace officer... to make arrests without a warrant when he has reasonable ground to suspect that a felony has been committed. In this case a felony has been actually committed."[31] With regard to Robins's theory that the officers might have confused lynch mob leaders with resisters, Lane remarked, "Mr. Robins' duty is that of a prosecuting officer." Lane found it therefore "unnecessary for the State's attorney to raise the defensive question of mistaken identity." "If arrested," Lane reminded the court, "I assume that each of the accused persons will be ably defended."[32]

When Governor Ritchie finally had the men arrested by the National Guard, Robins was no more helpful. The four indeed were ably defended. Their counsel sought a hearing on habeas corpus, questioning the detention of the men before a judge in Somerset County. The four men were returned from the jail with the support and assistance of Harry Martin, the warden of the Baltimore City jail, who'd permitted the men to stay in unlocked cells. Warden Martin said later that he "thought of [the four men] more as guests than as prisoners."[33] He personally escorted the prisoners back to Princess Anne. Taking only an unarmed aide with him, Martin and the prisoners ate lunch together on the ferry. Martin was cheered by the Princess Anne crowd after it was learned that the prisoners had been treated so well. At the habeas hearing before Judge Pattison and Judge Duer, Robins offered no evidence to support the arrest of the men, even though he was in possession of copies of the affidavit testimony from the state troopers. With no evidence offered by the prosecution, the men were released to a cheering Princess Anne crowd.[34]

At the grand jury hearing convened in January 1934, forty-two witnesses were called. The grand jury was able to hear and dispense with the case in one day. Although the very state troopers who'd identified leaders of the lynch mob by affidavit were called, no "true bill" was issued, and no indictments were handed down for anyone associated with the lynching.[35] The grand jury issued its report to Judge Duer, and the Armwood lynching case was over. The Armwood lynching may be the only one in the history of the United States in which nearly a dozen lynchers were identified based on the sworn affidavits of police officers, and in which four lynchers were arrested by the National Guard, and yet still no indictments were issued. And so the nine men identified by state police officers as leaders of the lynch mob lived out their lives, several in Princess Anne, for years thereafter, suspected by blacks and whites of being the men who lynched George Armwood and known, more importantly, as a symbol of the legal system's shameful alliance with white supremacy.

JUDGES

The lynching cases revealed a great deal about the state of the judiciary in Maryland in the early 1930s. The cases involved not just state judges, and not just judges on the Eastern Shore, but ultimately included judges from the federal bench, from the Maryland Court of Appeals, and from throughout the state. What emerges is a picture of legal minds both great and small, of judges courageous and reactionary, and of the critical leadership role judges play in fostering or undermining respect for and adherence to the rule of law.

A Fair Hearing on the Eastern Shore?

The judges to first rule on the Euel Lee case did not set the bar for judicial conduct very high. The principal issue before the judges of the First Judicial Circuit in November 1931 was whether to grant a change of venue sought by Lee's lawyer, Bernard Ades. Arguing that Lee could not get an impartial trial on the Shore, Ades sought to have the trial moved to Baltimore City. The First Judicial Circuit judges—Robert F. Duer of Somerset County, Joseph Bailey of Wicomico County, and John Pattison of Dorchester County—were all Eastern Shoremen. They rejected the defense argument that Lee, housed in the Baltimore jail after mobs gathered in Worcester County, could not receive a fair trial on the Shore. They concurred with the state's attorney's recommendation that the case be moved to Cambridge, Maryland, in Dorchester County, where Lee would be kept on a boat on the Choptank River during the course of the trial, guarded by state troopers and police officers. Bernard Ades appealed the decision. By the time the case reached the Court of Appeals, Matthew Williams had been lynched in Salisbury, confirming that not only would it be unlikely that Lee could appear before an impartial jury on the Shore but also unlikely that he would survive a trial there.

Even without the Williams lynching, the decision denying a change of venue from the Eastern Shore was indefensible. Lynch mobs had begun looking for Lee once word got out that he'd been arrested for the murder of the Green Davis family. A menacing crowd had surrounded Lee's lawyer, Bernard Ades, in Snow Hill. Lynch mobs had visited four Shore counties searching for George Davis in November. Nevertheless, Judges Duer, Pattison, and Bailey refused to move the case off the Shore. That the state's attorney envisioned housing Lee on a boat in the Cambridge harbor protected by armed guards should on its own have put paid to the notion that Lee's life was not in danger if he remained on the Shore for trial. But Eastern Shoremen and Shore papers clamored for having the Lee trial remain local. In the heated climate of hurled insults between Baltimore writers such as H. L. Mencken and various Shore newspapers, the question of a change of venue came to be more about the "honor of the Shore" than about whether a black defendant accused of the quadruple murder of a white family and chased from the Shore by lynch mobs could get a fair trial. The First Circuit judges, in what they must have regarded as the defense of the Shore's honor, issued a decision that simply could not withstand appellate scrutiny, especially after Matthew Williams was lynched.

The Court of Appeals' review of the case ultimately resulted in the change of venue that Ades had sought. It should be pointed out that technically, the Court of Appeals did not reverse the venue decision of the First Circuit judges. In fact, the Court of Appeals determined that it was without jurisdiction to consider whether the First Judicial Circuit's decision to keep the case on the Shore was legally sound.[36] The matter of venue, the court ruled, was one that could be appealed only after the case had gone to trial. Moreover, the Court of Appeals, even if it had jurisdiction to hear the matter, could not consider evidence related to whether the lynching of Williams supported the petition for a change of venue because that evidence had not been first presented to the Circuit Court. But the Court of Appeals predicted what would likely happen if Lee were tried and convicted on the Eastern Shore. A conviction of Lee by a jury impaneled on the Eastern Shore, the court warned, would probably result in a reversal on the grounds that Lee's constitutional right to appear before an impartial tribunal was violated. This kind of discussion in a judicial opinion is known to lawyers as *dicta*—a part of the court's decision that does not have the force of law and has no precedential value. But appellate courts sometimes use dicta to signal to a lower court how it is likely to respond to a particular decision should the matter come again before the court. The judges of the Court of Appeals put the First Judicial Circuit on notice that if they did not move the trial off the Shore, any conviction of Lee would be voided on appeal.

With no other option, the First Circuit judges decided on remand to move the Lee case off the Shore to Towson, in Baltimore County. The First Circuit judges were not humbled by the Court of Appeals' decision, however. In their order moving the case to Towson, the judges took pains to express their disagreement with the Court of Appeals' suggestion that the First Circuit had not perhaps fully examined and considered the threat of mob violence and the bearing of this violence on the question of whether Lee could receive a fair trial on the Shore. The judges reasserted their certainty that Lee could get a fair trail on the Shore—a position that was patently indefensible. Nevertheless, chastened by the apparent willingness of the Court of Appeals to overturn a conviction of Lee unless the trial was moved off the Eastern Shore, the First Circuit judges issued the order moving the case to Towson.

The initial decision by the local judges to deny the request for a change of venue in the Lee case is an important moment in the events that gripped the Shore over the next two years. The "us versus them" mentality that came to animate many of the worst decisions of Shore people during this period would have been undermined at the very outset if local Shore judges had been willing to acknowledge that mob action, rather than outside interference, undermined the likelihood that local courts would be able to hear the Lee case. What white Shore residents needed in December 1931 was for one of their own, for local leadership, to denounce mob rule. Instead, what they got was a decision by Judges Duer, Pattison, and Bailey that endorsed the fantasy that Lee could obtain a trial before an impartial jury on the Eastern Shore. That their decision would clearly have put Lee's life in danger—not just from execution after a guilty verdict but, more than likely, at the end of a lynch mob's rope—makes the decision that much more indefensible.

Courage and Failures in Euel Lee v. State

Two of the great judicial decisions that the Maryland Court of Appeals issued in the 1930s were in *Euel Lee v. State.* The first of these important decisions was discussed earlier, when the Court of Appeals left the First Judicial Circuit judges no choice but to move the venue of the Euel Lee case off the Eastern Shore. That decision probably saved Lee's life—at least until his execution in 1933.

But the even more important and far-reaching decision by the Court of Appeals in *Lee v. State* came in the court's decision to reverse Lee's first conviction for the murder of Green K. Davis after his trial in Towson. The conviction was reversed on the grounds that blacks had been impermissibly excluded from jury service in Baltimore County, where the trial was held. The decision was great because it affirmed for courts throughout the state that excluding blacks from juries—a practice outlawed by the U.S. Supreme Court in a case involving a black defendant from West Virginia in 1888, but still very much in practice in many states in the 1930s—would be regarded by the Maryland Court of Appeals as a basis for throwing out an otherwise valid conviction. In other words, counties where blacks were excluded from juries would, if convictions were challenged by black criminal defendants, find themselves in the position of having to retry defendants, a costly practice.

It was impressive that the Court of Appeals was willing to make an example of this important constitutional principle in the high-profile and highly charged Lee case. Certainly the court could have wanted nothing more than to have the Lee case put to rest, with Lee convicted and executed. The decision to overturn the conviction would not win the judges on the Court of Appeals friends among the Eastern Shore constituency, nor in other white communities throughout the state where the exclusion of blacks from jury service was the norm. In deciding *Lee v. State,* the Maryland Court of Appeals judges revealed the strength of their commitment to the rule of the law.

Yet another interesting twist to *Lee v. State* is that it did not involve discriminatory practices in jury selection on the Eastern Shore. Lee's case had been moved to Towson, in Baltimore County. The county was strictly segregated, and certainly more rural than urban, but it was also regarded as more progressive than the counties on the Shore. Yet Bernard Ades's skillful lawyering revealed that in Baltimore County, blacks had not served on juries in at least one generation. Frank I. Duncan, the judge in charge of selecting juries in the county, had, in the previous twenty-five years, never appointed a black man to serve on a Baltimore County jury.

Judge Duncan was a Baltimore County man through and through. He'd lived there his entire life until his death at the age of eighty-eight. Although he was admitted to practice law in 1885, Duncan's legal career was initially sidelined in favor of a career in journalism. He bought a local newspaper, the *Baltimore County Herald,* which had been a Republican paper.[37] After changing the name of the paper to the *Baltimore County Democrat,* Duncan edited the paper until the turn of the century. As a lawyer, he was elected the state's attorneys of Baltimore County, served as counsel to the Board of County Commissioners, and even served a term in the legislature. Duncan held a number of public positions in the county, serving as a member and leader of several fraternal organizations and on the boards of public hospitals and schools. This immense and varied experience might have made Judge Duncan uniquely qualified to fill up the jury lists with the names of upstanding citizens in the county, except that Duncan, like everyone else in Baltimore County, lived in a segregated world.

Judge Duncan's method for selecting jurors was largely dependent on his contacts in the community. He testified that he "first procured the names of good men from suggestions" made by his outside contacts.[38] These would probably have been from among the fraternal organizations he was a member of, or the boards he served on. None of these was likely to put Duncan in touch with an appreciable number of black men. Duncan's own subjective view of prospective jurors appears to have been paramount in the selection process. Seemingly unaware that his jury selection practices might be constitutionally deficient, Duncan forthrightly explained his jury selection method to the court:

> A witness may impress me on the stand favorably; I may meet someone at some social gathering or church gathering; I make a memo-

randum of him. I go to the tax books and the registered voters list to see if he is there, and the next step is to inquire from people in the community in which he lives, whether he is a good man, whether he pays his debts, is honest, sober, and if he is thought well of in his community. These are the only qualifications I am looking for, and that is the way the jury is selected.[39]

Using this method over the course of twenty-six years, Judge Duncan never selected a black person for jury service in Baltimore County.

The Court of Appeals struck down Lee's conviction and ordered a new trial. Jury selection in the county would have to include the names of blacks in the jury venire. Careful to absolve Judge Duncan of any *intent* to exclude blacks from jury service, the Court of Appeals found, however, that "the mere failure to select persons of the colored race over that period of time raised what *appears* to be an irrebuttable presumption of such an intent or purpose on the part of the judge."[40] The decision was a landmark. It reaffirmed in Maryland the continuing significance of the 1888 Supreme Court's decision, in *Strauder v. West Virginia*, that the exclusion of blacks from jury service violates the Sixth and Fourteenth Amendment rights of black defendants. And the Court of Appeals' decision exposed the practice of racial exclusion from jury service—not on the so-called backward Eastern Shore but in Baltimore County.

That Lee was entitled to a new trial meant that his execution—the event that many Shore residents regarded as the only outcome that could provide justice for the murdered Green K. Davis family—would not happen in 1932. This "delay" in what Shore residents were certain would be Lee's execution (there seemed to be no question that he would be convicted and given the death penalty) was a principal reason that Shore residents cited for why the Matthew Williams and George Armwood lynchings occurred. Lynching was swift justice. No Shore newspaper or commentator of the period publicly conceded that discrimination in the state's own criminal justice system had "delayed" Lee's execution. Instead, the reversal of Lee's conviction was described contemptuously as evidence of Bernard Ades's Communist-backed manipulation of legal technicalities. Adherence to the Constitution was merely a legal technicality when a black man was accused of an interracial crime.

The Court of Appeals' opinion authored by Judge Carroll Bond courageously and forthrightly swam against the tide of white public sentiment on the Shore (and no doubt other parts of the state, where jury selection practices were probably similar to that used by Judge Duncan), berated (albeit gently) the jury selection practice of an old and well-liked Baltimore County judge, and insisted that even a black criminal defendant accused of a heinous crime against a white family was entitled to the full protection of the Constitution.

Majority Doubts and a Dissenting Voice in the George Davis Case

Although George Davis was sentenced to sixteen years for attempted assault—a sentence impossible to imagine today—the judges who imposed this term on the twenty-three-year-old black farm laborer stand out as virtual profiles in courage compared with some of their judicial colleagues on other courts during this period. Davis's trial had been moved sixty-six miles north, from Kent County to Cecil County. The change of venue was granted on December 7, 1931, only days after the lynching of Matthew Williams. Lynch mobs had visited four Eastern Shore jails looking for Davis after his arrest.

Stephen Collins, the state's attorney for Kent County, had made the extraordinary decision to seek the death penalty against Davis, even though the crimes he was charged with, attempted criminal assault, involved no actual physical harm to the victim. Given the heated emotions on the Shore in late 1931 had Davis's case been tried before a jury, he might well have been executed for frightening Mrs. Lusby in her bedroom on an early November morning in 1931. Elkton was only thirty miles north of Chestertown, and although not part of the Lower Shore, it was still technically part of the Eastern Shore. But Davis's appointed counsel, in addition to seeking a change of venue, had the presence of mind to request a trial before a judicial panel rather than a jury. This decision most likely saved Davis's life.

Davis's case was heard before Chief Judge William Adkins, Judge Lewin Wickes, and Judge Thomas J. Keating. Two judges on the three-member panel, Adkins and Wickes, found Davis guilty. But rather than accept the death sentence recommended by the state's attorney, they chose to sentence Davis to sixteen years in the state penitentiary. But by far the most courageous of the three-judge panel was Keating, who took the extraordinary step of dissenting from the conviction. The refusal of two of the three judges on the panel to accept the state attorney's recommendation that Davis receive the death penalty for attempted assault, coupled with Judge Keating's dissent from the conviction, strongly suggests that all of the judges on the panel had doubts about Davis's guilt.

Chief Judge Adkins was nearing the end of an illustrious career on the bench. He'd first been appointed to the bench in 1906 and became chief judge of the Second Judicial Circuit in 1919. When Davis was tried in Elkton, Adkins was just three years shy of retirement from the bench.[41] His leadership, foresight, and good judgment had avoided the lynching of a black defendant named Isaiah Fountain in 1919, in a case involving the rape of a young white girl. Fountain escaped and fled from custody after a two-thousand-member lynch mob had assembled on the courthouse lawn in Easton, Talbot County, on the first day of his trial. Adkins managed to undermine efforts to lynch Fountain, deftly handling the local population and posting a $5,000 reward for Fountain's safe return. Fountain was found and returned to Talbot County unharmed. The case of Isaiah Fountain and Judge Adkins's participation are discussed at greater length in chapter 1.

Judge Lewin Wickes was a lifelong resident of Chestertown in Kent County who'd been appointed to the bench in 1919—the same year Adkins had been elevated to chief of the Second Circuit. By the time of the Davis trial, Wickes was seventy-five years old and would have only a year left to live. Judge Thomas J. Keating was sixty years old and had been serving on the Second Judicial Circuit for ten years when he issued his extraordinary dissent in the Davis case. Keating came from a prominent political family in Queen Annes County.[42]

In January 1932 the Shore was deep in the throes of postlynching self-protection. The battle of words between Shore newspapers and H. L. Mencken was in full swing. Paranoia ran rampant as well, with white leaders fearing a black uprising and white extremists insisting that Communists were instigating blacks to interracial violence. Armed guards surrounded the courthouse in Elkton where George Davis's trial was being held.

Davis's appointed counsels were two well-known and well-regarded white attorneys. Bernard Ades had sought to represent Davis, using Euel Lee as the conduit for messages in the Baltimore City jail. Ades attempted to obtain permission from Davis to enter an appearance on his behalf. Warden Harry Martin at the Baltimore jail refused to give Ades permission to meet with Davis. But Davis's attorneys, R. Hynson Rogers and J. H. C. Legg, were well-known Eastern Shore lawyers who took seriously their representation of Davis. Legg was a former state senator. Without question, they did not raise the kinds of issues that Ades would probably have raised. But they first sought a trial before a judicial panel, rather than a jury. Accounts of the trial suggest that the legal team took great pains to ingratiate itself with the judges, commending the bench on its fairness to their client.[43] The two defense lawyers acquiesced to the request to have Lusby testify in private, outside the presence of the public and outside the presence of George Davis, the defendant. It seems unlikely that Ades would have permitted Davis to waive his constitutional right to confront the main witness against him. Davis's attorneys also appear to have conceded that the attack had occurred but suggested that Davis was intoxicated and thus not in control of himself.[44] This again seems an unlikely course for the defense had Ades been Davis's counsel.

But the evidence against Davis was weak, and the judges must have known it. Although Lusby testified that Davis had tried to rape her, the judges, in explaining their sentencing decision, speculated that perhaps Davis had no intention of harming Lusby when he entered her room to ask her for assistance in getting his job back. Instead, Judge Adkins suggested, Davis may have entered her room for legitimate purposes but under the influence of alcohol become aroused by seeing Lusby in her nightdress.[45] Given the fact that Davis did not testify in his own behalf, the court's speculation about Davis's motives was unusual. The implication of the court's imaginary reenactment—the details for which there appeared to be no support in the record—was that the judges did not believe Davis had attempted to assault the young farm wife. To cast doubt on Davis's motive challenged Lusby's testimony, at least implicitly.

The majority went on to note that Davis should be credited for coming back after the "attack," "call[ing Lusby] politely by name, and [seeking] to apologize."[46] The court then found that "[t]o inflict the death penalty in such a case ... would not be in the interest of public policy... [and would] place the accused beyond redemption."

Davis was taken to the Maryland Penitentiary under heavy guard. The last record for Davis at the penitentiary shows that he was transferred to the prison farm at Hagerstown in 1942.

Judge Robert Duer and the Lynching of George Armwood
Perhaps no judge emerged from the lynching cases as roundly denounced as Judge Robert F. Duer. Born and raised in Princess Anne, Duer was a rare Republican judge on the largely Democratic Eastern Shore. In fact, when he was first elected to the bench in 1917, Duer became the first Republican judge to serve on the Eastern Shore since the Civil War. When his fifteen-year term was complete, he was appointed by Governor Albert Ritchie to serve until the next general election in 1934.[47] Duer's ignominious role in the Eastern Shore lynching cases began with his participation in the first significant decision of the First Judicial Circuit, the decision denying the motion to move the venue of the Euel Lee trial from the Eastern Shore. Nevertheless, it was Duer's conduct in the George Armwood case that was the most egregious. Duer reportedly endorsed the order returning Armwood from the Baltimore City jail to Princess Anne, although he claimed not to remember whether he was asked to endorse it.[48] And it was Duer who failed to warn the governor that mob lawlessness appeared imminent on the night of October 18. Of his failure to apprise the governor that conditions were unsafe for Armwood, Duer said after the lynching that he had been "badly mistaken" in believing that the crowds he addressed were harmless.[49] To be fair, Duer's failure to realize that the mob that had formed outside the jail in the evening of the 18th were not just curiosity seekers, but were in fact intent on violence, was a "mistake" made by Sheriff Luther Daugherty and Chief of Police Charles Dryden as well. But unlike the two law enforcement officers, Duer had addressed the crowd. His impotence before them and their cavalier dismissal of his pleas to disperse were most certainly evidence that this crowd was one with a fixed intention and with little regard for the trappings of the law.

Despite his close connection to the case, including his address to the lynch mob, Duer presided over or participated in subsequent hearings and closed-door judicial meetings related to the lynching. Along with Judge Pattison, Duer participated in the habeas corpus hearing when the four lynching suspects arrested by the National Guard were returned to Princess Anne after one night in the Baltimore City jail. The four men

The Law In All Its Majesty

The Baltimore Sun *ran a political cartoon titled "The Law in All Its Majesty," showing a beleaguered and impotent Judge Duer after the Armwood lynching.*

were released in a hearing that lasted only a few minutes. Outraged that the four suspected lynchers had been taken back to Princess Anne from the Baltimore jail just a day after the melee with the National Guard, Governor Ritchie called Judges Duer and Pattison before the hearing to urge a postponement until Attorney General Lane could provide the state witnesses who had identified the suspects. Neither the governor nor Attorney General Lane had been informed by State's Attorney Robins that the men would be arraigned. This action was surely an embarrassment to the gov-

ernor, who had expended tremendous political capital in calling out the
Guard to make the arrests. Governor Ritchie made clear to Judge Duer
that State's Attorney Robins had in his possession the evidence that supported the arrest of the men and had been in possession of the information
for more than a week. Governor Ritchie suggested that Judge Duer compel State's Attorney Robins to produce the evidence that had been furnished to him by the attorney general—including the affidavits of state
police officers positively identifying the suspects as active members of
the lynch mob. Alternatively, the governor noted that it was within Judge
Duer's authority to postpone the habeas hearing until Attorney General
Lane could come forward and present the evidence to the court himself.
Governor Ritchie sent a telegram to the judges reiterating his views. But
Judges Duer and Pattison pressed ahead with the hearing despite this
communication from the governor and the unwillingness of State's Attorney Robins to use the evidence furnished to him by the attorney general. The four suspected lynchers were released based on a lack of evidence
supporting their arrest and detention. The crowd of several thousand
townspeople (and, as no doubt Judge Duer was aware, voters) that packed
the courtroom broke out in cheers. Governor Ritchie publicly concluded
that Attorney General Lane had not been apprised of the hearing or
given an opportunity to present evidence for the simple reason "that the
Attorney-General's witnesses were not wanted and the Attorney-General
was not either."[50]

Judge Duer was a witness in the grand jury hearing into the lynching,
in which, after receiving the testimony of forty-two witnesses, the grand
jury found no true bill—Maryland's way of saying no cause for indictment—against anyone associated with the lynching. Oddly enough, the
grand jury made its report for the January term to Duer, who thanked the
jury and discharged them on January 25, 1934. The grand jury did report an
indictment against Sam Johnson, a black man accused of killing a white
woman in Somerset County on New Year's Eve. In a repeat of the now-
familiar pattern, Johnson had been removed to Baltimore for safekeeping. Duer announced that it would be unnecessary to bring Johnson back
to Princess Anne immediately for arraignment.[51]

Duer lost his reelection bid the next year, but his colleagues provided a
balm to his pride by selecting him as chair of the Somerset County Bar

Association. He went into practice thereafter with his son, E. McMaster Duer, and with Charles Hearne, who as a law student had observed the lynching of Matthew Williams from the balcony of the Wicomico Hotel in 1931. The firm of Duer, Hearne, Duer was located in Salisbury at the intersection of Main and Division Streets—across the street from the courthouse, just yards from where Matthew Williams was lynched.

CHAPTER 5

"SERVING THE PENINSULA": LOCAL NEWSPAPERS AND LYNCHING

As in most small towns in the 1930s, local newspapers on the Shore were more than just sources of news. They were a key means by which communities learned about the goings-on in adjacent towns and through which communities polished their image. Stories in local papers most often showed the "best face" of the town. Shore papers were no exception. There was a kind of "booster" quality to the reporting. Bad news—about the failing Shore economy, for example—was downplayed. Positive, upbeat stories about charity drives and local civic activity were prominent. National news included one or two stories about the rise of Nazism in Germany and Winston Churchill's ill health but tended toward the more mundane. The impending repeal of Prohibition was a big story, which papers large and small never seemed to tire of. But for the most part local papers were a conduit through which Shore towns could reflect their best self-image.

A plethora of local papers chronicled life on the Shore—the *Democratic Messenger* in Worcester County, the *Marylander and Herald* in Somerset County, the *Star-Democrat* in Talbot County, and the *Cambridge Banner* in Dorchester County. In Wicomico County, the local paper was and still is the *Salisbury Times,* known today as the *Daily Times*. Purchased by the Truitt brothers, Charles and Alfred, in 1923, the *Salisbury Times* provided a daily diet of national news and chronicled life in Wicomico County, from the trivial to the monumental. No community event was too small to escape mention in the *Times*—garden club meetings, engagements, charity drives, were all given the careful and supportive attention that only a local paper, steeped in the community, can give. Unless of course the event in question took place in the black community. News about the new black high school, about black church fund-raisers, and about the doings of black civic groups did not appear in the pages of the *Times* in the early 1930s, and if they did, they were relegated to small announcements buried in the back pages of the paper.

This is not to say that stories about blacks never appeared in the *Times*. They did. These stories, however, were invariably accounts of black criminality. Historian Cezar Jackson opens his study of local media responses to the lynchings in the 1930s with an observation that a month before the murder of the Green Davis family, the *Salisbury Times* ran a front-page story describing the flogging of a black man convicted of domestic assault.[1] The flogging was administered with a whip by the Wicomico County sheriff Murray Phillips and was attended by Levin C. Bailey, the state's attorney for the county. Although the flogging was held inside the jail, three hundred people stood outside and did not disperse until the beating had been completed.

When a black person was accused of a violent crime against a white person, local papers placed these stories prominently on the front page. For this reason, the *Times* and other local Shore papers were full of stories about blacks from the fall of 1931 until the same time in 1933, when Euel Lee was finally executed.

It is easy to see why the murder of the Green Davis family and the case of Euel Lee would garner a great deal of media attention. The news that a black laborer had murdered a white family riveted the residents not only of Worcester County, where the crime occurred, but of the entire Shore. The crime was an ominous one. Many white families relied to some extent on black labor. The prospect that a black farmhand, who perhaps merited little attention or notice, might strike out violently and with staggering brutality against a white employer raised a million fears among Shore whites. Thus whites read about the Lee case with rapt attention. And the papers encouraged this attention by serving up the Lee story in dramatic and vivid description.

From the very beginning, when papers described the killing as an "axe murder," a consistent pattern of inflammatory disinformation plagued coverage of the story. This hyperbolic and inaccurate reporting in the local papers of the Shore had dire consequences, however. The more brutal the crime alleged to have been committed by a black assailant, the more whites could feel justified in subjecting the black defendant to the barbarity of a lynching.

Race was an explicit dimension of the local papers' report on interracial crimes. Black defendants were expressly identified by race, and their guilt in local papers seemed a certainty. The names of black defendants were optional. A black defendant could just as easily be referred to as a "confessed Negro slayer" as by his name. When Matthew Williams allegedly shot D. J. Elliot, the headline in the *Salisbury Times* simply read, "Negro Kills D. J. Elliot Then Self."

The local papers were unabashedly partisan. Their interest in presenting Shore whites in the best possible light was openly admitted. When Matthew Williams was lynched, this protectiveness went into overdrive. The *Salisbury Times* took the extraordinary step of deciding not to report on the lynching. Both publishers of the newspaper, Charles and Alfred Truitt, observed at least part of the lynching. Charles Truitt, in particular, saw Matthew Williams hung outside the courthouse. Charles Truitt was the AP correspondent for the Shore and dutifully wired his story to the AP describing the lynching of Williams. But he refused to publish what he saw on the night of December 4 in his own paper.

On December 5 the headline of the lead story in the *Salisbury Times* was about the lynching, although that word was never used. The headline read, "Coroner's Jury to Investigate Slayer's Death." The first paragraph provided only a bare-bones account of what had happened: "Matthew Williams, confessed slayer of D. J. Elliot at his office yesterday afternoon, was removed from the Peninsula General Hospital last night and hanged in the Courthouse yard. The hanging was witnessed by hundreds of people."[2] That account is the only description of the lynching that ever appeared in the *Times*. Instead, on the front page of the same paper, the Truitt brothers published a statement, which read as follows:

This paper is omitting the details of the demonstration here last night when Matthew Williams, confessed slayer of D. J. Elliot, was hanged in the Courthouse square for the very obvious reason that almost every reader of our paper had had an opportunity to learn of them first hand from eyewitnesses.

The facts which formed the background for the demonstration

and the direct causes are also well known and a repetition of them would be superfluous.

The slaying of Mr. Elliot was deplorable as was also the mob scene.

Every person living on the Eastern Shore, realizing the background, should use his best judgment and pay little heed to the overdrawn pictures that will be painted by metropolitan newspapers who have no obligation to this peninsula and whose only purpose is that of so preparing news as to increase their circulations. It becomes a contest among the larger papers to see which one can bring out new excitable features of such a story.

This paper is a part of the Eastern Shore, and always tries to serve the best interests of the peninsula. We at all times deplore violence, either of an individual or a congregation of individuals, but when violence is done, it behooves every one of us to co-operate in speeding up a return to absolutely normal and harmonious conditions.[3]

The statement was extraordinary for several reasons. Besides the obviously unusual step of refusing to cover what was the most important event to have happened in the county in some time, the Truitts' statement operated as a charge to the public. Quite unabashedly, the Truitts instructed whites in Salisbury to remain silent about the lynching, for the good of their communities. The prime directive from the leadership of the local paper was that whites should "return to absolutely normal and harmonious conditions." With this statement, the *Times* articulated for the community the expected code of behavior. According to his own account, publisher Charles Truitt genuinely believed that there might be a "Negro uprising" in Salisbury. He insisted, even years after the lynchings, that there really was Communist infiltration of black communities on the Shore, and that the Elliot murder was part of a larger plot by blacks to assassinate white leaders in the town.[4] For these reasons, Truitt regarded it as his obligation to maintain peace and calm in the town. No evidence of a "Negro uprising" or of Communist influence in the death of D. J. Elliot was ever found to corroborate Truitt's suspicions. And Truitt declined to report on or identify the sources of his view in the paper. The statement certainly gives no indication that Truitt was doing anything more than accommodating the sensibilities of white townspeople, who did not want to face the reality that a lynching had occurred in their town. The use of the word "demonstration" rather than "lynching" was itself a kind of avoidance, an effort to assist whites in minimizing what happened on the night of December 4.

The decision not to cover the Matt Williams lynching in the *Salisbury Times* warrants examination, discussion, and analysis. The news blackout on the Williams lynching enabled whites to minimize the significance of this hideously violent racial act. Christmas shopping continued apace in the town. Discussions about the lynching by Baltimore papers or the national media were regarded as "outside interference." As a leading institution in the community, the *Times* "Statement," signaled to whites that the town's leadership had determined how the lynching was to be handled. Townspeople were ominously warned to "use [their] best judgment and pay little heed" to the way Williams's murder would be characterized by off-Shore papers "who have no obligation to this peninsula." The publishers advised their readers that "it behooves every one of us to co-operate in speeding up a return to absolutely normal and harmonious conditions." Any white person who departed from the course set by the *Times* had good reason to believe that he or she would be ostracized, and perhaps worse, for exposing neighbors to prison and the community to national censure. Townspeople received the paper's message. Although more than one hundred witnesses were called before a grand jury, none recognized any of the lynchers. The predictable result was a finding that Williams died "at the hands of persons unknown." The long-term consequence was a stain on the entire community, which by its actions licensed the public murder of a black man.

Other Shore papers also failed to forthrightly condemn mob action. Instead editorials offered "explanations" for the actions of local lynch mobs. When a mob tried to attack Euel Lee's lawyer in Snow Hill in 1931, editors of the *Democratic Messenger* from Worcester County explained that the mob "was composed of residents of Delaware, Virginia and from that section of Worcester County where the murdered Davis family lived."[5] The paper then reprinted an editorial written by Charles Truitt in the *Salisbury Times* on the "demonstration" in Snow Hill, in which Truitt described the lynching attempt as "Worcester's answer to those who would interfere with the progress of court justice and retard the trial of a man who has twice confessed to the commission of the most atrocious crime in the county's history. No one can say that Worcester's answer to such tactics was not expressive."[6]

A week after George Armwood was lynched, the Somerset *Marylander and Herald* devoted its principal editorial to asking "Who Took Armwood to Baltimore?" The editors regarded Armwood's removal to Baltimore as "the cause of the lynching." "We honestly believe," wrote the editors, "that had Armwood been lodged in the Somerset County Jail that night [when he was arrested], without State, or local protection, there would have been no lynching." The editors also offered the assurance that the lynchers were not from Somerset County, insisting that "had there been built around Somerset County that night a fence that would have excluded all outsiders, there would have been no lynching."[7]

The local news reporting could also be outright misleading. The December 29, 1931, edition of the *Salisbury Times,* for example, issued a banner headline reading "Court of Appeals Lee Case Must Be Conducted in Cambridge." The subheadline read, "State's Highest Tribunal Decides Trial Shall Be Conducted in Cambridge." This was simply not true, and the editors of the *Times* must have known it. In its review of the First Judicial Circuit's decision to move the venue of the Lee trial only as far as Cambridge, Maryland, rather than off the Eastern Shore, the Court of Appeals determined that it could not order a change of venue based on evidence that had not been before the Circuit Court.[8] That new evidence was the lynching of Matthew Williams, which had occurred after the First Circuit's decision denying a change of venue off the Shore and the hearing before the Court of Appeals on the First Circuit's decision. Moreover, the Court of Appeals ruled that the decision on the venue was an interlocutory order, meaning that it could not be reviewed on appeal until after trial on the merits. The Court of Appeals went out of its way, however, to suggest that if Lee were tried and convicted on the Shore, the verdict would probably be overturned as unconstitutional, given the atmosphere of mob violence that pervaded the Shore. In essence, the Court of Appeals declined to review the appeal of the decision denying a change of venue but foreshadowed the likelihood that if the venue were not moved from the Shore, a verdict against Lee would not survive appeal. The First Judicial Circuit a week later moved the venue of the trial off the Shore to Towson, Maryland.

But the December 29, 1931, article in the *Times* suggested that the Court of Appeals had affirmed the decision of the First Judicial Circuit and had conferred legitimacy on the decision to hold the trial in Cambridge. This interpretation was directly contrary to even the most rudimentary review of the court's decision. Yet the *Times* chose to placate its readership, rather than report that the mob atmosphere, which much of its readership had at least tacitly endorsed, had tainted the ability of Lee to get a fair trial on the Shore.

The responsibility for skewed racial coverage of the events during this period does not fall entirely on the local media. The *Baltimore Sun* also had its limitations. It failed to report on black lynching victims and communities in ways that sufficiently conveyed their humanity and complexity. The *Sun*'s postlynching news coverage, while clearly more balanced than that of local Shore papers, focused exclusively on the perspectives and viewpoints of whites. Despite the extensive reportage following the Williams and Armwood lynchings, no story in the *Sun* included interviews with the family of either man or of residents of the black communities who were terrorized by the lynchings. The *Washington Post*, in its reportage, similarly devoted no attention to Williams as a man. His age was listed as thirty-five, his name was often spelled incorrectly, and for the most part Williams was just "the Negro" in the pages of both the *Post* and the *Sun*. The *Afro*, by contrast, took pains to create a complex picture of Matthew Williams and George Armwood. The *Afro*'s description of Williams's weakness for processed or straightened hair, and his trips to the Apex Beauty Shop to get "touch-ups," added the kind of human dimension to the story of his death that helped *Afro* readers "recognize" Williams not just as a victim but as a man. Armwood, whose background was much darker than Williams's, received similar treatment. His strength as a field laborer, his separation from his family at the age of fifteen after his services were requested by a white couple, the circumstances surrounding reports that he had attacked a black woman the previous year—all of this was explored in detail in the *Afro*, giving readers an opportunity to gain a sense of Armwood's life as an unskilled and uneducated laborer on the Eastern Shore.

The rich and multilayered reporting on the effect of the lynchings on the community and family of the lynched men in the *Afro-American*, and the *Afro*'s insistence on doing investigative rather than just passive reporting on the lynchings, highlight the shortcomings of the *Sun*'s coverage. The *Afro* included a front-page interview with Armwood's mother, as well as interviews with young men who had grown up and worked with Armwood. Photos of Armwood's extended family also appeared in the paper. Likewise, the *Afro*'s coverage of Williams's death included a front-page photo of Williams's sister Olivia Simmons, who returned from her home in Philadelphia after receiving word of his death.[9] A photo of the relatives with whom Williams grew up appeared in the paper as well, attesting to the fact that Williams had been raised in a close-knit, middle-class family in Salisbury.

By contrast, on the day after Williams was lynched, the front page of the *Sun*, under the caption "Mob Took Negro from Her Custody," featured a large above-the-fold photograph of Helen Wise, the white nurse who was on duty at Peninsula Hospital when Williams was taken by the mob.[10] On the day after Armwood was lynched, the front page of the *Sun* featured yet another large above-the-fold photograph of a white "bit player" in the lynching, Capt. Edward McKim Johnson of the state police. The studio photo of Capt. Johnson in full dress uniform ran under a small caption, "Among 9 Injured by Shore Mob."[11] This photographic emphasis on white players in the story diverted readers' attention away from the real victims of the lynching—the black men, their families, and the communities where they lived.

One of the most important aspects of the *Afro*'s reportage of lynchings during this period was its insistence on questioning whether the lynched or nearly lynched man actually had committed the crime for which white townspeople had judged him guilty. The *Afro* challenged the "official story" and introduced the possibility of the black men's innocence. Some of this was accomplished by the *Afro*'s interviews with the family of the lynching victim. An extensive interview with Matthew Williams's sister, as well as with his cousin, who described his behavior on the day of the murder and lynching, for example, raised serious questions about whether Williams had any motive for or intention of killing Daniel Elliot on December 4. The fact that Williams cautiously guarded his money and was missing a fairly large sum of money on the day he died made it only into the pages of the *Afro*.

Certainly the *Sun* enabled its readers to feel a kind of political outrage about the lynchings, but it failed to provide the information needed to fully comprehend the scope of the human tragedy and the lynchings' devastating effect on the community. The *Afro* reported on how community members continued to suffer violent reprisals, and even that another black man was found dead and mutilated only a week after the Williams murder, in what some blacks suspected was another white mob killing.[12] And readers were never given information by the *Sun* that might have led them to question whether the black lynching victims had in fact committed the murder or sexual assault of which they were accused.

The *Salisbury Times* might have been able to continue its vow of silence in the days after the Williams lynching had it not been for a stinging column penned by Baltimore satirist H. L. Mencken in the *Baltimore Sun.* Entitled "Eastern Shore Kultur," the column appeared on December 7, 1931, and ignited a two-year battle of words between Eastern Shore papers and the *Baltimore Sun,* and a decades-long boycott of the *Sun* by many Shore people. The column described the Shore as an example of "what civilization can come to in a region wherein there are no competent police, little save a simian self-seeking in public office, no apparent intelligence on the bench, and no courage and no decency in the local press." The people of the Shore, wrote Mencken, "are stupid enough, God knows, but they are probably less stupid than merely misinformed. There are no agencies of civilized opinion among them. They must depend for their ideas upon clowns in the pulpit, clowns on the stump, and clowns in the editorial chair." Mencken singled out the *Salisbury Times* for contempt, deriding the paper for going to "the almost incredible length of dismissing the atrocity as a 'demonstration.'"

Eastern Shore papers exploded in outrage. On December 8, 1931, the *Times* reprinted Mencken's entire column and offered only an editor's note in which it defended its reportage and insisted that its "handling of the situation has occasioned the congratulations of hundreds of Eastern Shore people, white and colored . . . who have said that we did the very best thing any newspaper could possibly have done in a similar position."

Over the next few months, and then years, Mencken and Shore papers continued to fire shots at each other. Shore people began a boycott of the *Baltimore Sun,* and later a boycott of products coming from Baltimore. Truck drivers and deliverymen from Baltimore became wary of bringing their goods into Salisbury after several trucks were attacked by local townspeople, who trashed the goods and burned Baltimore newspapers. The boycott of the *Sun* continued for many Shore people for decades, and well into the 1970s Shore residents refused to buy the *Sun*.

In sum, local papers on the Shore reinforced the sense of many Shore people that the lynchings of Williams and Armwood and the near lynchings of Lee and Davis were justified. Rather than providing an educational function or modeling the kind of self-reflection that would have served the Shore communities well during this period, local Shore papers reinforced for their residents a sense of self-righteous outrage. Although Baltimore papers voiced outrage at the lynchings, they did little to humanize the victims or to explore the effect of lynching on the local black community. This skewed and deficient reporting by white-owned papers left only the *Afro* to speak to and about blacks, who experienced firsthand the consequences of lynching. The result was the creation and perpetuation of a segregated account of the lynching, which has lasted for decades.

PART 2

TRUTH AND RECONCILIATION FOR LYNCHING IN THE TWENTY-FIRST CENTURY

CHAPTER 6

RECONCILIATION AND LYNCHING IN INTERNATIONAL CONTEXT

The dawning of the twenty-first century has been marked by urgent and intense calls for reconciliation. All over the world, from South Africa to Bosnia, from Cambodia to Chile, victims of systematic racial and ethnic violence and genocide have demanded an investigation and acknowledgment of crimes committed by state actors. Typically these demands have centered on three themes: an accounting (truth-telling), compensation for victims (reparations), and healing (reconciliation). Reconciliation can be said to encompass all three goals. It is the effort to create terms for respectful and humane coexistence between conflicting groups. Truth-telling and reparations are indispensable ingredients in reconciliation.

Without question, the highly publicized and compelling work of the Truth and Reconciliation Commission (TRC) in South Africa in the mid-1990s invigorated the international focus on and debate about reconciliation. The TRC has been called "the most carefully thought out and meticulously planned truth commission that has emerged as an alternative or as a complement to trials."[1] TRC hearings, in which black victims testified to unimaginable suffering and white perpetrators dispassionately confessed to committing unspeakable acts of terror, gripped television audiences. The dignity of the hearings, the eloquence of the committee's chair, Archbishop Desmond Tutu, and the tremendous forbearance of South Africa's majority black population, who learned the depths of the depravity behind the white supremacist forces of that country, inspired observers all over the world to embrace the TRC model as the gold standard for conflict resolution in the aftermath of racial and ethnic violence.

Despite international fascination with the TRC, criminal trials have also been at the center of this robust international conversation about reconciliation. The war in the former Yugoslavia marked by "ethnic cleansing," mass rape, forced removals, and other human rights violations on the European continent revived the long-dormant war crimes tribunal process in The Hague. Using the Nuremberg tribunals of 1948 as a guide, international legal experts fashioned procedures and a charter for an International Criminal Tribunal for the former Yugoslavia (ICTY). When 800,000 minority Tutsis were killed over a four-month period by Hutus in Rwanda, there was little doubt that a tribunal would also be created to address the genocide. The killing in Rwanda presented particular challenges. The sheer number of perpetrators alone—perhaps 100,000—and the fact that most were not government officials but average people presented the International Criminal Tribunal for Rwanda (ICTR) with a dilemma never faced before in the genocide context.

The postapartheid, post-Yugoslav war, and post-Rwandan genocide period of the mid- and late 1990s coincided with the then-upcoming turn of the century, creating additional momentum to confront historic acts of systematic racial, ethnic, and religious violence. In preparation for the Jubilee in 2000, the Vatican prepared expressions of regret or apology for a number of actions, from the Crusades and the Inquisition to the failure of the Catholic Church to oppose the Holocaust.[2] As the century turned, the German government and six thousand German companies agreed to pay $4.5 billion in reparations to those forced to work in slave labor camps and factories. Historians, politicians, activists, and even filmmakers explored and exposed the decades-long policy in Australia of cultural genocide by forcibly taking half-caste aboriginal children from their homes and putting them in state-run orphanages.[3] The national and heated debate that followed culminated in the refusal of Prime Minister John Howard to apologize on behalf of Australia for the systematic decimation of the aboriginal families.[4] But these are just a few examples of the scores of reconciliation initiatives that emerged at the close of the twentieth century.

The United States has not been immune to the wave of "reconciliation talk" that marked this period. The nearly three-hundred-year-old movement by black Americans seeking reparations for slavery was undertaken and continues to be pursued with renewed rigor, as prominent lawyers and skilled researchers have used a new array of resources—including DNA testing—to prove the harm caused by particular perpetrators and beneficiaries of slavery. The successful effort to expose the Rosewood Massacre in Florida and the Tulsa Race Riot of 1921 has been a critical part of this reawakening. Investigation into both pogroms unearthed a history forgotten and deliberately obscured: that of marauding white mobs who destroyed thriving and (in the case of Tulsa) highly prosperous black communities in the South. The Rosewood investigation ultimately resulted in the allocation by the Florida legislature of funds to compensate victims of the massacre.[5] In Tulsa legislative reparations have not been forthcoming, and survivors have had their litigation dismissed by the federal courts.[6] The Supreme Court declined to review the case.

Reconciliation initiatives focused on slavery are not limited to reparations litigation. The City Council of Chicago passed a resolution requiring that companies bidding on city contracts describe their company's involvement with or profit from slavery. Other similar measures have been introduced in other cities. Brown University, under the direction of its first black president, herself a great-granddaughter of slaves, has undertaken a full investigation of that university's connection to slavery and whether Brown should pay reparations for its profits from slavery.[7] Alfred Brophy, in addition to his fine work on the Tulsa Race Riot reparations efforts, which was chronicled in his book *Reconstructing the Dreamland,* has spearheaded efforts at his own school, the University of Alabama, to come to terms with its participation in and profit from slavery. The university recently issued an apology to the descendants of slaves who worked at the school or were owned by faculty members.[8] The University of North Carolina has followed suit with research and an exhibit chronicling the role of slaves in constructing buildings on campus and in working for faculty members and students.[9]

President Clinton, ironically, botched efforts to offer an unequivocal apology for slavery before embarking on a trip to Africa. Wavering back and forth on whether to issue the apology, Clinton ultimately became convinced that African Americans were not unified in their support for an apology. Instead, Clinton offered less than an apology and something more than a mere acknowledgment of the U.S. role in the trafficking and profit from the sale and labor of African slaves.[10]

All of these efforts, both internationally and in the United States, have created a complicated and sometimes tense conversation about race, reparation, and reconciliation. The scope of the discussion has been broad —perhaps too broad—reaching out to encompass genocide, ethnic cleansing, slavery, internment, and cultural dislocation. The scale of violence included in reconciliation discussions has ranged from crimes against one hundred thousand to nearly a million people, and from forced removal and internment to slaughter by machete. The means of reconciliation explored in all these instances have included apology, financial compensation for slavery, criminal prosecution, and truth commissions.

The literature that has accompanied this upsurge in "reconciliation talk" increasingly has criticized the effectiveness of criminal prosecutions and civil reparations claims that seek punishment, retribution, or compensation in promoting reconciliation and providing meaningful justice. Instead, a broad segment of academics and rights activists have emphasized and exalted alternative means of reconciliation that focus on healing for both victims and perpetrators, and that create opportunities for victims and perpetrators to rebuild a fractured society. This embrace of "restorative" rather than retributive justice increasingly has been regarded as both a process and a goal, essential to rebuilding broken nations and to creating multiracial democracies.

CHALLENGING RESTORATIVE JUSTICE

Restorative justice has not been without its critics. Not everyone has been infatuated with the South African TRC. Some scholars and activists critiqued what they regarded as the narrow focus of the "truth" that the TRC pursued. Rather than define the inhumanity of apartheid principally in terms of its greatest excesses—the murder and torture of activists by violent white perpetrators—Mahmood Mamdani lamented the failure of the TRC to implicate the beneficiaries of apartheid.[11] Apartheid was targeted at communities, not just individual activists, argued Mamdani. Thus the victims of apartheid are the millions of black and brown South Africans who suffered under the regime, not just their charismatic leaders or activists. The beneficiaries of apartheid, average whites who pretended or chose not to know about the atrocities being committed in their name, must also reconcile with victims. For Mamdani, the TRC "suffocate[ed] a much-needed social debate on how to go beyond the political reconciliation between state agents...and political activists...to a social reconciliation between beneficiaries and victims."[12] Mamdani's critique of the TRC is instructive for the discussion below about reconciliation and lynching.

Victims and their families have made a compelling case for the enduring importance of criminal prosecution and civil litigation to reparation efforts. In the most famous challenge to restorative justice, the Azanian People's Organization (AZAPO) and the family of Steve Biko, the charismatic founder of the Black Consciousness Movement who was killed by members of the South African security police in 1977, sued to challenge the amnesty provisions of the South African Truth and Reconciliation Commission. The provision in question immunized from prosecution anyone who came before the commission and fully confessed to having committed human rights violations in furtherance of "a political objective."[13] Amnesty provided by the commission extended to both criminal and civil liability, and it was even available to anyone who had already been convicted in the criminal courts for the act that formed the basis of the amnesty provision. AZAPO and the Biko family argued that state actors who systematically terrorized black activists should be tried criminally and be subject to civil liability for their crimes. The newly formed Constitutional Court of post-apartheid South Africa upheld the constitutionality of the TRC, deferring to what it termed "the deliberate choice" of "those who negotiated the Constitution" to seek "understanding over vengeance, reparation over retaliation, *ubuntu* [a recognition of shared humanity] over victimization."[14] Biko's murderers sought but ultimately were denied amnesty.

Gacaca tribunals in Rwanda have been critiqued on the very grounds that the Biko family cited in the AZAPO case. Gacaca, which literally means "justice on the grass," is a procedure based on a traditional form of dispute resolution in Rwanda that addressed conflicts between neighbors. Traditionally, a dispute would be presented to an elder and a coterie of community members, who together would propose solutions. The procedure would end with the disputing parties sharing a drink of banana beer from a common vessel. After the genocide, leaders in Rwanda embraced gacaca as a process that would enable community members to actively participate in fashioning punishment and reconciliation for crimes committed during the genocide. There was also a pragmatic reason to use gacaca tribunals. The sheer volume of perpetrators in the Rwandan genocide, coupled with the decimation of the justice system, meant that it might take nearly a decade to bring to trial all of the perpetrators languishing in Rwanda's prison at the end of the war. Given this reality, gacaca was regarded as an alternative means of meting out justice for human rights violations committed during the war.[15] That community members, laypersons respected by their peers, would play an active role in gacaca by determining the facts of disputed incidents and meting out sentences suggested that gacaca would also serve a reconciliatory function. Sentences imposed by gacaca courts can range from prison terms to reparation to victims and community service, with the latter emphasized in many cases. The local nature of the proceedings, attended by community members assembled in an open space, is a deliberate contrast to the distant and formal war crimes tribunal process of the ICTR taking place in Arusha, Tanzania. That gacaca is based on a traditional dispute-resolution procedure provides a sense of indigenousness and local control to the process as well.

But as some commentators suggest, gacaca may simply be inappropriate for addressing the challenges of genocide. Paul Rusesabagina offers perhaps the most cogent critique: "Justice on the grass was never designed to address something as grave as genocide. It was designed to solve cases of missing goats and stolen bananas." Rusesabagina takes issue with the very idea that gacaca will promote reconciliation between victims and perpetrators of the Rwandan genocide. "[T]he entire point of gacaca," concedes Rusesabagina, "was not punishment but reconciliation. You were supposed to apologize to the man you had wronged and share a bowl of banana beer as a sign of renewed friendship." Imagining such symbolic reconciliation for genocide and mass murder strikes Rusesabagina as impossible. He asks, "How in God's name can a man 'reconcile' with people he has raped, tortured, and murdered? How can things ever be put right with the parents of a baby who has been ripped limb from limb? Gacaca is a well-intentioned idea, but punishing crimes of genocide requires the authority, stature, and rigor of a state-sponsored court with impartial judges and firm rules of evidence."

Others lament the "local" nature of gacaca, which emphasizes "responsibility purely at the local individual level."[16] Deemphasizing the political dimension of genocide and focusing on local actors mean that "the Hutu will remain killer and the Tutsi victim."[17]

But the most compelling critique of both reconciliation and restorative justice processes, however, may be that the terms are simply misnomers. *Re*conciliation and *re*storative justice, as well as *re*paration, suggest or imply a return to a previous period of peaceful coexistence or oneness in a community recently fractured by racial or ethnic division and violence. This assumption belies what is often the reality. In most instances, communities in the throes of reconciliation or restorative justice work were never really unified. South Africa, for example, since the arrival of Jan van Riebeeck from the Dutch East India Company in 1652, has been a racially stratified society built on white supremacy. There was no former period to return to—that is, a period when blacks and whites lived as equals. It is even hard to make the case for historical unity for Tutsis and Hutus. Although the idea of Hutus and Tutsis as distinct ethnic communities may be the fantastic creation of German and Belgian eugenicists, there is certainly strong evidence to suggest that Hutus and Tutsis have been distinct *political* communities for some time, whose divisions probably predate, at least to some extent, the egregious exploitation of these divisions by colonial powers in the nineteenth and twentieth centuries.[18] Likewise, the unity of different ethnic and religious groups in the Balkans was forged recently, after World War II, by General Tito, the Communist leader of Yugoslavia. Tito served as a unifying figure for Serbs, Croats, and Muslims. But his insistence on a unified Yugoslav identity paved over deep conflicts and differing "emotional memories" that were ripe to be exploited by power-hungry politicians and demagogues.[19] Within ten years of Tito's death, Yugoslavia had exploded into violence based on ethnic divisions. Thus the illusion of preconflict unity may present its own challenge to reconciliation. Confronting this illusion can be profoundly painful and destabilizing for communities deeply invested in the idea that racial conflict and even violence are aberrant, rather than endemic to a community's history.

The promise of reparations may also be misleading. Law professor Naomi Roht-Arriaza identifies a

> paradox at the heart of the idea of reparations: they are intended to return victims to the state they would have been in had the violations

not occurred—something that it is impossible to do. They are also supposed to be the physical embodiment of a society's recognition of, and remorse and atonement for, harms inflicted. . . . But what could replace lost health and serenity, the loss of a loved one or of a whole family. . . the destruction of culture or an entire community?[20]

Thus one must begin with the understanding that reparations cannot fully "repair" the damage done by racial and ethnic violence; nor can reparations "return" a victim or a victimized community to the state it would have been in but for the violence. At best, reparation is a symbolic effort to balance the scales and an articulation of responsibility for the harm done. Both of these efforts help set the conditions for communities of victims, perpetrators, and beneficiaries to move forward toward reconciliation.

In sum, achieving reconciliation is a more daunting task than the word implies, precisely because in reality it is an effort to create something new —not to return to something old. Reconciliation efforts are focused on fashioning out of a community plagued by division and racial/ethnic violence "a new community," rather than returning a community to a pre-conflict state of unity.

Despite these challenges, the demand for truth, and the need for communities to become reconciled with a complicated and often ugly past of racial violence, continue to press communities in the twenty-first century to struggle toward reconciliation. The alternatives—silence, lies, disconnection, and continued cycles of violence—make the project of reconciliation an urgent one.

RECONCILIATION AND LYNCHING

Not only are reconciliation and reparation efforts increasing, they are also diversifying, as individuals, community groups, and activists look beyond slavery and genocide to focus on other forms of violent white supremacy and their lingering effects. Lynching has increasingly emerged as the focus of reconciliation projects. To date, the focus has been almost exclusively on truth-telling, although, as I discuss in chapter 9, a number of communities throughout the South where lynchings took place are looking expansively at lynching reconciliation. The 1998 lynching of James Byrd in Jasper, Texas, unleashed and coincided with a new wave of scholarship and study on lynching.

A startling exhibit of photographs, postcards, and "souvenirs" from lynchings titled *Without Sanctuary* premiered in New York in 2001 and has toured cities throughout the United States, sparking renewed conversations about, and memories of, lynching. After viewing the book accompanying the exhibit, Louisiana congresswoman Mary Landrieu sponsored a resolution in the U.S. Senate in 2005 to apologize for that body's refusal to pass antilynching legislation.[21] The question of which senators failed to co-sponsor the resolution (ultimately seven senators—all Republican) consumed media outlets and black community conversations for a week. Descendants and relatives of lynching victims converged on Capitol Hill to be in attendance during the vote.[22] The resolution passed unanimously, but the controversy surrounding senators who refused to cosponsor the measure continued. Congressman Thad Cochran of Mississippi reportedly stated that he did not feel he should apologize for something he did not do.[23] When it was pointed out that he had cosponsored measures apologizing for the government's treatment of Native Americans and Japanese American internees during World War II, his spokesperson offered the incredible explanation that those resolutions had been undertaken "on behalf of all America," not just the U.S. Senate.

The history of lynching presents particular reconciliation challenges. Lynching was a crime targeted at communities. It involved at some level the approval or tacit support of the white community. As Mamdani suggests in his critique of the TRC, when the community is the victim, a reconciliation process should not focus only on the perpetrators who were active participants in the violence. The beneficiaries of this violent white supremacy, who by their silence and acquiescence offered tacit approval of the violence, must also be key participants in the reconciliation process.

And there are other challenges. The participation of ordinary people in watching, cheering, or condoning lynching has created deep wells of distrust in black communities where lynching has occurred. This sense of distrust is not unusual, but it presents a formidable obstacle to reconciliation. Studies suggest that in the former Yugoslavia, "the *inability* of and *unwillingness* of their neighbors from other national groups to acknowledge that they stood by as other members of their group committed war crimes in their name was one of the biggest hindrances to reconciliation."[24]

Moreover, the complicity of local institutions such as the media and the legal system in lynching promoted black distrust of and disconnection from these institutions, which continues to have contemporary resonance. In addition, the public nature of lynching and its proximity to symbolic public sites, literally "on the courthouse lawn" in many instances, has rendered the public space in communities where lynching occurred racialized sites.

In the remainder of this book, I explore, through the Eastern Shore lynchings, how a reconciliation process targeted at lynching might contend with some of these challenges. I draw heavily on what we have learned from international reconciliation efforts in South Africa, Rwanda, and Bosnia and from the particular history of white supremacy in the United States.

I do not offer this discussion as a step-by-step handbook. Instead I contemplate how a local community might begin to approach the very serious and long-term work of racial reconciliation for specific incidences of racial/ethnic violence. Without question, the approaches I contemplate have their pitfalls. Some will work in some communities and others not at all. The specific history and the contemporary political, social, economic, geographic, and cultural reality of a community will greatly inform those processes likely to have the greatest success. In all cases, however, reconciliation is a task that must be undertaken for the long haul. No single conversation, criminal prosecution, or form of reparation can by itself produce reconciliation. Instead reconciliation is a process, one that should become part of the daily fabric of the community. Reconciliation should influence local public policy decisions, school curricula, law enforcement policy, land use and planning, and cultural resource allocations—in short, all of the decision making that shapes the future direction of a community.

Although my prescriptions are not formulaic, I do offer three principles for the promotion of reconciliation in communities where lynching has occurred, each of which is informed by the experience of international and local reconciliation efforts. They are quite simple, and I expand on them below. First, racial reconciliation efforts are principally local. Second, any meaningful reconciliation effort must emphasize dialogue. Third, reparations must be viewed expansively. This last principle is key. Criminal prosecution of perpetrators should be pursued where appropriate. Financial reparations should not be excluded. But reparation should not be focused solely on those initiatives. Whether criminal prosecutions or reparations are warranted must be determined by the local community. But other forms of reparation must be pursued as well. Naming and reconfiguring public spaces to acknowledge the history of lynching, expunging the record of black men wrongly accused of violent crimes against whites, including the history of local lynching in school curricula, providing gravestones for the unmarked burial sites of lynching victims, creating advisory boards to monitor the portrayal of African Americans in local print media, and eliciting apologies from institutional leaders for a history of complicity in lynching should all be considered and examined as useful forms of reparation as well.

Reconciliation Is Local

Reconciliation cannot be achieved at the national level. Historically, racism was felt, lived, and perpetrated locally. Reconciliation, therefore, must also be local. In his study of the war crimes tribunal for the former Yugoslavia, Eric Stover, director of the Human Rights Center at the University of California at Berkeley, writes that "history constantly reminds us, memories of wartime atrocities, like all memories are local; they are embedded in the psyche of those who have experienced the events." As a result, Stover cautions that "so-called 'impartial' or 'objective' outsiders who try to recast localized memories to fit a larger truth will always be viewed with suspicion."[25]

Lynching is local. No presidential apology or Senate resolution can heal communities where violent pogroms or lynchings took place. No "national conversation" can take the place of a locally based dialogue in which members of a discrete community come together to talk about how specific instances of racial violence affected their community. The chances of reconciliation are best realized through a locally driven process because those who live in a community will ultimately be most invested in finding ways to improve the quality of life there. Local residents also will know best what forms of reparation can heal the particular harms suffered in that community and will be accountable to one another for ensuring that agreed-upon reparation initiatives are implemented.

Breaking the Silence

Dialogue between and among blacks and whites in communities where lynching occurred is essential to any reconciliation process. It is precisely because silence was used to compel complicity and to enforce the terror of lynching that public speaking and truth-telling about the violent events that gripped the community are so important.

The silence that follows lynching, when newspapers fail to report on the events that transpired, when witnesses refuse to identify lynchers, when clergymen fail to address lynching in their sermons, has been imposed on both the black and the white community. Blacks fear speaking of the lynching because of the ever-present threat of violent reprisals. Silence can also be a coping mechanism, a way to move forward without becoming consumed by a potentially overwhelming situation. The loss of language is part of the experience of being a victim of violence, argues Teresa Godwin Phelps, a law professor who has studied truth commissions. In her work *Shattered Voices: Language, Violence and the Work of Truth Commissions,* Godwin Phelps contends that "appropriation and manipulation of language and of people's ability to speak...in their own voices are major weapons in an oppressive regime's arsenal."[26] Speaking the truth and openly challenging the official story are therefore part of the reconciliation process. As Godwin Phelps argues, "The restoration of the ability to speak in one's own voice can...go a significant way in balancing the harm done."

Silence must also be broken in the white community. Silence by white newspapers, witnesses, jurors, clergymen, teachers, parents, and children is the means by which the larger community becomes complicit in lynching. Whites who continue to maintain their silence about lynching remain uncritically bound to the violence of lynching. And because whites are the repositories of the most accurate information about the lynching itself (most blacks were not present at lynchings for obvious reasons), their continued silence withholds from the entire community key pieces of information, essential parts of the lynching story that is a part of the community's history. Whites must be willing to share what they know, to unburden themselves of the secrets of lynching, and to disconnect themselves from complicity with lynching.

Viewing Reparations Expansively

Reparations litigation can be an important feature of reconciliation. But even successful reparations litigation will not break down walls of silence between blacks and whites in communities where racial violence has oc-

curred. Certainly reparations litigation will produce important and positive results: a public record of the acts and actors giving rise to the claim for
reparations, the use of the legal system to vindicate the rights of victims,
and the redistribution of critical financial resources from perpetrators and
beneficiaries to victims of white supremacy. Thus, reparations litigation
plays a key role in the overall reconciliation process.

But financial reparation cannot take the place of other, more holistic
reconciliation efforts. Litigation has its limitations. The ability of victims
to tell their story is limited by rules of procedure and evidence. The relief
sought must be described in terms recognized by law—usually money or
some other form of injunctive relief. The participants in litigation are usually a narrow slice of the community affected by the relevant events. All
of these features of litigation can be a hindrance to the kind of dynamic
interaction between and among blacks and whites that is critical to any
meaningful reconciliation effort.

Criminal prosecutions, like reparations litigation, are a key component
of many reconciliation processes, but they are not enough to promote
reconciliation. Victims frequently report a sense of detachment from international war crimes prosecutions for both the former Yugoslavia and
Rwanda. The process is long, the trials are not held within the country
where the violence occurred, and the targets of the trials are most often not
the individuals who swung the machete or burned the home. The perpetrators brought before war crimes tribunals tend to be the high-level planners and organizers of genocide. Although the idea of pursuing high-level
actors may suit a kind of ideal of equality in the war crimes tribunal process, victims are often deeply wounded by seeing the person who committed the violent act against their family continue to walk freely in their
village, while the war crimes tribunals pursue leaders and generals whom
victims have never seen. How did the four-year effort to prosecute Serb
leader Slobodan Milosevic, an effort that ultimately ended with his death
from a heart attack in a jail cell in The Hague, promote reconciliation in a
town where women were raped by local militiamen and residents were
beaten by their neighbors? Moreover, how can a war crimes tribunal address the intense sense of betrayal that many feel when their former friends
observed or participated in the violence?

Neither the ICTR nor the ICTY is equipped to undertake the enormous task of exposing and confronting the underlying attitudes, stereotypes, resentments, and history of violence that made the ethnic cleansing and genocide of the Bosnian and Rwandan conflicts possible. In this sense, "reconciliation" remains elusive and largely unexamined in Rwanda and in the former Yugoslavia. Paul Rusesabagina sees this as a real danger. When asked what he found most frightening about Rwanda today, he replied, "My answer is this: It frightens me to death when my countrymen are not talking... my country today is packed with a lot of angry people not talking to each other. We could be witnessing the roots of a future holocaust."[27]

In the U.S. context, recent efforts to criminally prosecute those responsible for civil-rights-era murders are clearly a critically important component of reconciliation. The failures and in some cases collusion of the legal system in the South during those years of violence against civil rights leaders and activists is deeply felt by members of the black community and by the families of victims. Who can forget a jubilant Myrlie Evers, the widow of Medgar Evers, crying out "Medgar" in triumph and vindication after his murderer, Byron de la Beckwith, was finally convicted in 1994?[28]

Elie Dahmer, the widow of Mississippi voting rights activist Vernon Dahmer, sat through four trials in the 1970s and watched the man who masterminded the firebombing that killed her husband go free. Finally, in 1998 Dahmer was on hand for the conviction of Klansman Sam Bowers.[29] But why did it take so long for Dahmer to see the conviction of one of the killers? In most civil-rights-era murders, the failure of witnesses to come forward, of police officers to diligently investigate the murders, of prosecutors to zealously prosecute the cases, and of white jurors to convict made the legal system complicit in the violence against black communities. At a conference in 2006, Dahmer, referring to the white community's complicity in creating the men who killed her husband, explained: "They raised them up that way." Reconciliation efforts must get not only at the men who killed but at the communities who created killers and who condoned violence by permitting these violent murderers to live free in their midst for decades.

But even successful prosecutions do little to unearth and transform the deeply embedded and long-standing prejudices that often exist in communities where racial murders occur. Only a few months after the last of the three white supremacists were convicted for the 1998 lynching of James Byrd, blacks found that things began to return to "normal" in Jasper, Texas. In the immediate aftermath of the horrendous murder, white Jasper residents publicly committed themselves to improving race relations and went out of their way to demonstrate to blacks in the small East Texas town that they condemned the lynching. But in the view of many blacks, after the final conviction,

> The small courtesies, the racial hypersensitivity that emerged right after the murder began to fade. Once again, black customers at the variety store had to wait longer than whites, just as they had for decades. All the talk about job opportunities, industrial parks, and training centers began to dry up. Whites figured the black community got what they wanted—a death sentence for Bill King—so this bending over backward to be polite did not seem as necessary as it had in the weeks after the murder.[30]

Thus, reparations must focus on meaningful change in the community and on ongoing dialogue and action. An overreliance on legal action—whether criminal prosecution or reparations litigation—may short-circuit a reconciliation process once the legal case produces a result. Reparations, like reconciliation, must be regarded as a process, not an event. Communities engaged in reconciliation efforts must pursue forms of reparation that will provide the best and most effective support for reconciliation. Where criminal trials or reparations litigation is pursued, community members must emphasize that these measures do not in and of themselves constitute reparation. They are, at best, a gesture, not a substantive solution.

With these three cautions in mind, in the following chapters I return to the story of the Eastern Shore lynchings and imagine what forms a contemporary reconciliation process might take. Again, my goal is not to instruct but to suggest, and perhaps to inspire those with a will to address the past and to confront the future with honesty and courage.

CHAPTER 7

BREAKING THE SILENCE: "WORDS ARE THE MOST POWERFUL TOOLS OF ALL"

*And was it shame that prevented anyone from talking of
such terrible matters? Yes. Shame and fear. Fear had made
it happen and shame had enforced the silence.*
ELLEN DOUGLAS, Truth: Four Stories I Am Finally Old Enough to Tell

Talking about race and racism is never easy. Talking about the violence of racism—murder, lynchings, bombings—is even more challenging. When President Clinton issued his 1997 call for a "national conversation on race," he could not possibly have imagined the scope of what he was inviting Americans to do. His One America Commission indeed worked diligently to facilitate meaningful conversations about race throughout the country. The lynching of James Byrd in 1998 set off yet another wave of race talk. But the truth is that this country is always talking about race in one way or another. Public policy discussions about failing schools, welfare reform, immigration, criminal sentencing, teen pregnancy, family values, and personal responsibility are, in part, all conversations about race in disguise. Undoubtedly, what Clinton meant was an explicit conversation on race, in which the goals were greater mutual understanding and perhaps the beginnings of reconciliation.

Imagining this kind of talk at a national level was, in retrospect, overly ambitious. The truth is that talking about race is challenge enough within families, within communities, and within cities. The idea of a conversation involving the entire nation, with communities from coast to coast grappling with the immensely complex and alienating topic of race (within one four-year presidential term, no less), was naively ambitious, although admirable.

Certainly Clinton's instincts were right. He recognized the centrality of conversation—of talking—to racial reconciliation. Paul Rusesabagina, who as manager of the Hotel Mille Collines used persuasion, argument, flattery, and his wits to save the lives of a thousand people during the Rwandan genocide, wrote, "Words are the most powerful tools of all."[1] Thus breaking the silence has been recognized as a key step in overcoming oppression. Silence is, as law professor Teresa Godwin Phelps has observed in her book on language and truth commissions, "a crucial component of the technology of oppression."[2] The oppressor demands silence of both the victims of the oppression and of the passive beneficiaries. Only one story may be told—the one constructed by the oppressor. Counternarratives threaten the power of the oppressor. Godwin Phelps argues that a "critical ingredient of rebalancing, then, is . . . a retold story, a reconstruction of the shattered voice."[3] No racial reconciliation process can succeed without providing this opportunity for truth-telling.

But merely providing victims and their descendants the opportunity to tell their stories is not enough. The stories must be heard. It is in the telling *and hearing* of formerly silenced stories that communities can re-create themselves. In addition, local government officials and the leaders of a community's institutions must hear the stories and publicly acknowledge them. As Godwin Phelps cautions, reconciliatory "storytelling cannot be private or confidential."[4] The real challenge of truth-telling is the willingness to engage with fellow community members in the hard work of constructing a new community based on a full accounting of the past. The "new community" is one in which formerly excluded stories become part of the history, identity, and shared experience of all of the residents. At its core, reconciliation is just this: the creation of a new community, "a community that can hear and acknowledge the stories"[5] of both victims and perpetrators, of beneficiaries and bystanders.

Lynching, as discussed earlier, was almost inevitably followed by silence. The news blackout in the *Salisbury Times* the day after the lynching of Matthew Williams, the decision by white clergymen to exclude the lynchings from their Sunday sermons, the refusal of witnesses to come forward and identify lynchers, the determination of black witnesses like Howard Purnell to never speak of the lynching—all of these are examples of the silence imposed by the terror of lynching. And the silence of lynching can last for decades. As a result, even seventy years after the 1930s lynchings and near lynchings on the Shore, the ability of whites and blacks to talk openly, honestly, and productively about what happened and about the legacy of those violent events is likely to be difficult.

As many communities have discovered, interracial conversations about lynching inevitably reveal the deep fissures and conflicts that often lie beneath the now relatively peaceful coexistence of black and white communities. It is not difficult to imagine why these conversations are so daunting. Whites fear or resent being branded as racist, or they simply refuse to see themselves as responsible in any way for incidents in which they were not directly involved. But interracial conversations do not present the only challenge. The silence imposed by lynching is strong and powerful within single-race communities as well. Whites do not talk about historical incidents of racial violence even among themselves. The reasons for maintaining this silence are plentiful. Some whites simply do not regard these incidents as having continuing relevance in the twenty-first century. For them, discussing lynching is merely an exercise in dredging up the past, and an unpleasant past.

Other whites may fear that breaking the silence on these violent events will place them on the defensive, that blacks will be accusatory and will try to compel whites to take responsibility for actions that many will claim they knew nothing about. The more complex issue of what it means to be a beneficiary of a violent or oppressive regime may remain unexplored as white participants insist on their own "innocence."

For racial crimes for which perpetrators may still be alive, whites may fear that they will be called as witnesses in a reopened investigation or prosecution of an elderly perpetrator. In states like Mississippi and Alabama, where prosecutors have made a commitment to retrying cases involving civil rights murders, whites must decide whether to provide information that they have kept to themselves for decades, to see that white bombers and murderers are brought to justice.

Even more complicated is the discovery by young family members of the complicity of their parents and grandparents in violent racial oppression. Whites may find themselves deeply conflicted by the realization that family members were Klansmen, present at lynchings or deeply implicated in racial murder or assault. Author Cynthia Carr recently explored the emotions she experienced upon finding her deceased grandfather's Ku Klux Klan membership card and realizing that he was probably present at a double lynching in Marion, Indiana, in 1931.[6] Carr's essay, describing her decades-long sense of guilt and shame, supports the importance of truth-telling. After finally confessing to a black friend the truth about her grandfather's past, Carr was surprised to discover that her friend was relieved rather than repulsed by the revelation. The story of Carr's grandfather confirmed for the friend the truth she already knew. "White silence," Carr realized, "is often just a refusal to acknowledge what black people have been through."

Issues of guilt and responsibility also figure into whites' reluctance to revisit episodes of racial violence. In her fascinating collection of essays about war criminals and victims in the former Yugoslavia, Croatian writer Slavenka Drakulic puts it this way: "It is easier, and much more comfortable, to live with lies than to confront the truth and with that truth the possibility of individual guilt—and collective responsibility."[7] Thus evading the truth becomes a means of evading responsibility. But the project of reconciliation at its core demands of individuals and communities the willingness to acknowledge painful truths and to take responsibility for injustice. And so some whites may seek to minimize or dismiss the importance of truth-telling as a pointless rehashing of the past precisely because such truth-telling demands responsibility and accountability in the present.

Whites' reluctance or refusal to openly address and acknowledge historical racial violence can be enormously frustrating for blacks. Most often, blacks have been told stories about the lynching, usually as cautionary tales, by their parents or grandparents. The stories were related as a way of ensuring that the children knew the potential for violent reprisals by whites if they crossed racial mores or boundaries. In cases where blacks were not told directly, they overheard the whispered conversations of their grandparents and drew their own conclusions about the threat of violence from whites in their community.

When whites dismiss the significance of these incidents of violence, insisting that "it was in the past" or "things are different now," blacks may become tremendously frustrated. Those who suffered or whose parents suffered under racial oppression and violence want first to tell their story, then to have the truth accepted, and finally to ensure that contemporary conversations about race are placed in a historical context. For truth-telling to have reconciliatory benefits, it must be heard, understood, and accepted. When understanding and acceptance are not offered, communication can be deeply undermined.

There is yet another complicating factor in truth-telling. To their surprise, victims will discover that perpetrators and beneficiaries have a story to tell as well. Listening to, understanding, and accepting the story of the perpetrator or the beneficiary is one of the greatest challenges of any truth and reconciliation process.

Some blacks, to be sure, will also resist revisiting incidents of racial violence. They may fear that such a conversation will be racially polarizing, undermining progress painstakingly made over decades, giving whites a reason to fear that blacks might seek retaliation or reparation of some kind for past injustices committed by whites. And in the twenty-first century neither blacks nor whites can be expected to share a common view about these events. Many different perspectives may be contained within one racial community.

In sum, race talk can be a messy business, at least initially. The outcome may seem uncertain. But what is the alternative? Is it perhaps preferable to just continue the silence? As first-person witnesses increasingly die out, will the racially violent history of communities throughout this country be forgotten? It seems unlikely. Stories of traumatic events have proven tremendously resilient. The stories live in the cautionary tales still passed down from black parents to their children and grandchildren. They emerge when children and grandchildren search through the private papers and photographs of dead relatives. They live on, as patterns of racial silencing and marginalization are passed down generationally in communities. As Paul Rusesabagina of Rwanda has observed about his own country, "History dies hard." There is a particular stubbornness to memories of racial trauma. Unaddressed and unresolved, they continue to have power over the lives of whites and blacks, as the stories below illustrate.

A STORY ABOUT CONVERSATION AND TRUTH TELLING: SILENCE IN THE WHITE COMMUNITY

During a trip to the Shore to search for 1930s pictures of the town of Salisbury, I visited the Wicomico County Historical Society. My guide was a very helpful middle-aged white man named Jim Parker (not his real name). He was friendly, informative, energetic, and willing to meet with me on very short notice. I confess I did not explain specifically that I was writing about lynching. I rarely do when I first meet someone on the Shore. I said something more vague, that I was writing about the county in the 1930s. He did not press for more specifics, and I did not volunteer. I later thought that my instinct not to reveal the more specific focus of my research was right.

I met Parker in one of the beautiful old historic homes of Salisbury. The home is on the walking tour of historic places sponsored by the Historical Society and is filled with antiques in marvelous condition. As I often did when I met whites of a certain age on the Shore, I casually mentioned to Parker that I'd heard about some lynchings that had happened in the 1930s. He looked at me penetratingly for a moment and then airily confirmed that there had been two lynchings in the early 1930s. He seemed impatient with the subject. Then he paused, and for reasons I still cannot fathom, told me an interesting story. About a decade or so earlier, Polly Stewart, a local professor from Salisbury State University, had made a presentation about the lynching of Matthew Williams to the Historical Society. I recognized Stewart's name. In the course of my research, a number of folks at the Salisbury State Nabb Center, which contains historical records, research materials, and papers on the local area, had told me that I should talk with her. In fact, I think that my students had contacted her years before to confirm some historical data we were using in the civil rights case challenging the location of the Route 50 bypass. I knew that she was white and that she was expected to retire shortly from the university.

Parker stated that he had attended this gathering of the Historical Society, and what he described sounded like a very unpleasant and hostile meeting. Stewart presented her research describing the lynching of Matthew Williams in 1931. When she had finished, Stewart's presentation was met with icy silence. According to Parker, Stewart tried to "blame whites in Salisbury" for the Williams lynching. As this did not strike me as an absurd conclusion, I just looked at him and nodded. Parker's disapproval of Stewart's presentation was still apparent. The idea that whites should be blamed or feel responsible for the lynching "just wasn't going to go over with this group," he said. Stewart, he said, should just have presented the facts of what happened and not tried to assign blame or to interpret the events as indicative of the attitude of whites in the county. He and others like him saw the lynching as an aberration, a foul act committed by a few marginalized whites who may have been from out of town. Stewart treated the lynching as a kind of defining racial event for Salisbury and seemed to put the responsibility for the lynching on all whites. Parker spoke with such vehemence that I began to wonder if perhaps he did not know what my research was about. But a moment later, he moved on to another subject, suggesting places where I might find some good 1930s photos of homes in the county. He later drove me out to an old farmhouse and very kindly permitted me to sift through boxes of pictures for several hours.

But I was haunted by the story of Polly Stewart's presentation. I questioned what now seemed like my naive idea to promote truthful and productive conversations about the lynchings in this town. Stewart was not an outsider in the sense that I was. She lived on the Shore—had been living there for more than a decade and taught at the local university. Moreover, Parker was quite careful to tell me that he and others in the group had considered Stewart a friend. But apparently Stewart's presentation was not met with friendly politeness. If whites had reacted so negatively to the presentation of their "friend," what did I, a black woman from New York, a civil rights lawyer, and a Baltimore law professor think I could accomplish in trying to talk with whites about reconciliation and restorative justice? Why did I think that they would talk with blacks in the town about the lynchings? I resolved to talk with Polly Stewart.

As fate would have it, about six months later I came upon an essay written by Stewart in a book of edited selections called *A Sense of Place: American Regional Cultures.*[8] In her essay, Stewart argued that the geographic isolation of the Eastern Shore has created a regional consciousness among its people that made them deeply suspicious of outsiders. She used the Eastern Shore lynchings and the reaction of local Shore people in the 1930s to what was perceived as the intervention of outsiders to support her discussion about regional consciousness. Then came the shocker for me: in the last four paragraphs of her essay, Stewart described her experience of making a presentation about the lynching to the local historical society, an event that she, like Parker, described as a presentation before her "friends." I learned that Parker had not exaggerated his description of the evening. Stewart's account of what happened at the meeting, of the hostile reaction of the group, was nearly identical to Parker's. What Stewart conveyed in her essay, though, and what Jim Parker did not see or was uninterested in was the deep pain Stewart felt at being so harshly rejected by a group of colleagues. "Years afterward," Stewart wrote, "it is still hard to write about this." She continued, "I was hurt and mystified at the vehemence of their reaction, horrified at the irrationality of their anger. These people were my friends, and they were turning on me. Some responded with more anger than others, but it was clear that everyone there was really upset with me. Some of them still are."[9]

It was difficult for me to reconcile Stewart's obviously genuine pain with the tight-lipped scolding I had heard in the voice of Jim Parker when he explained that he and his colleagues were not going to sit there and listen to Stewart try to blame all whites for the lynchings.

Stewart's essay convinced me that I was on the right track. Reconciliation is urgently needed among and between whites, just as it is between blacks and whites. Whites are often unable, even among themselves, to engage honestly and openly in conversation about the meaning of their community's history of racial violence. In her article, Stewart attributed the negative reaction of the group to the fact that she was an outsider, not a native Shorewoman. But I do not think Stewart's thesis fully explains the vehemence with which the members of the society rejected not only her presentation but Stewart herself, long after the incident.

When in 2004 I spoke with Stewart, who has since retired and returned to her home state of Utah, the Historical Society presentation was still fresh in her mind. She told me that she was "snubbed for years after" the incident.[10] She even recalled being at an outdoor fair or festival in Wicomico County some time after and approaching a member of the Historical Society only to have him turn his back on her. Yet another prominent citizen who was present at her talk left the receiving line of a relative's wedding when he saw Stewart approaching. And these were people who had been her friends before her presentation. It was clear, in our conversation, that Stewart was still nursing the hurt of her rejection.

Whites are often deeply confused and conflicted about how to manage their feelings about their community's participation in racial violence. Community leaders, clergy, parents, and teachers build and maintain walls of silence. Southern writer Ellen Douglas remarked, after learning of the public execution of a group of slaves in her family's community in Mississippi during the Civil War, "I had never heard one hint, one breath, one word regarding these matters." She wondered, "Was it that such happenings had never been interesting to any of us, never worth passing down, worth talking about?"[11] Unlike Douglas, many whites nurture and sustain those walls without ever questioning why they were built and whether they still serve the purpose for which they were created. But behind those walls some whites are also confused, conflicted, and hungry for a safe space in which to share their memories or to raise their questions.

The confusion can be particularly acute when whites have witnessed racial violence in their communities as children. In *Bitters in the Honey*, Beth Roy wrote about interviewing white students who attended Central High School in Little Rock, Arkansas, during the pitched battle surrounding the integration of that school.[12] The book provides an intriguing window onto the mass of contradictions that white children face when racial violence, condoned or sanctioned by their parents and neighbors, erupts in their communities. "Betsy," one former white Central High School student, describes a startling scene that she observed from her classroom window and that many of us have seen on the television documentary *Eyes on the Prize*. As cameras rolled, whites chased a black reporter for the New York–based *Amsterdam News*. The reporter, a tall, well-built man, looked as though he could have taken on any of the whites who taunted him in a fair fight. But he was smart enough to know that collectively and on their own turf, these white men could easily kill him. And inside Central High School, Betsy knew it too. As her teacher dutifully led the students in a recitation of the Pledge of Allegiance, Betsy looked out her window "and saw this mob of people chasing what to a sixteen-year-old girl was an elderly black man."[13] Betsy continued, "I was watching them chase him across the yards . . . and I knew, I really believed, that if they caught him they would kill him." And then, in a moving description of the fundamental contradictions America presents to its children, Betsy recalled: "In that moment, while I'm watching this, saying the Pledge of

Allegiance, hand on my heart, I'm thinking, there's something wrong here. How can this be happening in a country that we're pledging allegiance to? What's wrong with this picture? And that left an indelible—I can see it today, I will never, ever forget that."

In Spike Lee's brilliant and moving documentary *Four Little Girls*, former *New York Times* editor-in-chief Howell Raines described a similar sense of disconnect in the white Birmingham of his childhood. Raines recalled watching the news in the midst of the 1963 bombing crisis in which police were interviewed about whether they'd been able to apprehend a group of whites who had beaten up a black man. The white assailants were caught on film, and the reporter asked whether the police had been able to identify the men. As Raines recalled, the police officers in the interview insisted that they had not been able to identify the men. Raines remembered that he knew that the police officers were lying. Raines himself recognized the men from the photographs. He had seen them in a restaurant called Cash's Barbecue. And Raines knew that the police must have recognized the suspects as well because Cash's was a popular hangout for police officers. In a moment, watching the police lie to protect a violent white suspect, Raines learned that everything is not as it appears. And as a boy, he must have wondered why.

The effect of lynching on children presents an urgent need for truth-telling. Children who witnessed lynchings were often exposed to the most hideous kinds of human torture and degradation. The smell of burning flesh is, by all accounts, repulsive. The agony of the victims, the mutilation, the fear, the terror, and the jubilation of the crowd must have created a uniquely terrifying set of memories for young children. The questions raised for the children who witnessed these acts—questions about violence, law, truth, decency, compassion, and race—cannot be answered because the silence that falls soon after a lynching is so complete. Thus child witnesses to lynching can be left traumatized and confused. After James Byrd was lynched in 1998, one man, in a letter to the editor published in the *Dallas Morning News*, described the lingering effects of the lynching on his childhood:

As a boy of 12 growing up in Shreveport, La, in the summer of '56 I witnessed the dragging of a black man tied to the back of a pickup truck. This event took place because the black man was thought to be living with a white woman, a fact I can't affirm. It happened in a very small black community across the bayou from where I lived in a white neighborhood. I don't even know if the man survived the dragging, but I doubt it from what I saw.

I had a friend, a year younger than I and black, who would help me cut yards in my neighborhood. After this happened, I was terrified to be seen with my black friend, not fully understanding the situation, for fear they would come after me or my friend. I was also the neighborhood paperboy and the next morning there was not a word of any kind about what had happened. . . .

All these years later I can still see those four men in that truck and I am still terrified by that scene.[14]

The writer's description demonstrates the deeply internalized fear and confusion that can be engendered in children who witnessed a lynching. Even the experience of Judge Truitt, whose young black friend would no longer walk on the sidewalk with him after the Matthew Williams lynching, reflects how racial violence changed the world for children in ways that they were incapable of understanding. Truth-telling and conversations about lynching provide an opportunity for whites to unburden themselves of the weight of silence and to "work out" for themselves the effects of witnessing racial violence on the development of their own attitudes and perceptions.

THE LEGACY OF TERROR IN THE BLACK COMMUNITY

I interviewed Dr. Clara Small in early 2006. A fixture at Salisbury State University, she's known in both Princess Anne and Salisbury as an expert on the history of African Americans. Originally from North Carolina, Dr. Small is a "come here," as folks on the Shore call nonnative Shore residents. She arrived in 1977 and since then has been a keen observer of the slow racial progress on the Shore.

Small and I spent quite a bit of time talking about race, about the prospects for black and white economic and educational advancement, and about lynching. When I asked her about whether the history of lynching continued to resonate in the attitudes of blacks toward whites, Small told me this story. She was in a meeting of whites and blacks at which a very controversial matter was being discussed. Small expressed her concern toward white participants at the meeting that certain matters were being left out of the conversation. Her remarks were respectful but forceful. Later, Small talked about the meeting with a black female acquaintance from Salisbury. After Small described her objections to the discussion at the meeting and her expression of displeasure toward the white participants, the black woman said to her: "Aren't you afraid you'll be lynched?" This conversation took place in 2000, Small recalled.

Now clearly, the woman who cautioned Small did not mean to suggest that Small would be physically lynched. But "lynching" was the metaphor this woman used to signify the reprisal she thought was sure to follow Small's outspoken censure of whites. This kind of thinking—what Small frankly called a "slave mentality"—is a by-product of the intense pressure placed on blacks during the Jim Crow years, when "the place" for blacks was narrowly proscribed and violently enforced. It is perhaps time to explore the deep psychological and social wounds that lynching and racial terrorism inflicted on blacks.

The memory of lynching is indelibly engraved on the collective psyche of blacks. Even blacks who never witnessed a lynching can describe one—whether it is the lynching of Emmitt Till or James Byrd. This effect was intentional. Lynch mobs, as in Salisbury, often dragged the body of the lynching victim to or through the black community, or they insisted that the body of the victim remain displayed for hours or in some instances days. When Jesse Washington was lynched before a crowd of fifteen thousand in 1916, his "charred body was put in a sack and dragged behind an automobile to Robinson, where it was hanged to a telephone pole for the colored populace to gaze upon."[15] In 1917 the decapitated head of lynching victim Ell Persons was left on Beale Street, then the heart of the black business district in Memphis, Tennessee.[16]

In many cases, blacks heard the lynchings as they happened. White crowds numbering in the hundreds often shouted their approval or cheered. Shooting hundreds of rounds of bullets at the victim's hanging body was a routine practice. Although shuttered in their homes, blacks could no doubt hear the horrible cries of lynching victims who were tortured. Descriptions of lynching torture rituals often include the victims' cries for mercy, which could be heard from far away. Certainly, the sickening smell of burning flesh would linger long after the lynching.

In some instances, explicit notes were attached to the body. One note, reading "Beware all darkies! You will be treated the same way," was affixed to a Georgia lynching victim.[17] The display of the murdered and mutilated black body reinforced the message of lynching throughout the black community. Black children, who on their way to school observed George Armwood's body thrown carelessly in a lumberyard, could never remove the picture of his burnt flesh from their mind's eye. Nor could they ever forget the powerlessness of their families and their community in the face of this violence.

Lynching provided a disincentive for blacks in many communities to try to prosper economically or educationally because lynching was often motivated by white fear of black advancement. Ida B. Wells-Barnett took up her lifelong commitment to the antilynching crusade after three prosperous black businessmen—one of them a good friend of hers—were lynched in Memphis, Tennessee, by jealous white competitors.[18] When her own life was threatened for speaking out against the lynching in her newspaper, Wells-Barnett left Memphis for good. In yet another reported lynching in Tennessee, a black farmer, "who had by his prosperity aroused the jealousy and enmity of poor whites, was ambushed as he drove to town with his daughters to sell a load of cotton. The three were killed, the two girls by hanging and the father by shooting; the wagon was driven under the tree on which the girls' bodies hung, and fire was set to it, burning the bodies to a crisp."[19] In these communities, black prosperity was a form of racial insubordination, which could provoke violent reprisals.

The arbitrary nature of lynching must have enforced a sense of insecurity and fear among blacks. Because any act perceived as racial insubordination could trigger violence, lynching imposed social, educational, and political controls on black life. But while laws restricting the civil rights of blacks were external prohibitions on advancement, lynching encouraged blacks to curb their own ambitions, to turn away from opportunities for advancement, and to restrict their individual and communal growth and development.

The psychological effect on black individuals who witnessed or experienced lynching is immeasurable. Even those who observed the mutilated bodies of victims in the aftermath of lynching must have been deeply traumatized by the image. The black men who worked at the Wicomico Hotel and saw the lynching of Matthew Williams carried with them the horrible images of a helpless and bandaged Williams strung up before a howling mob and burned. Walter Black recalled that his grandfather James Harrison Webb, a cook at the Wicomico Hotel, heard one white man shout as Williams's body was dragged in front of the courthouse, "Anybody want a nigger sandwich?" The scene must have been of such overwhelming debauchery and inhumanity that the young black men who worked at the Wicomico Hotel and who knew Williams were probably deeply traumatized in ways that shaped their lives and those of their families. That the men undoubtedly feared for their own lives as well could only have added to the horror of the night.

The families of lynching victims were devastated by the death of their sons and husbands (and occasionally mothers and sisters) and doubly wounded by their inability to seek or obtain justice for the lynching of a loved one. Family members could be required to retrieve the mutilated bodies or charred remains of their lynched relative. In 1921 August Turner, "father of [a] mob victim, was summoned to the park to remove his son's charred remains."[20] The sight and smell of the tortured remains of one's child or sibling must have remained deeply embedded in the memory of a family member. In other cases family members were too frightened to collect the remains or attend the funeral of a lynched relative. The cavalier treatment by authorities of lynching victims' remains could be an additional source of pain and trauma for families. Etta Armwood was not visited by local authorities after the lynching of her son, George Armwood, or told where his body was. She learned this information from *Afro* reporters, who located her on October 19.[21] Once the mob had completed its ritual, Matthew Williams's burning body was collected by city officials, loaded into a truck, and dumped on the outskirts of town.[22] The body was returned to town only after the urgent request of Williams's uncle.

Many black children, even those who only heard about the lynchings, were deeply affected. Eastern Shore poet Adele Holden recalled her emotions after hearing from her parents about the lynching of Matthew Williams:

Fear saturated our lives, and even we children felt the strange uncertainty that had invaded our world. Parents tried in vain to shield children from the gruesome details that were being circulated around town. Children brought tales to school—accounts of the horrors overheard in their parents' work places and discussed when their children were supposed to be sleeping. And I was not the only child whose "lynching nightmares" alarmed the restless slumber of many parents.[23]

For those children who saw the victims' bodies or saw part of the lynching, the effects would be even more devastating. The memory of the lynching would form an indelible picture etched forever on a young mind. Civil rights lawyer James Nabrit, one of the attorneys on the *Brown v. Board of Education* case, remembered vividly how as a child he saw the burning body of a black man lynched for bragging about the victory of black boxing champion Jack Johnson over white challenger Jim Jeffries.[24] Child witnesses of violence often suffer lifelong psychiatric effects. According to physicians specializing in the treatment of children and adolescents, "Children who witness violence early in life, come to see the world as dangerous and unpredictable, and their own place in it as tenuous."[25] The problems these children suffer can affect their ability to function normally in their home and at school. Sleep disturbances, flashbacks, and emotional detachment are all the routinely reported symptoms of children who have been exposed to acts of violence.[26] Yet black children were discouraged from talking about lynching, and few opportunities would have existed for children or adults to talk through their emotional reaction to the violence of white supremacy. Without a space in which to process their emotions, many blacks exposed to lynching were left to deeply internalize the lessons of violent white supremacy in ways that affected their sense of how to manage racial boundaries.

In sum, blacks may underestimate the nature and scope of trauma suffered by their parents and grandparents who were exposed to the violence of lynching and the effect of this trauma on how blacks regard contemporary conflicts and their interaction with whites. The silence that followed a lynching denied blacks the opportunity to confront their fears, anger, and confusion. The lynching became more powerful because it was a taboo.

Tulani Salahu-Din, a native of Salisbury and now a professor at Morgan State University, remembered the tales about the lynching of Matthew Williams that her father told her, which took on the air of a "ghost story."[27] The political, social, and legal dimensions of the lynching were never publicly aired. What remained was the private horror of the event.

And in some families, the lynching was never discussed. The Reverend David Briddell, a retired Methodist minister, was born in Peninsula Hospital a few days before Matthew Williams was lynched. Because his mother had a cesarean section, she was still in the hospital on the night of the December 4 lynching. Yet Rev. Briddell never heard his mother or anyone in his family talk about the lynching, and in fact he did not hear about it until as an adult he began working on a family history.[28] Even during my research for this book, some elderly residents agreed to talk about the lynching, only to change their minds as the interview began. Others would talk about it only if their names were not used. And of course still others, like Howard Purnell, refused to revisit the horror of the lynching. The power of these events could silence a whole generation.

TRUTH-TELLING: RECLAIMING LOST POWER AND AFFIRMING HISTORY

A community conversation about the lynchings would also provide an opportunity to explore and examine the rich and diverse history of blacks' struggle for advancement on the Shore. After a lynching, blacks did not simply acquiesce to white supremacy. Instead, they responded in ways that they believed would strengthen their communities. Some tactics were accommodationist, others more confrontational and progressive. It is important for blacks on the Shore to reclaim this history. Few blacks know, for example, about the meeting of nineteen black leaders in Salisbury in December 1933 and their letter to the *Afro* denouncing the effort by three other black leaders to shift blame for the lynchings away from Eastern Shore whites and onto "outside influences." Their demand for antilynching legislation, and the insistence that so-called leaders handpicked by the white establishment would not silence the black community, make the letter signed by the nineteen leaders a shining example of the kind of courageous and activist leadership that existed in the black community alongside a more reactionary and cautious leadership.

The kinds of intragroup tensions reflected in the letter exchange between the three black accommodationist leaders and the nineteen signa-
tories to the *Afro* letter are typical of struggling black communities and
indeed any oppressed community. Certainly they were apparent in the
1990s during the litigation to challenge the construction of the Route 50
bypass in Salisbury. Distrust of church leaders, local NAACP chapters,
and elected leaders was apparent among some members of the black neighborhood group. The effort to determine who "spoke for" blacks in the
community was an ongoing source of controversy. This is not surprising
or even unwelcome. These are the dynamic building blocks and natural
growing pains of organized resistance. Moreover, oppressed groups have
always used multiple strategies of resistance. Some are more accommodationist, and others are confrontational. The open conflict between
Booker T. Washington and W. E. B. DuBois and between traditional civil
rights protesters and more militant activists during the 1960s and 1970s are
additional examples of this phenomenon. The experience of Eastern Shore
blacks is consistent with these ongoing intellectual and "movement" tensions. Rather than suggesting dysfunction, this kind of strategic and even
philosophical diversity is evidence of a dynamic and engaged community.

Conversations between and among black leaders about lynching provides an opportunity for community members to openly identify and
name ongoing sources of intracommunity tension and to reflect on and
about the role of churches in social justice movements, about how and why
some blacks are designated as "leaders" by white institutions and individuals, and about the responsibilities of "representing" or "speaking for" an
oppressed community. More important, these tensions can be seen as part
of an ongoing discussion dating from at least the 1930s.

In addition, the lynchings on the Shore played a key role in laying the
foundation for some of the most important civil rights gains in the nation.
This history also must be reclaimed. While Shore blacks attempted to negotiate a way to coexist with whites after the turbulent events of December 1933, blacks in Baltimore were growing increasingly radicalized. Rallies
and meetings were regularly held in churches throughout the city to address the question of lynching. The *Afro*, published by John Murphy, had
kept up a steady drumbeat against lynching and mob violence. Its interviews with the families of lynching victims, its investigative reporting, and
its consistent coverage of lynching had enabled blacks throughout the state

to follow closely and to share with Shore residents the experience and effects of racial violence.

Young Juanita Jackson had returned from college in Philadelphia to find only limited employment opportunities in Baltimore for a bright young woman used to competing in an integrated university environment. Her mother, the indomitable civil rights leader Lillie Carroll Jackson, thought that young people should stay busy. She encouraged her daughter to form an organization for youth that would enable them to become involved in the positive aspects of civil life and responsibility. The organization, the City-Wide Young People's Forum, took up lynching as its principal issue, and the meetings held at the Sharp Street Church in Baltimore were filled to overflowing. By 1934 Juanita Jackson had been selected to testify before Congress, representing the City-Wide Young People's Forum in favor of the Costigan-Wagner antilynching bill.

The NAACP and its general counsel, Charles Houston, were outraged by the Armwood lynching. Maryland was a border state, and two lynchings in two years had ominous implications for blacks everywhere. Houston, the mentor of Thurgood Marshall and the architect of *Brown v. Board of Education,* instructed NAACP president Walter White to "throw the whole weight" of the organization behind the Armwood lynching. Houston scolded then-governor Ritchie for his failure to avert the lynching, and later testified before Congress in favor of the Costigan-Wagner antilynching bill. Houston would later represent Bernard Ades in federal court in a disbarment proceeding. He successfully defended Ades, with the case resulting in a five-month suspension for Ades.

Antilynching activity stirred up the black community in Baltimore. The organizing by Juanita Jackson and others set in place a prepared and powerful black community that became a principal source of support for young Thurgood Marshall when he began to attack racial segregation in education two years later. His first case—and first major civil rights victory—was in the Baltimore courts, when he challenged and defeated the University of Maryland Law School's policy of excluding black applicants. The case was tried before Judge Eugene O'Dunne, a crusading white liberal lawyer who'd had some experience with lynching on the Eastern Shore. O'Dunne, as a young lawyer, had defended Isaiah Fountain, the black man who was nearly lynched by a mob of two thousand on the courthouse lawn in Talbot County in 1919 (this near lynching is discussed at length in chapter 1). In 1933 O'Dunne had some involvement with the Eastern Shore lynching cases as well. When lawyer Bernard Ades attempted to take custody of the body of Euel Lee after Lee's execution, it was O'Dunne who ruled that Ades did not have proper authority to take the body. His ruling came just a few days after the lynching of George Armwood, when rumors circulated that the Armwood lynchers would try to take Lee's body before it was buried. O'Dunne ordered Baltimore City sheriffs to guard Lee's body. And in a swipe at the local Princess Anne officers who had permitted the mob to storm the jail and take Armwood without firing a shot, O'Dunne reminded the Baltimore sheriffs that they were to shoot to kill if approached by a mob seeking to interfere with Lee's burial. O'Dunne saltily reminded the officers that "side arms are not provided the State Constabulary as a sex stimulant on the feminine mind of the fair daughters of the 'Free State,' but they are made to shoot with, and not intended as mere official ornament and decoration ... if justified in shooting to preserve authority and suppress disorder, you are also justified in shooting to kill."[29] When faced with the law school desegregation case two years later, O'Dunne ruled in favor of Thurgood Marshall's client Donald Murray.

With financial and editorial support from John Murphy at the *Afro*, and a mobilized and organized Baltimore black community, Marshall, over the next ten years, was able to challenge and mostly defeat Jim Crow in all aspects of education in the state of Maryland. These cases were the building blocks for *Brown*. And Marshall's success was due in large part to the mobilization of the black Baltimore middle class created by their activist response to the Williams and Armwood lynchings.

And the Eastern Shore lynchings contributed to the success of civil rights at the national level in one other way. Juanita Jackson's boyfriend and high school sweetheart, Clarence Mitchell, had been the *Afro* cub reporter who arrived on the scene in Princess Anne to report on the aftermath of the Armwood lynching. He too had been radicalized by the lynchings and went on to become a legendary lobbyist for the NAACP.

A CONVERSATION ABOUT LYNCHING: TRUTH-TELLING THROUGH COMMUNITY CONFERENCING

When fifteen teenagers unexpectedly showed up at Lauren Abramson's first neighborhood community conference, she did not panic. Abramson, the director of Baltimore's Community Conferencing Center, was facilitating a meeting involving complaints by several neighbors about a black female resident who appeared to leave her teenaged son unsupervised at home. The boy was alleged to be trouble in the neighborhood, intimidating neighbors and using foul language. The neighbors had called the police on several occasions. The conflict had both racial and class overtones. It was likely to be a tense conference.

But when the horde of unexpected teens showed up, Abramson did not turn them away. She explained the purpose and nature of the conference discussion and invited them in. Those teenagers, according to Abramson, ended up providing some of the most candid and productive contributions to the conversation. The conference ended up not really being about one mother's supervision of her son. Instead the conference, which by the end included thirty-five people, including neighbors, police officers, and a local elected representative, explored the desire of neighborhood teenagers for a safe place to play football, the heartbreak of a mother who'd lost her son to violence, and the struggle of a single mother to work two jobs to make ends meet.

Community conferencing is a facilitated discussion that enables those who have been "affected by behavior that has caused serious harm" to work together to find solutions and to repair harm. The conference is, in essence, a dynamic, open, and mediated discussion. Everyone gets to speak and to say what he or she wants, uninterrupted. Victims, perpetrators, their families, bystanders, and whoever else has been "affected" by the incident at the center of the discussion are participants. Abramson has identified three key features of the community conference: "Hearing what happened, letting everybody say how they've been affected by the situation and then having the group come up with ways to repair the harm and prevent it from happening again."[30] The conference ends with a contract—an agreement between all the parties on the contours of a reparation plan. Community conferencing has been used principally as a diversion program for juveniles facing incarceration and for neighborhood disputes. But conferencing may provide an excellent means of promoting truth-telling and conversation for communities where lynching has occurred. Its appeal is deceptively simple. As Abramson has said, "We do the radical thing of giving people a chance to talk to each other, and all at the same time."

Without question, conversations within communities about racial violence will have to take many forms. Some discussions may take the form used by the Truth and Reconciliation Commission in South Africa, in which witnesses come forward to give written or oral statements to a group of commissioners. In other instances, a form of town hall meeting may be appropriate. But productive conversations on race must provide opportunities for community members—black and white—to do what Abramson describes as "radical," that is, the opportunity *to talk to one another.*

The success of community conferencing and its promise for conversations about lynching lie in one other key feature. Conference participants themselves identify and agree to pursue forms of reparation that they have collectively determined will best repair the harm in their particular situation. This is a key concept to include in conversations on race. Reparations are often discussed and pursued at a macro level. But the harm caused by systematic racial violence was experienced locally. White supremacy has unique fingerprints. Its manifestations in New York or Chicago can be distinguished from its imprint in Walton County, Georgia, or Abbeville, South Carolina. For this reason, repairing the harm caused by racial violence is not a case of one size fits all. Nor can it be effectively imposed from the outside. Community members themselves must be in a position to identify and pursue appropriate forms of reparation that will mend the unique harm suffered by victims in that jurisdiction and that is responsive to and reflective of the unique cultural practices, geographic constraints, and racial realities of that particular jurisdiction.

Community conferencing compels community groups and residents to take responsibility for developing and implementing the contours of their own healing. Perhaps for this reason, community conferencing has had an extraordinarily high success rate in addressing neighborhood and school conflict. Ninety-nine percent of conferences have resulted in agreements. And in 90 percent of those cases, participants have complied with the terms of the agreement.

The conversations I am imagining for communities with a history of lynching are as diverse as the communities themselves. The multiple levels of complicity and harm experienced by those on the Eastern Shore suggest that no single conversation can effectively promote healing. Some conversations may be within churches or within community groups. Some will need to be intraracial, and others interracial. Yet still other conversations will most effectively be limited to schoolteachers, judges, or police officers and the communities they serve. In essence, truth-telling compels communities to engage in what Paul Rusesabagina calls "the conversation that will never end."[31] In the context of racial reconciliation, this is a commitment to keep talking, to keep listening, to be unafraid of the truth, to honor the past, and to work hard for the promise of the future.

CHAPTER 8

CONFRONTING THE ROLE OF INSTITUTIONS IN RACIAL/ETHNIC VIOLENCE

Given our modern fixation with personal responsibility and individual autonomy, it is almost irresistibly tempting to lay the full weight of responsibility for racial and ethnic violence at the feet of ordinary people. Movies such as *Schindler's List, To Kill a Mockingbird,* and *Hotel Rwanda* celebrate and lionize the willingness of individuals to resist the tide of genocide or ethnic violence, often at great peril to themselves. The heroes in these films show us that whatever the weapons of a racist government or faction, each person can use his or her individual humanity to counter collective or state-sponsored inhumanity. One man, one woman, can make a difference —save a life.

But there is a danger to our fascination with these solitary heroes. The danger lies in our inclination to see systematic racial and ethnic violence in purely individual terms. *If just one soldier had protested orders to shoot, perhaps others would have followed. If one member of the mob, one jailer, one sheriff, stood up to the mob, then a lynching could have been averted. If one witness testified that "yes, I recognized my neighbor as the one who hoisted the rope,"* then perhaps justice would have been done. Of course, these are not mere fables. There is certainly truth and persuasive evidence that just one bold, humane individual can derail the driving force of violence. But often, as in the Matthew Williams lynching, one man resisting a mob cannot save a life. Unlike the moving scene in *To Kill a Mockingbird* when young Scout Finch arrives outside the town jail and unwittingly stumbles on a lynch mob, there is no record of any lynch mob being shamed into dispersing.

More important, the humane individual who intercedes may prevent one act of violence, may save one life, or divert one mob. But the individual does not—indeed cannot—single-handedly disrupt the repeated pattern of racial violence and terror in a community. The truth is that systematic racial terrorism is, at its core, not individualized. It is, instead, institutionalized. By this I mean that lynching, genocide, and other forms of systematic racial or ethnic violence cannot flourish without the active participation and support of a community's institutions and institutional actors. In fact, it is the institutionalization of racism that creates the conditions in which individuals are prepared to commit acts of genocide or racial violence. The individual actor is emboldened because he believes that his community's institutions—its legal system, the media, and the business community—will ultimately support or condone his actions.

Thus, the project of addressing institutional complicity in racial and ethnic violence is a critically important one. It can also be overwhelming. Our willingness to see racial and ethnic violence solely in terms of individual accountability may reflect our unconscious desire to reduce the project of racial reconciliation to manageable proportions. For example, it is by no means easy, but perhaps less difficult, to seek out and prosecute the individuals involved in bombing the Sixteenth Street Baptist Church in Birmingham, Alabama, after thirty-five years than it is to examine and confront the conditions that existed in that city enabling the Klan members—all known to local law enforcement officials—to commit such an act with almost certain impunity. Nor is it easy to confront and root out the vestiges of racism in Birmingham's legal and social system that permitted racial bombings to become so routine that even before the Sixteenth Street Baptist Church bombing, the city had become known as "Bombingham."

Unearthing and exposing the complicity of institutions in systematic racial and ethnic violence are more than just difficult. In some countries, the attempt to delve too deeply into institutional complicity can have dangerous consequences, particularly when those institutions and the actors who run them continue to hold considerable power. Even where there is an opportunity to explore institutional complicity, the question remains, how does an institution accept responsibility for its role in perpetrating racial/ethnic violence? An institution is not a person with a soul who can be convicted or compelled to demonstrate empathy or transformation. Can institutions be held to standards of morality and humanity? How can such standards be imposed? Ann Bernstein, former head of the Center for Business Development and Enterprise in South Africa, sought to exculpate the business community from responsibility for apartheid. She argued, "Corporations are not institutions established for moral purposes. They are functional institutions created to perform an economic task.... This is their primary purpose. They are not institutions designed to promote some or other form of morality in the world."[1]

Yet another difficulty in holding institutions accountable for their role in perpetrating racial/ethnic violence is their sheer power. Institutions by their very nature are among the most powerful forces in a community. They protect and reflect the interests of the most successful and influential members of a community. The viability of a community is often judged by the strength of its economic, social, and cultural institutions. This is particularly true for communities that have emerged from the devastation of systematic racial or ethnic violence. The potential economic and political viability of South Africa, for example, was judged in large part by how soon and how well the country's institutions began operating again after the transition from apartheid to democracy. Powerful and sorely needed international benefactors—financial investors, for example—sought reassurances that South Africa's institutions were up and running and were protected against destabilizing challenges. So it is often the case that institutions—the media, the legal system, the business community, and so on, as well as the actors within those institutions—are subjected to the *least* scrutiny in a reconciliation process. They are too sorely needed to be simply turned out as part of the "old order." Where a country's very future hangs in the balance, challenging and potentially weakening the authority and legitimacy of its key institutions may be regarded as an untenable threat. Even the victims of racial and ethnic violence may find themselves unable to impose hard forms of accountability on institutional actors simply because of the pragmatic need to maintain functioning institutions in the aftermath of societal disruption. The South African TRC is itself the product of a compromise between the black leadership, those who represented the victims of apartheid, and the leadership of the white apartheid National Party. The compromise was born of the pragmatic recognition by Nelson Mandela and others that a new South Africa needed whites to remain.

In essence, in a society recovering from the effects of systematic racial and ethnic violence, institutions are, to coin a phrase, the eight-hundred-pound gorilla at the tea party. They get to sit wherever they want. Given this power, societal institutions have proven particularly adept at avoiding responsibility for their role in racial or ethnic violence—dodging apologies, suppressing truth, and using institutional channels to avoid liability, both financial and criminal. Institutional actors who sanctioned and advanced institutional support for racial or ethnic violence have often been able to retain their institutional positions and to continue to vigorously participate in the institutions where they served. Postwar Germany saw local political leaders and judges who by their actions or inaction had aided and abetted the Nazi regime return to public life and to leadership in key societal institutions.

Nazi-era judges proved to be remarkably resilient. Within ten years of the war, even judges who had served on the People's Court, described by historian Ingo Muller as the "supreme summary tribunal for the suppression of every hint of opposition to the [Nazi] regime,"[2] were restored to positions of authority and influence in the judicial system in Germany. Judge Gunther Schulz, who during the war had decided cases brought under the notorious "Race Laws" in Hamburg, was appointed in the 1950s as the presiding judge on a board hearing reparations claims for victims of the war and of the Race Laws tribunals in that city. In a shocking and blatant betrayal of victims brutalized by the legal system in Hamburg, Judge Schulz "decided claims filed by the survivors of his own earlier trials, and by the relatives of those he had sentenced to death."[3] After a decent interval had elapsed, still other Nazi-era judges and prosecutors joined the new Federal Ministry of Justice, served as criminal court judges and prosecutors, or became influential legal scholars in post–World War II Germany.

South Africa's old-order judges, business managers, and media owners remained largely unchanged in the postapartheid era. Countries such as Argentina, Chile, and most recently Liberia have faced a similar reality. Rwanda, of course, is different. Many of the country's institutional actors, such as judges, are not returned to former positions for the simple reason that they were massacred.

Despite these difficulties, the complicity of institutions in perpetrating racial and ethnic violence must become a critical focus of inquiry in a meaningful reconciliation process. Until institutional leaders commit to examining how the practices and values of the institutions they serve promote or contribute to racial prejudice and violence, and to recognizing that community institutions function as moral actors, racial reconciliation efforts will fail. In particular, institutions must be pressed to examine how conceptual cloaks that appear morally neutral can mask institutional complicity with inhumanity. The very concept of "impartiality," for example, can serve as a conceptual cloak for judges whose "neutral" decisions may uphold or enforce inhumane laws. The notion of "freedom of the marketplace" can be used to shield the business community from taking responsibility for promoting economic strategies or practices that perpetuate disparities between racial or ethnic groups or that have devastating consequences for particular members of the community. Both are examples of what I contend can be "conceptual cloaks" or "theoretical covers" that enable institutions and institutional actors to justify disconnection from or irresponsibility for systematic racial or ethnic violence. Conversations that explore the scope and meaning of these terms in a human rights context compel institutions and the actors that serve them to redefine institutional missions and to constantly and rigorously examine the effects of institutional practices on communities. In sum, institutional transformation should be an explicit and fundamental goal of any racial reconciliation process.

Nevertheless, the question remains, how can a reconciliation process address institutional complicity in historical racial and ethnic violence? Let us take the media, for example. In the aftermath of the genocide in Rwanda, journalists for the first time faced indictments by the United Nations' International Criminal Tribunal for Rwanda (ICTR). After a three-year "media trial" followed closely by media institutions all over the world, the tribunal convicted a journalist and two media executives of inciting to genocide. The exhaustive 361-page decision rendered by the court found the three guilty of inciting the death of thousands.[4] The conviction of the journalist and two media executives in the ICTR sent an important message to journalists all over the world. The power of the opinion and conviction lay in its insistence that journalists and media institutions are moral actors. The court rejected the contention that the right of free speech protected the journalists from moral responsibility in a society beset by the threat of racial/ethnic violence. That the institutional actors did not themselves raise machetes or guns to kill thousands did not remove their criminal or moral culpability for the genocide. By inciting Hutus to commit these murders, the journalist and media executives had participated in the genocide.

Nevertheless, the ICTR decision had the limitations of any criminal conviction. Like any prosecution, it was targeted at individuals. Certainly journalists beyond the borders of Rwanda and within the international community were collaterally touched by the decision. But the conviction of the journalist and two media executives could not compel media institutions in Rwanda or anywhere else to engage in self-analysis and to apologize or make amends to individuals or communities who were targeted. Nor could their criminal conviction compel media institutions to identify and articulate journalistic standards designed to ensure that the kind of abuses perpetrated by the convicted journalist and media executives could not happen again. Thus, although the ICTR decision punished individual institutional actors, it could not approach or challenge the institutions themselves.

Perhaps the most ambitious effort to address the role of institutions in this regard was undertaken by the South African Truth and Reconciliation Commission (TRC). The TRC held institutional hearings that sought to call to account key institutions in South African society—the media, the legal system, the business community, faith communities, the health sector, and the prison system—for their role in supporting apartheid. The decision to hold these hearings was among the most courageous and groundbreaking made by the commissioners. Curiously, the commission's institutional hearings were also the most underappreciated and underreported aspects of the TRC process. The victim-offender hearings, with their riveting and devastating personal stories of loss, torture, and courage, were intensely dramatic and were, without question, the most important part of the TRC hearings. The power of these hearings came to define the work of the commission. But the institutional hearings were, in their own way, compelling and dramatic as well. These hearings demonstrated the critical role institutions played in creating and supporting an environment in which the kinds of abuses so wrenchingly described in the victim-offender hearings could take place over decades.

Letters from the chair of the commission went out to leaders of the business community, the legal community, the media, the faith community, the prison system, and the health sector, seeking their participation in TRC hearings. Specifically, the TRC wanted to find out "how these institutions saw themselves and how, brought together with those who had opposed them, a part of the enigma of the South African evil could be unraveled."[5] Representatives of these institutions were asked to provide live and written testimony and submissions. These hearings were not intended to be adversarial. Instead, the hearings would offer a chance for institutional actors to engage in self-examination, to explore the dimensions of their own complicity with apartheid, and to share with the TRC their findings. Panels of experts from outside the institutions would thereafter comment on the submissions and testimony offered by the institutional representatives.

The TRC's institutional hearings offer helpful direction for communities engaged in reconciliation efforts. Two of the hearings in particular are instructive for contemporary reconciliation efforts in the United States. The legal-system hearings that focused on the role of judges are worth examining because of the refusal of the judges to participate. The other instructive hearing was the media hearing. The media hearings, by contrast, reflected the kind of transformative self-analysis that is the goal of reconciliation.

THE TRC'S LEGAL-SYSTEM HEARINGS

The TRC's invitation to judges and other members of the legal system to participate in the institutional hearings offered assurances that the hearings would not be adversarial and that it was "not the purpose of the hearing to establish guilt or hold individuals responsible." Instead, the goal of the hearings was "to attempt to understand the role the legal system played in contributing to the violation and/or protection of human rights *and to identify institutional changes required to prevent those abuses which occurred from happening again.*"[6] This forward-looking goal bears emphasis. The TRC recognized that the institutional hearings provided an opportunity for institutions to not only look back at their role in legitimizing and perpetuating apartheid. Institutions were invited to engage in rigorous self-examination and then to transform themselves in both purpose and operation, in ways that would guard against future complicity in human rights abuses.

Despite these assurances—that the process was nonadversarial and not judicial in nature, that it was forward-looking and did not seek to identify guilt or innocence—the judges refused to come. In fact, no judicial officers attended the hearings.[7] A few offered written submissions. The refusal of judges to attend the hearings was startling. Even President Nelson Mandela had regarded himself as subject to the authority of the TRC and responded to their request to testify. Former National Party Leader and Prime Minister F. W. DeKlerk appeared and testified before the commission, as did Winnie Mandela.

There appeared to be three principal reasons for the judges' refusal. Some judges from the apartheid era, "old-order judges" who continue to serve on the bench, simply dismissed the TRC process as unimportant and stood by the role they had played during the apartheid era. Others, including the then–chief justice of South Africa, Michael Corbett, argued in a written submission that for judges to appear before the TRC would compromise judicial independence. He also contended that examining the record of judges would require an "impractical" review of every particular proceeding that might be questioned. "The mind boggles at what all of this would involve," stated Justice Corbett.[8] Even those old-order judges regarded as liberal, who made attempts to resist the harshest and most draconian interpretations of apartheid law in their decisions, refused to appear before the commission. What became apparent from both the absence of live presentations by the judges and from the few written submissions that were presented to the commission was perhaps best summed up by David Dyzenhaus, a law professor who closely watched the hearings and testified about the conduct of apartheid-era judges: "Judges of the old order, even those who had a reputation for commitment to the rule of law, were deeply unwilling to confront their past."[9]

Perhaps most striking was the failure of even "new-order" judges—those appointed after the fall of apartheid, including several judges of color—to appear before the TRC. These judges had devoted their careers to fighting against apartheid in the South African courts. They had witnessed gross miscarriages of justice, including judicial misconduct, yet they also declined to appear. Most prominent among these was Arthur Chaskalson, president of the Constitutional Court, who submitted a joint written submission with Ismail Mahomed, head of the Supreme Court of Appeal. Chaskalson had been part of the legal team defending Nelson

Mandela at the Rivonia trial in 1964. Both Chaskalson and Mahomed, who is of Indian descent, were perhaps the most distinguished human rights lawyers in South Africa. Both were, by the time of the collapse of apartheid, recognized throughout the world for their antiapartheid work. In an article authored five years before the end of apartheid, Chaskalson wrote about the role of judges under the apartheid system. Dyzenhaus contends that Chaskalson's writing assumed a prominent role at the TRC hearings on judges. In the 1989 article, Chaskalson argued that "little is to be gained by lamenting the past." While acknowledging that old-order judges "could have done better than they did," Chaskalson also credited the judges with having "kept alive the principles of freedom and justice which permeate the common law."[10] During the TRC process, many old-order judges took great comfort from Chaskalson's magnanimous statements. Indeed, Chaskalson unwittingly provided a "cover" for most old-order judges who refused, as Dyzenhaus wrote, to confront their past.

But clearly animating what must have been the difficult decision of new-order judges not to appear before the TRC was a more pragmatic concern. They feared that if they appeared before the TRC and testified about the mostly shameful record of old-order judges, the fragile collegiality of the newly integrated South African courts would be destroyed. Dyzenhaus agrees that "for either [Chaskalson or Mahomed] to criticize judges of the old order would risk much."[11] That is, new-order judges, many of them former human rights lawyers and activists who had suffered under the apartheid regime, were undertaking the enormous challenge of integrating themselves on a bench with old-order judges, many of whose records bore witness to their abdication of principles of justice and humanity. Old-order judges felt threatened not only by the TRC process but by these new-order judges as well. In fact, some old-order judges had shamefully and publicly challenged the appointment of new judges. For example, one Afrikaner judge serving on the Supreme Court of Appeal openly denounced the appointment of Judge Mahomed to head that court and suggested that Mahomed should withdraw his name from nomination to the court.[12]

And tempting as it might have been, these old-order judges could not simply be dismissed. They represented a form of stability that encouraged white South Africans to believe the African National Congress's promise that the new South Africa would be a country for everyone, not just blacks. This was a principal concern of President Mandela and other ANC negotiators who worked on the transition. In fact, this desire—to discourage white flight from the country—was one of the reasons for the creation of the TRC. Turning out the entire white apartheid-era judiciary would surely have been regarded by whites in the first days of the new democracy as a betrayal of the ANC's promise of inclusion. And it is not entirely clear that constitutionally the judges could have been removed from office without some prolonged process that demonstrated cause for the removal of each judge.

Moreover, apartheid had created a virtual racial monopoly on technical and professional skills. Although there were and are many highly competent and indeed brilliant black lawyers in South Africa, the white, old-order judges had the experience and skills that would be needed to maintain the functioning of the legal system during and after the transition of power. They could not, as a practical matter, simply be turned out of office—certainly not before a sufficiently trained and experienced class of black lawyers could be prepared to fill judicial benches throughout the country. Entrenched racism over time protects itself by ensuring that the day-to-day functioning of a community's institutions is dependent on old-order actors. Here, then, is the kind of pragmatic reality that, as I suggested earlier, protects institutions from undergoing radical examination and transformation in the postgenocide or postracial violence period.

In any case, the sum of these concerns was the failure of judicial officers to appear before the commission. The commission's final report on the legal hearings concluded with a restrained, yet blistering condemnation of the judges' refusal. It predicted that "[h]istory will judge the judiciary harshly."[13]

The few written submissions offered by some judges were telling as well and largely unsatisfactory. Some interpreted their obligation under the constitution to interpret laws narrowly, based solely on the intention of the legislature. This line of thought of course leads to the obvious question: what is the moral obligation of judges when the intention of the legislature is to discriminate, to subordinate, and to deny human rights? Should judges resign? Denounce unjust laws? How can judges legally act to bring about just results when the laws at issue are fundamentally unjust?

All of these questions have been the subject of analysis following the legal-system hearings. The commission's findings based on the legal-system hearings were harsh. "The organized legal profession," the commission found, "generally and subconsciously or unwittingly connived in the legislative and executive pursuit of injustice."[14] Ironically, the refusal of judges to appear before the commission ultimately generated more and perhaps richer dialogue about the role of judges in a democracy, and the scope of judicial responsibility for protecting fundamental human rights, than perhaps would have been generated had the judges consented to appear. Can judges, unlike any other actor in a democracy, be exempt from accountability for complicity in human rights violations? Does judicial independence mean freedom from accountability? If not, what is the scope of accountability that can be reasonably asked of judges?

The testimony of legal organizations like the Black Lawyers' Association, the Legal Resources Center, and academics at the hearings on the judiciary provided further support for critical questioning of the judiciary —both for their nonappearance and for their actions during apartheid. The organizations argued that "judicial independence was a myth that had been exploded in the daily experience" of South Africa's courts.[15] Such an excuse, therefore, could not legitimately be asserted as a reason for failing to appear at the TRC hearings.

In sum, the nonappearance of judges, as well as the written submissions, provided a wealth of material from which members of the legal community and indeed the community at large could begin and sustain a conversation about the appropriate role of the judiciary in a society where injustice was legal. In the absence of institutional legal hearings, these conversations would have been private ones—limited to law review articles and obscure academic conferences. The TRC's legal-system hearings enabled the entire country to participate in this discussion. Ongoing struggles surrounding racial diversity on the bench in South Africa are animated and informed by the debate that began at the legal-system hearings.

THE TRC'S MEDIA HEARINGS

The media hearings at the TRC were also illuminating. The conclusion reached by many who made submissions to the TRC was that the media "had provided a 'cloud of cover' under which gross human rights violations were possible."[16] The hearings directly questioned the relationship between the media and the state, the ethical obligations of individual journalists, and the narrow framework within which even the English press "opposed" apartheid. Representatives of the Afrikaans press, the print media recognized as the most conservative and supportive of the apartheid regime, made no submissions to the TRC and failed to appear.[17] Testimony about the complicity of the South African Broadcasting Corporation (SABC) in supporting the National Party and in serving as "a tool of the government" was in some ways unsurprising. The extent to which the SABC answered to and took instructions from the National Party and the control that the Broederbond (an influential Afrikaner secret society) held over SABC were alarming. Among the most disturbing revelation was that black staff members who were subject to disciplinary action at the SABC could consent to being whipped by superiors instead of being fired from their jobs.[18]

Interestingly, some of the harshest criticism was leveled at the English press, generally regarded as liberal. By all accounts, white reporters were stunned to discover that black journalists were particularly angry about their working conditions at white papers and at what they regarded as an insufficiently oppositional stance by white liberal reporters toward apartheid.[19] This exchange seems particularly important and relevant to contemporary racial reconciliation efforts in the United States. It is quite likely that many white media outlets in the United States that regard themselves as liberal would find that blacks share a very different opinion. In fact, blacks may hold the so-called liberal media to higher levels of responsibility than they do the conservative press for the failure to forthrightly address racial injustice in their communities.

INSTITUTIONAL HEARINGS FOR A LYNCHING TRC

Any meaningful attempt at reconciliation for racial violence must include some form of institutional accountability. In the case of lynching, an examination of the legal system and media is critically important. As discussed earlier, the role of the legal system and of the media was critical to creating, maintaining, and condoning the conditions in which lynching occurred on the Eastern Shore of Maryland. This was no less true in other regions of the country. There is no account anywhere in the United States of a white person being tried and convicted for the lynching of a black person until the James Byrd case in 1998. Given the public nature of lynching, this can only mean that the legal systems in countless jurisdictions throughout the country were complicit in lynching.

Jurisdictions where lynchings occurred are often characterized by continuing disparities that reflect the long-term effects of racial exclusion. On the Eastern Shore, the absence of black lawyers and judges, even in counties with large black populations, shows that similar disparities continue to exist. In fact, it was only in 2006 that the first black judge was appointed to the District Court bench on the Eastern Shore.[20] No black had ever run for or been appointed to fill an unexpired term on the Circuit Court bench on the Shore before the twenty-first century. Even more remarkable is the fact that Somerset County, where 41 percent of the population is black, has no practicing black lawyers. In fact, only six black lawyers practice law on the *entire* Eastern Shore. In states from Mississippi to Delaware, African Americans have made extraordinary gains in the legal profession in the last seventy years. Yet this progress has simply passed by many Eastern Shore counties. Black lawyers attribute this to the fact that blacks who wish to become lawyers know there is little opportunity for them to advance on the Shore. The first black judicial law clerks were hired here in 2005. The established white firms in Salisbury have never hired a black associate. The first black person to serve in the state's attorney's office on the Eastern Shore was Gerald Purnell, who became a deputy state's attorney in 2002. There is currently only one black prosecutor on the Eastern Shore.

Moreover, controversy over how race influences the legal system— particularly the criminal justice system—has been an ongoing concern in some Eastern Shore towns for decades. Judges have not been immune from the focus of these concerns. The peak of this concern was most certainly in early 1963, when police responded to civil rights protests in several Eastern Shore communities with a display of ferocity widely viewed as disproportionate. During this period, some judges also imposed draconian criminal sentences on black civil rights protesters. One such judge, ironically, was

E. McMaster Duer, the son of former judge Robert Duer, who played such an ignoble role in the George Armwood lynching. Duer served on the Circuit Court bench for twenty-three years, after years in private practice with his father. If the name Duer had become synonymous with a racially indifferent and insensitive Eastern Shore judiciary in the 1930s, then E. McMaster Duer solidified that reputation within the black community during the Cambridge Riots of 1963. When two fifteen-year-old black activists were arrested for protesting the exclusion of blacks from a local bowling alley and movie theater and engaged in a series of nonviolent forms of civil disobedience outside segregated establishments in Cambridge, Maryland, Duer found them to be juvenile delinquents and remanded them for indefinite incarceration in juvenile detention facilities.[21] Duer's harsh sentencing of the two youths suggested to blacks that orderly peaceful protest would not be handled justly and thus encouraged some young blacks to adopt a more militant stance.[22] By the end of the summer, violent battles broke out on the streets of Cambridge between armed whites and blacks, and the National Guard was called out and positioned on Race Street, the eponymously named dividing line between the black and white communities in Cambridge.[23] The National Guard's presence in Cambridge—which ultimately lasted a year—is reputed to be the longest peacetime military occupation of a community in the United States since Reconstruction. Ultimately, the sentencing of the two young civil rights protesters was overturned on appeal after NAACP lawyers took up the case. Concerns about excessive use of force by police and diversity on the police forces on the Shore have continued to this day.

Institutional hearings on the role of the legal system in lynching would generate a much-needed and potentially productive discussion on the Shore. In addition to the historical truth-telling aspect of the hearings, a forward-looking discussion might confront several important questions. What accounts for the paucity of black lawyers and judges on the Shore? How do blacks regard the criminal justice system? How sensitized are actors in the criminal justice system to black perceptions of fairness and the rule of law? Are white police officers, state's attorneys, and judges sufficiently educated about and sensitized to the concerns of black litigants, defendants, and witnesses who appear in a legal system that is largely all-white? What level of comfort and inclusion do black litigants experience when they enter a legal system that is dominated almost entirely by whites? What effect does the dearth of black lawyers and judges on the Shore have on the respect and opportunities afforded the few black lawyers who do practice on the Shore? What efforts have been made by Shore bar associations to support the efforts of black lawyers who practice on the Shore? Does the appointment of the first black judge on the Shore reflect a new beginning for black lawyers in the region? Which counties on the Shore have had the greatest success in developing and retaining black lawyers? Which counties the least? Why?

Likewise, the media in many jurisdictions helped set the conditions in which lynchings could happen and in which they could go unpunished. Similar practices on the Eastern Shore have already been discussed. Newspapers on the Shore closed ranks after lynchings occurred and encouraged the communities they served to do the same. Local papers decried the involvement of "outsiders" as lawyers (such as Bernard Ades or even Attorney General Preston Lane) and as commentators and journalists (such as H. L. Mencken and the *Sun* papers). They absolved their local leaders of responsibility and in the first days after a lynching cued potential witnesses and jurors in to what would become the consensus story: the lynchers were "outsiders" who could not be recognized.

Perhaps more important, newspapers on the Shore were among those institutions principally responsible for dehumanizing the black population in the minds of many whites. The failure to report on the "ordinariness" of black people's lives on the Shore undermined the ability of whites to see their black neighbors, servants, and laborers as human beings. Thus Shore newspapers completed the process created by segregation. Whites could at best ignore the conditions in which most blacks lived and at worst develop a sense that blacks did not lead normal lives in which education, work, and family were paramount and central. Instead, blacks could be seen as "other," "different," not possessed of the same humanity as whites. These perceptions enabled whites—when confronted with lurid stories about interracial rape and murder—to imagine black men as beasts who could be controlled only by violence. The complicity of ordinary whites, who stood and watched a lynching without interfering, was made possible by the dehumanizing choices the media made in their coverage of blacks.

The lingering remnants of these dehumanizing portrayals of blacks in the media have modern currency. The overincarceration of black men in our nation's prisons, the ability of many whites to turn a blind eye to police brutality committed against black men, the continuing harsh reality of "driving while black" in some communities and on some highways, all attest to the continuing perception of blacks as dehumanized which pervades the thinking of many whites. And the media continue to play a role in furthering these perceptions. Front-page coverage of black-on-white crime—particularly murder—is still the norm in the *Baltimore Sun,* whereas black-on-black murder is often relegated to the paper's "Maryland" section, suggesting that the loss of a black person's life lacks the tragic content and public significance of the loss of a white person's life.

And what of H. L. Mencken's columns denouncing the Shore? His condemnation of the lynching of Matthew Williams and his outrage over the Shore's reflexive self-protection were perhaps right on target. But did Mencken's inflammatory language help or hinder the protection of Eastern Shore blacks from racial violence? More likely, Mencken's columns provided a welcome rallying point for Shore people, even those who might otherwise have condemned the lynching but were driven by a kind of regional pride to close ranks with their more extreme neighbors after Mencken's tirade. The Shore people's sense of "us versus them," most strongly demonstrated on the streets of Salisbury, when Shoremen faced off against the National Guard in November 1933, only further set back the cause of blacks on the Shore, who after 1931 were more cut off from the progressive action of their counterparts in other parts of the state. By 1937 Thurgood Marshall had won his first major civil rights victory, striking down segregation at the University of Maryland Law School. By the mid-1940s, the Baltimore NAACP successfully struck down Jim Crow on golf courses in Baltimore City. But on the Eastern Shore, blacks who wanted to enjoy the beach at Ocean City were still limited to only three days a year until well into the 1960s. The virtual ban of the *Sun* on the Shore for decades similarly cut off Shore whites from exposure to the more moderate views and policies pursued on the Western Shore. Certainly responsibility for the Shore's racial reactionaryism in the decades following the lynchings cannot be laid at the feet of Mencken or the *Sun.* But a candid and forward-looking reconciliation process could not help but recognize the way in which the Mencken columns played a role in the Shore's further withdrawal from the increasingly progressive norms of the rest of the state. Institutional hearings on the role of the media might well include discussion of the responsibility of columnists and the newspapers in which they write during times of violent racial conflict. Should columnists be driven purely by their First Amendment right to write what and how they see fit? Or are newspaper columnists also obligated to assess and take some measure of responsibility for the likelihood that their writing might promote or inflame human rights abuses? When the consequences for the escalation of inflammatory rhetoric are likely to be borne not by the columnist or the newspaper but by the victimized population, does the media bear a heightened responsibility?

Recent controversy over the decision of a Danish newspaper to publish cartoons that mocked the Prophet Mohammed suggests that these are highly relevant questions for local, national, and international media. Of the nearly one hundred people killed during violent protests condemning the cartoons throughout the Middle East and Africa, none was Danish or even European. The Danish cartoonists in question certainly have been the object of fatwas, which threaten their lives. But the principal cost of the inflammatory cartoons has been borne by average people living outside Europe. Ongoing discussions about the dangers of censorship, and cultural sensitivity in a globalized media world, suggest that the kind of questions that would be raised in institutional media hearings for lynching bear directly on contemporary conversations about the scope of media responsibility for the impact of their reporting on violence.

The *Salisbury Times*—now the *Daily Times*—has become essentially the local paper of record for all of the Shore. The *Baltimore Sun* performs a similar function at the statewide level. The continuing importance of both the *Daily Times* and the *Baltimore Sun* on the multiracial communities they serve suggests that institutional hearings on the role these papers played in the events that unfolded in the 1930s would be critical to a meaningful and productive reconciliation process.

One southern newspaper recently engaged in a reconciliatory act related to its failure to cover civil rights protests during the 1960s. In 2004, after a former editor in a speech remarked on the *Lexington Kentucky Herald-Ledger*'s "blackout" of news about the civil rights movement, editors at the paper undertook an exposé of the paper's practices during the civil rights movement.[24] Appearing on its front page, and accompanied by "previously unpublished black-and-white photographs," the exposé revealed the paper's refusal over two decades—while sit-ins, boycotts, and marches were taking place on the streets of Lexington—to report on these events for readers. The paper's editors conceded in the exposé that the lack of coverage was an effort " 'to play down the movement' in the hopes that it would wither away." Whatever the reasons, the story presented an opportunity for blacks and whites to talk about the effect of the paper's decision to "ignore the Civil Rights movement in Lexington" on civil rights progress in that city.[25] Some blacks who were active in local civil rights activity revealed that they simply stopped reading the paper for decades because of its refusal to cover the movement.

Local Shore papers might well consider conducting similar studies of the way in which their coverage of blacks during the 1930s contributed to a dehumanized picture of blacks and discouraged whites from taking responsibility for the violence of lynching. Certainly the *Salisbury Times,* which imposed a news blackout on the Matthew Williams lynching, should be prepared to articulate to the public its current position on the paper's editorial decisions during this period. In 1998 George Roache, a columnist for the former *Salisbury Times,* wrote a three-part series on the lynching of Matthew Williams and described the newspaper's role in the events that surrounded the outbreak of violence in the town.[26] At the time his column appeared, Roache was the only black reporter at the paper. Printing these revelations in the *Times* made an important statement about the paper's willingness to confront its past. But a columnist's initiative cannot take the place of editorial and managerial willingness to take responsibility for the past shortcomings of the paper's coverage of racial conflict. The urgent need for a more official review of the history of the *Times*'s coverage of the Lee, Williams, Davis, and Armwood matters was reflected in hate mail Roache received for the column, including a letter from a resident of nearby Fruitland, Maryland, who still insisted that Communist interference was the cause of the Williams lynching.[27]

Of course the media and the legal system are not the only institutions that should be part of a reconciliation process. Churches would be important institutions to participate in self-examination as well. The unwillingness of local churches and pastors, black and white, to take a stand after the lynchings can serve as a centerpiece for discussion about the contemporary moral obligations of religious institutions in a community where racial and ethnic violence or terrorism is present. A diverse cross section of representatives of the faith community participated in the TRC's institutional hearings on the role of religious institutions in apartheid. The hearings and the submissions were strikingly candid and painful, and the discussions productive and dynamic. Churches, many of which had promoted the ideology of apartheid, came under particular and harsh scrutiny. While acknowledging the work that many churches did to resist apartheid and to support apartheid dissenters, the TRC ultimately urged religious communities "to accept moral and religious culpability for their failure as institutions to resist the impact of apartheid on the nation."[28] The commission ultimately concluded that "the failure of the churches... contributed not only to the survival of apartheid but also to the perpetuation of the myth, prevalent in certain circles, that apartheid was both a moral and Christian initiative." But because religious institutions can play such a critical role in uniting diverse people—victims, perpetrators, and beneficiaries—through the bond of a common faith, the TRC recognized that "[r]econciliation within [faith] communities could have a leavening effect for the whole society."[29] This is no less true than for faith communities in the United States.

Educational institutions would be key players as well. It was not unusual for African Americans I spoke with in Somerset and Wicomico Counties to express alarm and frustration that the details of the events surrounding the lynchings had been "kept from them." Several remarked, "We were never taught about this. It's our own history." Schools have an important role to play in helping a community create opportunities for truth-telling in their curriculum. But all of these institutions must stand ready and willing to reexamine and redefine their role as moral agents in the community.

CHAPTER 9

RECONCILIATION IN THE
TWENTY-FIRST CENTURY

On June 12, 2004, five hundred people gathered in downtown Greensboro, North Carolina, to witness the swearing in of the seven members of the Greensboro Truth and Reconciliation Commission. The Greensboro TRC is the first TRC created in the United States. Its mandate is to examine the murder of five activists and the wounding of ten other people by Klan and Klan-affiliated individuals on the morning of November 3, 1979. Despite the fact that the murders were caught on videotape, after two trials no one has been convicted of the murders.

The Greensboro TRC is one of a growing set of initiatives in communities throughout the United States where residents are undertaking the project of racial reconciliation for historic incidents of racial violence. The Greensboro TRC's final report was released on May 25, 2006. Its recommendations included a call on individuals involved in the 1979 murders to "reflect on their role and apologize . . . to those harmed," as well as institutional reforms such as antiracism training for all city and county employees, the creation of a community justice court to handle misdemeanor cases, the development of a curriculum for the county's public schools that would include the events surrounding the murders, and the issuance of annual reports on race relations in the city.[1] The impetuses for the projects are as diverse as the initiatives themselves. The Greensboro TRC was born from discussions surrounding the twentieth anniversary of the Greensboro killings. The exhibit of lynching photos, *Without Sanctuary,* helped renew and reinvigorate conversations about lynching in Georgia, including the lynching of Leo Frank. The reopening of investigations into civil rights–era murders in Mississippi has contributed to a period of reflection and reconciliation in that state. Even the Senate's apology for failing to pass antilynching legislation inspired a community in Abbeville, South Carolina, to open a conversation about the lynching of Anthony Crawford in 1916.[2]

Perhaps the most ambitious effort to date is that of Southern Truth and Reconciliation (STAR). STAR is a regional network of individuals and organizations focused on examining the history of lynching in the South and on working toward reconciliation in communities where lynchings have occurred. The creation of STAR ironically derives from a challenge issued by Archbishop Desmond Tutu, the chair of the South African TRC, during his two-year visiting professorship at Emory University in Atlanta. After listening to academics and community leaders offer critiques of the South African TRC, Tutu issued a challenge: "Stop studying our TRC and begin your own reconciliation process."[3] Community leaders and academics took up the challenge and began to formulate what became STAR in 2003. STAR held its first annual conference, "Racial Violence and Reconciliation," at the University of Mississippi in March 2006.

What is most compelling about these reconciliation initiatives is their sheer diversity. Some have sought merely to open dialogue, others have focused on reopening old cases, and still others have created commemorative sites where lynchings took place. Leaders in Duluth, Minnesota, for example, commissioned the creation of a memorial to commemorate the 1920 lynching of three young black men in that city. The bronze sculptures, unveiled in October 2003, have formed the centerpiece of a three-year effort to, as one leader said, "tell the truth . . . [and] make history right."[4] On the day designated to commemorate the lynching victims, twenty-five hundred residents walked from a downtown site to the memorial.

A number of reconciliatory efforts have focused on the 1946 lynching of two young black men and their two girlfriends in Walton County, Georgia. The four were killed near the Moore's Ford Bridge. The case attracted the attention of President Harry S. Truman, in large part because one of the murdered men was a veteran. Although federal investigators descended on Walton County within weeks of the lynching, no one was arrested or charged with the murder. In addition to unveiling a plaque describing the lynching on the site where it happened,[5] members of the Moore's Ford Committee have created four scholarships named for each of the lynching victims, to be awarded to graduating public high school seniors from the region. In perhaps the most innovative reconciliation activity, the group presented a reenactment of the lynching in the woods near the Moore's Ford Bridge, at an event attended by Jesse Jackson and other national civil rights leaders.[6] The reenactment was staged to encourage federal law enforcement officials to reopen the investigation into the case. The FBI has agreed to reopen the investigation.

In some instances, state officials have spearheaded reconciliation efforts by ordering investigations into long-forgotten unsolved racial murders. The North Carolina General Assembly commissioned a report on an 1898 incident in which a white mob intent on wresting political power from Reconstruction-era black leadership in Wilmington attacked the black community.[7] Black leaders were forced out of town into the nearby swamps. Nearly one hundred blacks are believed to have been killed in the melee. The report noted the long-term effects of the pogrom. After the murders, blacks were not active participants in local government in Wilmington until the civil rights era, nearly sixty years later. The report stated that the ability of white mobs to kill blacks with impunity in Wilmington let "everyone in the state, regardless of race, [know] that the white supremacy campaign was victorious on all fronts."

These many and diverse initiatives suggest that the time is ripe in America to confront our history of racial violence. As the first-person observers and participants who experienced these events begin to die out, stories about the history of racial violence will often survive on misinformation and rumor. Unless steps are taken forthwith to break the silence that has surrounded these events, we will have lost the valuable contribution of those who can tell what it felt like to bear witness to this aspect of community life in America.

There is no question but that these stories will survive. They may survive as inchoate snippets of information, shaped by time and embellishment. But the core of the stories will prevail. The lessons about race, trust, violence, and community will live on, even as the names of the participants and the details of the lynchings fade from memory. Now, in the first decade of the twenty-first century, we have the opportunity to confront twentieth-century racial violence and begin a long-overdue process of truth-telling and reconciliation. If Archbishop Tutu is right, and "the past does not lie down quietly," then we will have to confront this past and its lingering effects sooner or later.

ACKNOWLEDGMENTS

Many people have supported the completion of this book. I want to especially thank my colleagues at the University of Maryland School of Law, in particular my dear friend and mentor Taunya Banks, who believed in this project from the very beginning. The provision of research grants from the Law School and a sabbatical in 2001 were invaluable to the progression of my work on the book. The skill and professionalism of legal assistant Gynene Sullivan made it possible for me to focus on writing and to leave many of the details in her capable hands.

I am deeply indebted to all of those who assisted me in researching the events described in this book, including law students Tara Andrews, Dorcas Gilmore, Joe Lim, Matthew Renda, Pam Smith, Shontell Smith, Charles Sydnor, Lois Peterson at the Frederick Douglass Library of the University of Maryland Eastern Shore, research associates at the Nabb Center for Research at Salisbury State University, Walter Hill at the National Archives, Vivian Fisher at the Enoch Pratt Free Library, David Taft Terry at the Maryland State Archives, and Lisa Atkins at the Charles Chipman Center in Salisbury, Maryland. At the Thurgood Marshall Law Library of the University of Maryland, research librarian Maxine Grosshans is the best in the business. I could not do what I do without her invaluable assistance. I thank librarian Bill Sleeman for staying on the lookout for newly archived civil rights materials. My former legal assistant Diane Freeland started this journey with me and provided tireless commitment to our research, as well as great companionship on visits to the Shore.

I owe special thanks to the MacDowell Colony in Peterborough, New Hampshire, who awarded me a one-month residency to write in 2005. The best of my writing was accomplished during my stay there. I am grateful for the hospitality of Jay and Deborah Parker, at whose lovely Princess Anne bed and breakfast, Somerset House, I accomplished a good deal of writing.

Others who assisted my thinking about the subject of lynching and reconciliation include Derrick Bell, Alfred Brophy, Larry Gibson, Michael

Mitchell, the late judge William H. Murphy, Dumisa Ntsebeza, Paul Rusesabagina, and Eric Yamamoto.

There are many people from the Eastern Shore who talked with me over the years about the history of the Shore, race, and lynching, only a few of whom are specifically referenced in the text. Even if they are not specifically mentioned in the text, each helped shape my ideas about how a reconciliation process might work in that region. They include Chris Brown, the members of the Jersey Heights Neighborhood Association, the indomitable Commissioner Honiss Cane, the Honorable Rudolph Cane, Walter Conway, Evelyn and Bill Cottman, Rachel Polk, George Roache, Tulani Salahu-Din, Fran Starkey, Ed Taylor, Charles Whittington, and DeWayne Whittington.

I thank my editor at Beacon Press, Gayatri Patnaik, for her patience and for believing in this project, and the entire team at Beacon Press for their professionalism, enthusiasm, and support. I also thank Helen Lee for her encouragement, ideas, and support, and Jim Reische for making me believe that someone might want to publish this book.

Finally I thank my family—my husband, children, sisters, and brothers—who have listened to my incessant talk about lynching over the past eight years and have patiently waited out the birth of this book. I try always to make you proud.

CHAPTER 1: A CONVERSATION ON RACE:
LYNCHING AND THE COURTHOUSE LAWN

Details about the experiences of Frederick Douglass in Maryland can be found in *Douglass: Autobiographies*, ed. Henry Louis Gates, Jr. (New York: Library of America, 1994).

1. Chris Guy, "Veterans Pack Hearing on Abolitionist's Statue," *Baltimore Sun*, March 10, 2004, online version, http://pqasb.pqarchiver.com/baltsun/advancedsearch.html.

2. Walter Black, telephone interview March 10, 2004.

3. Chris Guy, "Douglass to Get Place by Easton Courthouse," *Baltimore Sun*, March 17, 2004, online version at http://pqasb.pqarchiver.com/baltsun/advancedsearch.html.

4. Ibid.

5. Gregory Kane, "Douglass Statue Deserves Display at Easton Courthouse," *Baltimore Sun*, February 11, 2004, online version at http://pqasb.pqarchiver.com/baltsun/advancedsearch.html.

6. Guy, "Douglass to Get Place."

7. Christian Davenport, "Battle Rages Over Tribute to Douglass," *Washington Post*, March 17, 2004.

8. Guy, "Douglass to Get Place."

9. Guy, "Veterans Pack Hearing on Abolitionist's Statue," *Baltimore Sun*, March 10, 2004, online version at http://pqasb.pqarchiver.com/baltsun/advancedsearch.html.

10. Ibid.

11. Gregory Kane, "Douglass Statue Deserves Display at Easton Courthouse," *Baltimore Sun*, February 11, 2004.

12. "Fountain May Be Reprieved," *Afro-American*, May 14, 1920.

13. "Fountain Found Guilty," *Easton Star-Democrat*, April 26, 1919.

14. Ibid.

15. Ibid.

16. Ibid.

17. "New Evidence Clears Fountain," *Afro-American*, June 6, 1919.

18. Ibid.

19. Ibid.

20. Ibid.

21. "Fountain May Be Reprieved."

22. "Many Deputy Sheriffs," *Easton Star-Democrat*, April 26, 1919.

23. *Fountain v. State of Maryland*, 135 Md. 77, 85 (1919); "Fountain Found Guilty."

24. Elliott Wheeler, "The Isaiah Fountain Affair," *Delmarva* 2, no. 3 (Winter 2003): 46. Wheeler was one of the local townspeople who were deputized to participate in the manhunt for Fountain.

25. Ibid.

26. *Fountain v. State of Maryland*, 135 Md. 77, 78–79 (1919).

27. Ibid., 81; "Wanted Militia to Come," *Easton Star-Democrat*, April 26, 1919.

28. "Wanted Militia to Come."

29. *Fountain v. State of Maryland,* 135 Md. 82.
30. Fountain's lawyer, Eugene O'Dunne, later cited the speed of the jury's deliberations as evidence that the atmosphere of mob violence had kept the jury from impartially weighing the evidence before them. See "O'Dunne Pleads for New Trial for Isaiah Fountain," *Afro-American,* June 27, 1919.
31. Wallace Shugg, *A Monument to Good Intentions: The Story of the Maryland Penitentiary, 1804–1995* (Baltimore: Maryland Historical Society, 2000), 90–121.
32. *Fountain v. State of Maryland,* 135 Md. 77 (1919).
33. Ibid., 77, 78.
34. Ibid., 85.
35. Ibid.
36. "Wanted Militia to Come."
37. "Fountain to Die Friday Morning," *Afro-American,* July 23, 1920.
38. "Fountain Hanged; Protests Innocence," *Baltimore Sun,* July 23, 1920.
39. Ibid.
40. "Mr. O'Dunne Replies," *Eastern Star-Democrat,* May 31, 1919.
41. Jim Auchmutey, "'Without Sanctuary': The Children of Lynching, Anguish Endures for Descendants on Both Sides," *Atlanta Journal-Constitution,* available through the archives at www.ajc.com.
42. Ibid.
43. "Duluth, Minnesota Pays Tribute to Three Black Men Lynched in 1920," *All Things Considered,* National Public Radio (June 8, 2001).
44. "Lynch, Shoot, Burn Negro," *Houston Post,* November 19, 1921, in *100 Years of Lynchings,* ed. Ralph Ginzburg (Baltimore: Black Classic Press, 1988), 155–56 (henceforth *100 Years*).
45. "University Students Help Mob Lynch Janitor," *New York World,* April 20, 1923, in *100 Years,* 169.
46. "Suspect Hanged from Oak on Bastrop Public Square," *New Orleans Tribune,* July 10, 1934, in *100 Years,* 219–20.
47. Ellen Douglas, *Truth: Four Stories I Am Finally Old Enough to Tell* (Chapel Hill, NC: Algonquin Books, 1998), 196.
48. W. Fitzhugh Brundage, *Lynching in the New South: Georgia and Virginia, 1880–1930* (Champaign: University of Illinois Press, 1993), 40.
49. Scott Thistle, "A Celebration to Remember," *Duluth News Tribune,* October 11, 2003; "Duluth, Minnesota Pays Tribute"; Larry Oaks, "Marches Honor Duluth Lynching Victim," *Minnesota Star-Tribune,* June 16, 2001.
50. Jay Apperson and Andrea F. Siegel, "Glendenning Pardons Black in 1919 Murder," *Baltimore Sun,* June 1, 2001.
51. Raymond Whitaker, "Carving Out a New View of History," *Independent* (London), June 21, 1998.
52. Chris Guy, "Shore Towns Embrace Growth," *Baltimore Sun,* November 30, 2003, online version at http://pqasb.pqarchiver.com/baltsun/advancedsearch.html.
53. See "Berlin Mayor Denies Riot Stories," *Afro-American,* October 24, 1931.

CHAPTER 2: MOB RULE ON THE SHORE, 1931–1933

The account of events surrounding the lynchings and near-lynchings in this chapter and the next has been derived from a review of newspaper articles, books cited below, witness accounts on file at the Nabb Research Center at Salisbury State University, interviews, and court records.

1. Denton L. Watson, *Lion in the Lobby: Clarence Mitchell, Jr.'s Struggle for the Passage of Civil Rights Laws* (Lanham, MD: University Press of America, 2002).

2. Information about the Salisbury Colored High (Salisbury Elementary) School was obtained from http://sailor.lib.md.us/docs/af_am/wico.html under "Inventory of African American Historical and Cultural Resources in 1994." Link no longer available online, copies on file at Enoch Pratt Free Library, African American Department, Baltimore, Maryland.

3. See "Babson Again Rates Salisbury 'Good' in Sales Forecasts," *Salisbury Times,* September 8, 1931. Much of the research regarding economic conditions on the Shore can be found in "A Comparative Study of Perceptions of the Media Relating to Lynchings on the Eastern Shore of Maryland, 1931–1933," by Cezar Jackson (master's thesis, History Department of Salisbury State University, 1996). The thesis can be found on file at the Nabb Center for Research at Salisbury State University, Wicomico County, Maryland.

4. T. H. Watkins, *The Hungry Years: A Narrative History of the Great Depression in America* (New York: Henry Holt, 1999), 60, 62.

5. "County Hit Hard by Storm," *Marylander and Herald,* August 25, 1933.

6. "Re-employment Office Opens Here Saturday," *Marylander and Herald,* September 29, 1933.

7. John R. Wennersten, *Maryland's Eastern Shore: A Journey in Time and Place* (Centreville, MD: Tidewater Publishers, 1992), 146.

8. See the *Afro-American,* November 29, 1933; the headlines read "Missouri Mob Hangs Negro: Burns Body"; "4 Arrested in Slaying of Aged Negro by Mob" (report on the arrest of alleged lynchers in South Carolina); and "Harvard Crimson Praises Governor Rolph's Stand" (discussing the remarks of the California governor that he would have joined the mob that lynched).

9. Sherwood Anderson, "Look Out, Brown Man!" *The Nation,* November 26, 1930, in *Burning All Illusions: Writings from the Nation on Race, 1866–2002,* ed. Paula J. Giddings (New York: Avalon Publishing, 2002), 60.

10. Kate Clifford Larson, *Bound for the Promised Land: Harriet Tubman, Portrait of an American Hero* (New York: Ballantine Books, 2004) (describing several narrowly averted lynchings in Dorchester and Caroline Counties during the late 1850s).

11. A gripping account of the execution was published in "Four Negroes Hung," *The World,* March 6, 1869.

12. Ibid.

13. See Judge Lynch's Statistical Tables, Maryland State Archives, official list of lynchings, www.ecpclio.net/megafile/msa/speccol. See also *16 Lynchings in Maryland,* compiled from *Baltimore Post,* October 20, 1933, found in Maryland Vertical files, Enoch Pratt Free Library, Baltimore.

14. "Garfield King Lynched," *Salisbury Times*, May 26, 1898.

15. "Stephen Long Murdered in Cold Blood," *Afro-American*, September 16, 1921; "2,000 Persons Attend Stephen Long's Funeral," *Afro-American*, September 23, 1921.

16. Adele Holden, *Down on the Shore* (Baltimore: Woodholme House, 2000), 170.

17. "O'Dunne Pleads for a New Trial for Isaiah Fountain," *Afro-American*, June 27, 1919.

18. Armwood reportedly left school when he reached the fifth grade. Levi Jolley, "Armwood Quit School in 5ᵗʰ Grade, Says Pal," *Afro-American*, October 28, 1933.

19. Levi Jolley, "Mother's Heart Is Broken from Lynch Tragedy," *Afro-American*, October 28, 1933.

20. Ibid.

21. Editorial, "Get at the Roots," *Afro-American*, October 28, 1933.

22. Ibid.

23. "Police to Rush Accused Negro Back to Shore," *Evening Sun*, October 17, 1933. Additional details of this account are derived from Wennersten, *Maryland's Eastern Shore*, 151–54.

24. "Robins and Daugherty Told Armwood Would Be Lynched," *Afro-American*, October 28, 1933 (affidavit of Frank Spencer, dictated to John Louis Clarke).

25. Charles Hamilton Houston and Leon A. Ranson to Colonel West A. Hamilton, October 20, 1933, in files of NAACP, Manuscript Division, Library of Congress, College Park, Maryland.

26. Wennersten, *Maryland's Eastern Shore*, 153.

27. "Judge Admits He Made Error in Denying Lynching Possibility," *Washington Daily News*, October 19, 1933.

28. Ernest V. Baugh Jr., "19 Witnesses Fail to Name Members of Lynching Mob," *Baltimore Sun*, October 25, 1933.

29. "Police Head Describes Mob Attack," *Baltimore Sun*, October 19, 1933.

30. "Robins and Daugherty Told Armwood Would Be Lynched."

31. Clarence Mitchell, "Mob Members Knew Prey Was Feeble-Minded," *Afro-American*, October 21, 1933.

32. Telephone interview with Roma Jones, June 25, 2002.

33. Shepard Krech III, *Praise the Bridge That Carries You Over: The Life of Joseph L. Sutton* (Cambridge, MA: Schenkman Publishing, 1981).

34. George A. Corddry, *Wicomico County History* (Salisbury, MD: Peninsula Press, 1981), 58.

35. "Mob Took Negro from Her Custody," *Baltimore Sun*, December 5, 1931.

36. See the interview with an anonymous informant, collected by Melva A. Brittingham on June 18, 1973, available at Nabb Research Center, Salisbury State University, Wicomico County, Maryland.

37. Corddry, *Wicomico County History*, 58.

38. Interview with Eugenie "Shanie" Shields, Princess Anne, Maryland, March 25, 2002.

39. Corddry, *Wicomico County History*, 59.

40. "Eyewitness Tells How Mob Acted," *Afro-American*, December 12, 1931.

41. Interview with Lemuel Brown, collected by Jane Brown, June 28, 1972, on file at the Nabb Research Center, Salisbury State University, Wicomico County, Maryland.

42. "Eyewitness Tells How Mob Acted." This account was confirmed in an interview with Helen Pusey in Salisbury, Maryland, on August 8, 1971; on file at the Nabb Research Center, Salisbury State University.

43. Interview with Eloise Buckley, June 15, 1973, available at the Nabb Research Center, Salisbury State University.

44. Levi H. Jolley, "Aunt Sobs, Declares 'Buddie' Mob Lynched Was a Good Boy," *Afro-American*, December 12, 1931.

45. Ibid.

46. "Salisbury Mob Played 5 Hours," *Afro-American*, December 12, 1931.

47. Testimony of Charles S. Howe, reprinted in *Transcript of Record from the Circuit Court of Baltimore County in the Case of* Lee v. Maryland, Court of Appeals, no. 46, appeal filed February 9, 1933, p. 75; available at the Library of the Maryland Court of Appeals.

48. Testimony of Coon Cooper, reprinted in *Transcript of Record from the Circuit Court of Baltimore County in the Case of* Lee v. Maryland.

49. Lee's confession is printed in the recently published work by Attorney Joseph Moore, *Murder on Maryland's Eastern Shore: Race, Politics and the Case of Orphan Jones* (Charleston, SC: History Press, 2006), 245.

50. See *In re Ades*, 6 F.Supp. 467 (1934).

51. Ibid.

52. "Berlin Mayor Denies Riot Stories," *Afro-American*, October 24, 1931.

53. *Lee v. State*, 163 Md. 56 (1932).

54. See William O. Player, "Shore Mob Lynches Negro," *Baltimore Sun*, October 19, 1933; Ralph Matthews, "Euel Lee Dies on Gallows," *Afro-American*, November 4, 1933.

55. A picture of George Davis and references to his boyish appearance appeared in "Convicted Man Whizzed Away to Foul Mob," *Afro-American*, January 9, 1931.

56. Andy Stritch of the Maryland Transition Center, a facility for prisoners preparing to reenter society, located this information in archives of the Maryland Penitentiary in the fall of 2003.

57. "Convicted Man Whizzed Away to Foul Mob."

58. See "Davis Trial at Elkton Begins Under Guard," *Salisbury Times*, January 5, 1932.

59. "Convicted Man Whizzed Away to Foul Mob."

60. A description of the mob's attempt to find George Davis can be found in "Mob in Kent Demands Negro Who Attempted to Assault White Woman," *Democratic Messenger*, November 28, 1931; "Crowds Visit Jails Seeking Accused Negro," *Salisbury Times*, November 24, 1931; "Negro Locked Up Here to Escape Mob That Visits 4 Jails," *Evening Sun*, November 24, 1931.

61. "14 Lynchings in State Since 1885, None Prosecuted," *Salisbury Times*, March 18, 1932.

CHAPTER 3: A CONSPIRACY OF SILENCE:
ORDINARY PEOPLE AND COMPLICITY IN LYNCHING

1. The epigraph by W. E. B. DuBois is from *Black Reconstruction in America* (Russell & Russell, 1935), 678; "15,000 Witness Burning of Negro in Public Square," *New York World*, May 16, 1916 (describing the public burning of Jesse Washington). According to this report, "Many women and children were among the 15,000."

2. "Minnesota Pays Tribute to Three Black Men Lynched in 1920," *All Things Considered: Duluth*, National Public Radio (June 8, 2001) (available at LEXIS, News File, National Public Radio File).

3. George H. Corddry, *Wicomico County History* (Salisbury, MD: Peninsula Press, 1981), 58.

4. Ibid.

5. Ibid.

6. "Lynch Mob Prosecution Promised," *Evening Sun*, December 5, 1931.

7. "Shore Mob Lynches Negro," *Sun*, December 5, 1931.

8. "Mob Members Knew Prey Was Feeble-Minded," *Afro-American*, October 21, 1933.

9. Walter White, *Rope and Faggot* (Salem, NH: Ayer Company, 1969), 1.

10. See James Allen, ed., *Without Sanctuary: Lynching Photography in America* (Santa Fe, NM: Twin Palms, 2000).

11. "Boy Unsexes Negro Before Mob Lynches Him," *Chicago Defender*, October 13, 1917, reprinted in *100 Years*, 113–14.

12. Interview with S. N. Pilchard, June 25, 1972, for Salisbury State Oral History Project. Copies of the interviews for this project are on file at the Nabb Research Library, Salisbury State University, Maryland.

13. The actions of Grier and Downing were reported by Broadus Mitchell of Johns Hopkins University, who conducted an investigation in Salisbury two weeks after Matthew Williams was lynched. See Broadus Mitchell Papers, Southern Historical Collection, Wilson Library, University of North Carolina at Chapel Hill.

14. "Man's Toes Cut Off by Mob at Salisbury," *Afro-American*, December 19, 1931.

15. "Glad They Lynched Him, Says Son of Alleged Victim," *Afro-American*, October 22, 1933.

16. "People of Town Discuss Lynching," *Evening Sun*, October 20, 1933.

17. David R. Roediger, ed., *Black on White: Black Writers on What It Means to Be White* (New York: Schocken Books, 1998), 16.

18. "Murder at Moore's Ford," *Atlanta Journal-Constitution*, May 31, 1992.

19. "A Statement," *Salisbury Times*, December 5, 1931.

20. Ernest V. Baugh Jr., "Investigation of Lynching Awaits Coroner's Inquest," *Sun*, October 22, 1933.

21. "Outsiders Blamed by Salisbury Clergy," *Evening Sun*, December 7, 1931.

22. H. L. Mencken, "The Eastern Shore Kultur," *Evening Sun*, December 7, 1931.

23. "State Blamed for Lynching by Ministers," *Baltimore Sun*, October 22, 1933.

24. Telephone interview with Judge Alfred Truitt Jr., June 26, 2002.

25. "People of Town Discuss Lynching," *Evening Sun*, October 20, 1933.

26. White, *Rope and Faggot*, 27, quoting a story in the *Memphis News-Scimitar*.

27. "Lynching Bad for Business," *Memphis Commercial Appeal*, August 5, 1913, reprinted in *100 Years*, 82.

28. Fitzhugh Brundage, *Lynching in the New South: Georgia and Virginia, 1880–1930* (Urbana: University of Illinois Press, 1993), 228–29.

29. Claudine Ferrell, *Nightmare and Dream: Antilynching in Congress, 1917–1922* (New York: Garland, 1986), 90.

30. Clarence Mitchell, "Mob Members Knew Prey Was Feeble-Minded," *Afro-American*, October 21, 1933.

31. "Salisbury Mayor Rounds Up the Town's Leaders," *Afro-American,* December 12, 1931.

32. "Coroner's Jury to Investigate Slayer's Death," *Salisbury Times,* December 5, 1931.

33. "Lynch Verdict Closes Probe," *Baltimore Post,* March 19, 1932.

34. "Witnesses Fail to Name Lynch Mob Members," *Sun,* October 25, 1933.

35. Adele Holden, *Down on the Shore* (Baltimore: Woodholme House, 2000), 144.

36. "Lynch Threat Used to Make Worker Quit," *Afro-American,* December 12, 1931.

37. "Shore Lynchers May Have Had Second Victim," *Afro-American,* December 12, 1931.

38. "Doctor Deserts Home After Seeing Mob," *Afro-American,* December 12, 1931.

39. "Colored People Blame Communists and Ades," *Marylander and Herald,* December 3, 1933.

40. "Three Uncle Jameses Speak" and "The Three Jimmies Glorify Lynching," *Afro-American,* December 16, 1933.

41. "Salisbury, Md. Citizens Hit the Three Jameses," *Afro-American,* December 16, 1933.

42. Ibid.

43. For a discussion of Dr. Chipman's fifty-year commitment to educational advancement for blacks in Wicomico County, see Corddry, *Wicomico County History,* 198–99.

44. Telephone interview with Alfred Truitt Jr.

CHAPTER 4: "THE LAW IN ALL ITS MAJESTY"

1. "Lynch Mob Prosecution Promise; Ritchie Back, Opens Inquiry with Lane," *Evening Sun,* December 5, 1921. According to the news account, Holland insisted that "the authorities had no indication that a lynching was planned and that his investigation during the night produced evidence that the mob developed spontaneously."

2. Ibid., 2.

3. Ibid.

4. Affidavit of Frank Spencer, reprinted in "Robins and Daugherty Told Armwood Would Be Lynched," *Afro-American,* October 28, 1933.

5. "Son of Victim Ready to Face Jury," *Evening Sun,* October 23, 1933.

6. Affidavit of Frank Spencer.

7. Ibid.

8. Testimony of Louis Azrael, associate editor of the *Baltimore Post,* February 20, 1934, in *Punishment for the Crime of Lynching, Hearings before a Subcommittee of the Committee on the Judiciary, United States Senate,* 73rd Cong., 2nd sess. on S. 1978 (Washington, DC: GPO, 1934).

9. "Sheriff Staves off Mob," *Montgomery Advertiser,* August 19, 1939, reprinted in *100 Years of Lynching,* 83.

10. "S.C. Lynchers Slay Negro: One Tells of Police Help," *Herald Tribune,* October 10, 1932, reprinted in *100 Years,* 199.

11. "Belleville Is Complacent over Horrible Lynching," *New York Herald,* June 9, 1903, reprinted in *100 Years,* 50–52.

12. "19 Witnesses Fail to Name Members of Lynching Mob," *Baltimore Sun,* October 24, 1933 (italics added).

13. "Unable to Identify Any Lynchers, Jailer Says," *Sun,* October 19, 1933.

14. "Witnesses Fail to Name Lynch Mob Members," *Sun,* October 25, 1933.

15. "Coroner Says Jury Will Make Inquiry," *Evening Sun,* October 19, 1933.

16. "Unable to Identify Any Lynchers."

17. "Duer Recalling Grand Jury to Seek Lynchers," *Evening Sun,* October 29, 1933.

18. "Coroner Says Inquiry Will Be Made by Jury," *Evening Sun,* October 19, 1933.

19. Ibid.

20. "Four in Maryland Held as Lynchers Freed by Court," *New York Times,* November 30, 1933.

21. "Sixteen Years Given Davis for Assault," *Salisbury Times,* January 6, 1932.

22. "'Against' Lynching, but for Saving Money," *Evening Sun,* November 24, 1931, reprinted from *Chestertown Transcript.*

23. "Lynch Verdict Closes Probe," *Baltimore Post,* March 19, 1932.

24. Ibid.

25. Statement of Officer (1st Cl.) C. C. Serman, in *Punishment for the Crime of Lynching,* February 20 and 21, 1934, p. 129.

26. Statement of Sgt. William Weber, in *Punishment for the Crime of Lynching,* 131.

27. Ibid.

28. Statement of Corp. J. F. Norris, in *Punishment for the Crime of Lynching,* 131.

29. Ernest V. Baugh Jr., "Lynching Investigation Awaits Coroner Inquest; Lane Will Help in Probe," *Sun,* October 22, 1933.

30. John B. Robins, state's attorney for Somerset County, to Hon. Preston Lane Jr., attorney general of Maryland, November 20, 1933, in *Punishment for the Crime of Lynching,* 121–22.

31. Attorney General Wm. Preston Lane Jr. to Hon. John R. Pattison, November 21, 1933, in *Punishment for the Crime of Lynching,* 122.

32. Ibid.

33. Harry C. Martin, "Baltimoreans Not Bad Lot, Martin Tells Folk on Shore," *Sun,* November 30, 1933.

34. A detailed account of the hearing can be found in "Judge Pattison Releases Four Lynch Suspects as Thousands Cheer Wildly," *Sun,* November 30, 1933.

35. See the list of Maryland state police summoned for the January 23, 1934, grand jury hearing, in *Punishment for the Crime of Lynching,* 23.

36. *Lee v. State,* 161 Md. 430 (1931).

37. For a detailed description of Judge Frank Duncan's professional career, see *Report of the Mid-Winter Meeting and Fifty-first Annual Meeting of the Maryland State Bar Association* (1946), available at Library of the Court of Appeals, Annapolis, Maryland.

38. Judge Duncan's testimony is quoted in *Transcript of Record from the Circuit Court of Baltimore County in the case of* Euel Lee v. State of Maryland, *Record No. 46 Appeal to the April Term, 1933 of the Court of Appeals of Maryland,* p. 56, available in Library of the Court of Appeals, Annapolis, Maryland.

39. Ibid.

40. *Lee v. State,* 163 Md. 56 (1932).

41. *Report of the Mid-Winter Meeting and Fifty-sixth Annual Meeting of the Maryland State Bar Association* 23.

42. James F. Schneider, *A Century of Striving for Justice: The Maryland State Bar Association, 1896–1996* (Baltimore: Maryland Bar Association, 1996), 40.

43. "Convicted Man Whizzed Away to Foul Mob," *Afro-American,* January 9, 1932.

44. Ibid.

45. Ibid.

46. Ibid.

47. "Former Judge Robert F. Duer Dies Here Sun.," *Marylander and Herald,* January 1, 1958.

48. "Robins Orders Sheriff to Get Mob Evidence," *Evening Sun,* October 20, 1933.

49. "Judge Admits He Made Error in Denying Lynching Possibility," *Washington Daily News,* October 19, 1933.

50. Louis J. O'Donnell, "Governor and Lane Deny Receiving Any Notice of Hearing," *Sun,* November 29, 1933.

51. "Lynching Case Is Closed by Somerset Jury," *Sun,* January 26, 1934.

CHAPTER 5: "SERVING THE PENINSULA":
LOCAL NEWSPAPERS AND LYNCHING

1. Cezar Jackson, "A Comparative Study of Perceptions of the Media Relating to Lynchings on the Eastern Shore of Maryland, 1931–1933" (master's thesis, History Department of Salisbury State University, 1996). The thesis can be found on file at the Nabb Center for Research at Salisbury State University, Wicomico County, Maryland.

2. *Salisbury Times,* December 5, 1931.

3. Ibid.

4. Corddry, *Wicomico County History,* 58.

5. "Unsolicited Notoriety," *Democratic Messenger,* November 7, 1931.

6. Ibid.

7. "Who Took Armwood to Baltimore?" *Marylander and Herald,* October 28, 1933.

8. "Shore Lynchers May Have Had Second Victim," *Afro-American,* December 12, 1931.

9. "Philadelphia Woman Mourns Brother Who Was Lynched," *Afro-American,* December 12, 1921.

10. *Sun,* December 5, 1931.

11. Ibid., October 19, 1933.

12. See *Lee v. State,* 161 Md. 430 (1931).

CHAPTER 6: RECONCILIATION AND LYNCHING
IN INTERNATIONAL CONTEXT

1. Jodi Halpern and Harvey M. Weinstein, "Empathy and Rehumanization after Mass Violence," in *My Neighbor, My Enemy: Justice and Community in the Aftermath of Mass Atrocity,* ed. Eric Stover and Harvey M. Weinstein (Cambridge: Cambridge University Press, 2004), 309.

2. See Peter Smith, "Vatican Considering a Number of Mea Culpas to Mark Jubilee," Religion News Service, January 8, 1999.

3. Human Rights and Equal Opportunity Commission, "Bringing Them Home: National Inquiry into the Separation of Aboriginal and Torres Strait Islander Children from Their Families," April 1997, available at http://www.austlii.edu.au//cgi-bin/disp.pl/au/journals/AILR/1997/36.html?query=%22Bringing%20Them%20Home:%20National%20Inquiry%22.

4. See Smith, *Vatican Considering a Number of Mea Culpas;* Roger Cohen, "Last Chapter: Berlin to Pay Slave Workers Held by Nazis," *New York Times,* May 31, 2001.

5. See C. Jeanne Bassett, Comment, *House Bill 591: Florida Compensates Rosewood Victims and Their Families for a Seventy-One-Year-Old Injury*, 22 *Fla. St. U.L. Rev.* 503 (1994).

6. *Alexander v. State of Oklahoma*, 382 F.3d 1206 (2004).

7. Pam Belluck, "Brown U. to Examine Debt to Slave Trade," *New York Times*, March 13, 2004.

8. "University of Alabama Apologizes to Descendants of Slaves," *Jet*, May 10, 2004.

9. "UNC–Chapel Hill Opens Up Records about Ties to Slavery," *Diverse Issues in Higher Education*, November 17, 2005.

10. John F. Harris, "Clinton Says U.S. Wronged Africa; President Cites Slavery," *Washington Post*, March 25, 1998

11. Mahmood Mamdani, "A Diminished Truth," in *After the TRC*, ed. Wilmot James and Linda Van de Vijver (Athens: Ohio University Press, 2001), 60.

12. Ibid.

13. Promotion of National Unity and Reconciliation Act, Act 95-34, July 26, 1995, Office of the President, no. 11111, no. 34 of 1995, available at www.doj.gov.za/trc/legal/act9534 .htm.

14. *AZAPO v. President of the Republic of South Africa*, decision of the Constitutional Court of South Africa, CCT 17/96 (July 25, 1996), 19.

15. For a detailed discussion of the formation of the gacaca tribunals, see Urusaro Alice Karekezi, Alphonse Nshimiyimana, and Beth Mutamba, "Localizing Justice: Gacaca Courts in Post-Genocide Rwanda," in *My Neighbor, My Enemy: Justice and Community in the Aftermath of Atrocity*, ed. Eric Stover and Harvey M. Weinstein (Cambridge: Cambridge University Press 2004), 69–84.

16. Ibid., 75, quoting Jennifer Balint, in *Law's Constitutive Possibilities: Reconstruction and Reconciliation in the Wake of Genocide and State Crime*, in *Lethe's Law: Justice, Law and Ethics in Reconciliation*, ed. Emilios Christodouldilis and Scott Veitch (Oxford: Hart Publishing, 2001), 141.

17. Ibid.

18. Mahmood Mamdani, *When Victims Become Killers* (Princeton: Princeton University Press, 2001), 49–60.

19. Slavenka Drakulic, *They Would Never Hurt a Fly: War Criminals on Trial in The Hague* (New York: Viking, 2004).

20. Naomi Roht-Arriaza, "Reparations in the Aftermath of Repression," in *My Neighbor, My Enemy*, ed. Stover and Weinstein, 122.

21. Avis Thomas-Lester, "Repairing Senate's Record on Lynching," *Washington Post*, June 12, 2005.

22. Ibid.

23. Terry M. Neal, "Symbolic Lynching Resolution Forced Concrete Political Choice," *Washington Post*, June 23, 2005.

24. See Eric Stover, "Witnesses and the Promise of Justice in The Hague," in *My Neighbor, My Enemy*, ed. Stover and Weinstein, 117.

25. Ibid., 116.

26. Teresa Godwin Phelps, *Shattered Voices: Language, Violence, and the Work of Truth Commissions* (Philadelphia: University of Pennsylvania Press, 2004), 55.

27. Paul Rusesabagina, with Tom Zoellner, *An Ordinary Man* (New York: Viking, 2006), 195.

28. "Beckwith Convicted of Evers Murder," *St. Louis Post-Dispatch*, February 6, 1994.

29. Larry Copeland, "After 5 Trials, Ex-Klansman Convicted in Miss.," *USA Today*, August 24, 1998.

30. Dina Temple-Raston, *A Death in Texas* (New York: Henry Holt, 2002), 237.

CHAPTER 7: BREAKING THE SILENCE:
"WORDS ARE THE MOST POWERFUL TOOLS OF ALL"

1. Paul Rusesabagina, with Tom Zoellner, *An Ordinary Man* (New York: Viking, 2006), 190.

2. Teresa Godwin Phelps, *Shattered Voices: Language, Violence, and the Work of Truth Commissions* (Philadelphia: University of Pennsylvania Press, 2004), 47.

3. Ibid., 44.

4. Ibid., 59.

5. Ibid., 60.

6. Cynthia Carr, "An American Secret," *New York Times Magazine*, February 26, 2006, 110.

7. Slavenka Drakulic, *They Would Never Hurt a Fly: War Criminals on Trial in The Hague* (New York: Viking, 2004), 16.

8. Polly Stewart, "Regional Consciousness as a Shaper of Local History: Examples from the Eastern Shore," in *A Sense of Place: American Regional Cultures*, ed. Barbara Allen and Thomas J. Schlerth (Lexington: University of Kentucky Press, 1998), 75–87.

9. Ibid., 87.

10. Telephone interview with Polly Stewart, July 8, 2004.

11. Ellen Douglas, *Truth: Four Stories I Am Finally Old Enough to Tell* (Chapel Hill, NC: Algonquin Books, 1998), 201.

12. Beth Roy, *Bitters in the Honey: Tales of Hope and Disappointment across Divides of Race and Time* (Fayetteville: University of Arkansas Press, 1999).

13. Ibid., 210.

14. Dennis D. Smith, "Shreveport, the Summer of '56" (letter to the editor), *Dallas Morning News*, February 2, 1999.

15. "15,000 Witness Burning of Negro in Public Square," *New York World*, May 16, 1916, reprinted in *100 Years*, 103.

16. "Grim Reminder" (picture caption), *Chi. Defender*, September 8, 1917, reprinted in *100 Years*, 112–13.

17. "Negro Burned Alive in Florida; Second Negro Then Hanged," *Springfield (Mass.) Weekly Republican*, April 28, 1899, reprinted in *100 Years*, 15–17.

18. *Selected Works of Ida B. Wells-Barnett*, ed. Trudier Harris (New York: Oxford University Press, 1991), 5.

19. Walter White, *Rope and Faggot* (Salem, NH: Ayer Company, 1969), 37.

20. "Lynch Victim's Father Called to Clear Away Son's Ashes," *St. Louis Argus*, November 25, 1921, reprinted in *100 Years*, 156. Turner's son William was only nineteen when he was lynched for having a fight with a white man.

21. "Mother's Heart Is Broken from Lynch Tragedy," *Afro-American*, October 28, 1933.

22. "Eyewitness to Lynching Tells How Mob Acted," *Afro-American*, December 12, 1931.

23. Adele Holden, *Down on the Shore* (Baltimore: Woodholme House, 2000), 146.

24. This account can be found in Richard Kluger, *Simple Justice* (New York: Vintage Books, 1977), 518.
25. Betsy McAlister Groves, "How Does Exposure to Violence Affect Very Young Children?" *Harvard Mental Health Letter* 11, nos. 7, 8 (1995).
26. Betsy McAlister Groves et al., "Silent Victims: Children Who Witness Violence," *JAMA* (1993): 269, 262, 262–65.
27. Interview with Deborah Tulani Salahu-Din, Baltimore, July 29, 2002.
28. Telephone interview with the Reverend David W. Briddell, August 7, 2002.
29. *Ades v. Brady,* Docket No. A-478–1933 (Circuit Court Baltimore City), reprinted in *Daily Record,* October 30, 1933.
30. Laura Mirsky, "The Community Conferencing Center: Restorative Practices in Baltimore, Maryland," Restorative Practices Forum, March 9, 2004. A publication of the International Institute for Restorative Practices. Additional information about community conferencing derived from discussions with Lauren Abramson between 2001 and 2006.
31. Rusesabagina, *An Ordinary Man,* 180

CHAPTER 8: CONFRONTING THE ROLE OF INSTITUTIONS
IN RACIAL/ETHNIC VIOLENCE

1. *Truth and Reconciliation Commission of South Africa Report,* vol. 4 (Bath, UK: Bath Press, 1999), 53.
2. Ingo Muller, *Hitler's Justice: The Courts of the Third Reich* (Cambridge, MA: Harvard University Press), 145.
3. Ibid., 215.
4. *The Prosecutor v. Ferdinand Nahimana, Jean-Bosco Barayagwiza, Hassan Ngeze,* Case No. IGTR-9952-T, Judgment and Sentence, December 3, 2003.
5. Ibid., 2.
6. David Dyzenhaus, *Judging the Judges, Judging Ourselves: Truth, Reconciliation and the Apartheid Legal Order* (Oxford: Hart Publishing, 1998), 95 (emphasis added).
7. Ibid., 93.
8. Corbett memorandum at p.1, quoted ibid., 37.
9. Dyzenhaus, *Judging the Judges,* 41.
10. Arthur Chaskalson, "Law in a Changing Society," *South African Journal on Human Rights* 293 (1989), quoted ibid., 20.
11. Dyzenhaus, *Judging the Judges,* 39.
12. Ibid., 40.
13. Ibid., 107.
14. *Truth and Reconciliation Commission,* 101.
15. Ibid.
16. Ibid., 165.
17. Ibid., 177.
18. Ibid., 172.
19. Ibid., 174.
20. Chris Guy, "The Shore's First African-American Judge Achieved His Goal with 'Quiet Endurance,'" *Baltimore Sun,* February 16, 2006.

21. Judge Duer's decision is discussed in the opinion by the Court of Appeals overturning the harsh sentence; *In the Matter of Dwight Cromwell,* 232 Md. 409 (1963).

22. See Peter B. Levy, *Civil War on Race Street: The Civil Rights Movement in Cambridge, Maryland* (Gainesville: University of Florida Press 2003), 80–82.

23. Ibid.

24. James Dao, "40 Years Later, Civil Rights Makes Page One," *New York Times,* July 13, 2004.

25. Ibid.

26. See George Roache Jr., "First Anniversary of Publishing Salisbury's Black History Is Noted," January 2, 1994; "Atrocities Continue Following Brutal Death of Lynching Victim," December 26, 1993; "Vigilantes Took the Law in Their Own Hands," December 12, 1993; all in the *Daily Times.*

27. Jerome W. Banks, letter to the editor, January 6, 1994.

28. *Truth and Reconciliation Commission,* 91.

29. Ibid., 59.

CHAPTER 9: RECONCILIATION IN THE TWENTY-FIRST CENTURY

1. The full report of the Greensboro TRC and the commission's entire list of recommendations can be found at www.greensborotrc.org.

2. Paul Alongi, "Churches Apologize for Lynching," *Greenville News,* July 13, 2005.

3. See www.southerntruth.org/aboutus/htm. I have served as an adviser to STAR and delivered the keynote address at their regional conference in March 2006.

4. Scott Thistle, "A Celebration to Remember," *Duluth News Tribune,* October 11, 2003.

5. Lee Shearer, "Site of Lynching Marked with Sign," *Athens Banner Herald,* July 26, 1999.

6. Jeffrey Scott, "Horror Revisited," *Atlanta Journal-Constitution,* July 26, 2005.

7. John DeSantis, "North Carolina City Confronts Its Past in Report on White Vigilantes," *New York Times,* December 19, 2005.

Made in the USA
San Bernardino, CA
12 March 2017